Children of the Drug War

Children of the Drug War

Perspectives on the Impact of Drug Policies on Young People

Damon Barrett, editor

International Debate Education Association
New York, London & Amsterdam

Published by

The International Debate Education Association
400 West 59th Street
New York, NY 10019

Library of Congress Cataloging-in-Publication Data

Children of the drug war : perspectives on the impact of drug policies
on young people / Damon Barrett, editor.
    p. cm.
  ISBN 978-1-61770-018-7
  1. Drug control. 2. Children--Drug use. 3. Children--Social
conditions. I. Barrett, Damon.
  HV5801.C494 2011
  362.29'13--dc22
                                    2011006930

Printed in the USA

Contents

Foreword

In 1971, U.S. President Richard Nixon officially launched a "war on drugs," declaring drug abuse to be "public enemy number one," and requesting Congress to commit nearly $400,000,000 to national and international efforts to address "drug abuse control." A key justification for this commitment? Protection of children. As Nixon stated in his Congressional address announcing the war on drugs,

> Narcotics addiction is a problem which afflicts both the body and the soul of America. . . . It comes quietly into homes and destroys children, it moves into neighborhoods and breaks the fiber of community which makes neighbors. . . . We must try to better understand the confusion and disillusion and despair that bring people, particularly young people, to the use of narcotics and dangerous drugs.[1]

Forty years—and more than $1 trillion later—there is widespread consensus that the war on drugs has failed, not just in the United States but also worldwide.[2] Notwithstanding, governments worldwide continue to support the same costly programs that do not work, and do so with policy support from UN drug control agencies. The justification, against all evidence of their effect to the contrary, continues to be child protection. As U.S. Department of Homeland Security Secretary Janet Napolitano recently stated,

> This is something that is worth fighting for because drug addiction is about fighting for somebody's life, a young child's life, a teenager's life, their ability to be a successful and productive adult. . . . If you think about it in those terms, that they are fighting for lives—and in Mexico they are literally fighting for lives as well from the violence standpoint—you realize the stakes are too high to let go.[3]

What Napolitano did not mention in her speech was that today, in the city of Juárez, Mexico, alone, there are 10,000 children who have been orphaned by the drug war violence.[4] Napolitano's comment highlights key flaws in drug war efforts to "protect" children. Not only has the war on drugs proved a costly failure in addressing drug addiction or use overall, including among young people, it has also caused significant harm to the health and lives of children and young people. Children are, indeed, "fighting for their lives"—but in many cases, due to the very drug control efforts that are adopted in their name.

As some of the essays in this book describe, and as Human Rights Watch's work in Cambodia, the United States, Russia, and Thailand has shown, children often experience a wide range of human rights violations linked to drug control efforts. These include torture and ill treatment by police; extrajudicial killings; arbitrary detention; and denial of essential medicines and basic health services. Existing drug control policies, and accompanying enforcement practices, often entrench and exacerbate systematic discrimination against people who use drugs, and impede access to controlled essential medicines for those who need them for therapeutic purposes.

In some countries, children are detained in compulsory drug detention centers together with adults, and denied appropriate health, education, and other social services. In 2008, nearly one-quarter of detainees in Cambodia's compulsory drug detention centers were aged eighteen or below. They were detained alongside adults, forced to work, and physically abused.[5] A sixteen-year-old detainee in one center reported "[A staff member] would use the cable to beat people. . . . On each whip the person's skin would come off and stick on the cable."[6]

Restrictive drug policies have not only had a pervasive effect on people who use drugs for recreational purposes or have a dependency on them, but also on those who need them for pain management. The World Health Organization estimates that 80 percent of the world's population, including tens of millions of people worldwide who suffer from moderate to severe pain, do not have adequate access to pain treatment. Much of their suffering could be prevented if morphine, an inexpensive, effective, and safe medication that is generally not difficult to administer, was available. However, in more than 150 countries around the world, access to morphine is virtually nonexistent,[7] in part due to excessively strict drug control regulations.[8] Children are doubly victimized by government failure to ensure access to pain relief: on the one hand, those who suffer pain cannot access direct relief and, on the other hand, children of parents denied treatment are denied parental support.[9]

Severe drug laws resulting in mass incarceration deprive thousands of children of their parents, and, in some cases, their access to social benefits, including public housing;[10] and in some countries, a disproportionate share of those incarcerated are poor racial or ethnic minorities.[11]

Scant attention has been paid to whether drug control efforts are consistent with human rights protections, or indeed, to what extent they affect children and young people. *Children of the Drug War* makes a critical contribution to addressing this gap. Its mix of academic, journalistic, and first-person essays, and the wide-ranging, often hidden, issues they cover illustrate the many ways in which the war on drugs affects the lives and health of children, from production and trade through use. By placing children and young people at the forefront of this inquiry, this book compels us to consider, in a comprehensive way, the diverse ways in which drug policies affect them. It should also foster critical thinking and debate about whether current policies are indeed protecting children as government officials claim, and if not, how this approach could prove important in shaping emerging policy and practices. Every policymaker and decision maker should read it before defending current drug policies in the name of children.

Rebecca Schleifer
Advocacy Director
Health and Human Rights Division
Human Rights Watch, New York

Endnotes

1. President Richard Nixon, "Special Message to the Congress on Drug Abuse Prevention and Control," www.presidency.ucsb.edu/ws/?pid=3048/.
2. See, for example, United Nations Office on Drugs and Crime, *Drug Control, Crime Prevention and Criminal Justice: A Human Rights Perspective*, E/CN.7/2010/ CRP.6–E/CN.15/2010/CRP.1, March 2010.
3. Martha Mendoza, "U.S. Drug War Has Met None of Its Goals," Associated Press, May 13, 2010, www.msnbc.msn.com/id/37134751/ns/us_news-security/.
4. Adriana Gómez Licón, "Juárez Violence Leaves Thousands of Children Orphaned, Traumatized," *El Paso Times*, October 10, 2010, www.elpasotimes.com/news/ ci_16301040/.
5. Human Rights Watch, *Skin on the Cable: The Illegal Arrest, Arbitrary Detention and Torture of People Who Use Drugs in Cambodia*, January 25, 2010, www.hrw. org/en/reports/2010/01/25/skin-cable/.
6. M'noh, aged sixteen, describing whippings he witnessed in the Social Affairs "Youth Rehabilitation Center" in Choam Chao (Phnom Penh, Cambodia), in ibid., 41.
7. Statement of Sevil Atasoy, president of the International Narcotics Control Board, to the United Nations Economic and Social Council, July 30, 2009, www.incb. org/documents/President_statements_09/2009_ECOSOC_Substantive_Session_ published.pdf.
8. See Human Rights Watch, " 'Please Do Not Make Us Suffer Anymore' ": Access to Pain Treatment as a Human Right, March 3, 2009, www.hrw.org/en/ reports/2009/03/02/please-do-not-make-us-suffer-any-more/.
9. See Human Rights Watch, *Needless Pain: Government Failure to Provide Palliative Care for Children in Kenya*, September 9, 2010, www.hrw.org/en/ reports/2010/09/09/needless-pain/; and Human Rights Watch, *Unbearable Pain: India's Obligation to Ensure Palliative Care*, October 28, 2009, www.hrw.org/en/ reports/2009/10/28/unbearable-pain-0/.
10. See, for example, Human Rights Watch, *Collateral Casualties: Children of Incarcerated Drug Users in New York*, June 22, 2002, www.hrw.org/en/ reports/2002/06/22/collateral-casualties-0/.
11. In the United States, for example, African-American men and women are sent to prison for drug charges at rates many times that of their white counterparts and the application of mandatory minimum sentencing often subjects them to equal or harsher penalties than the principals of the drug trade. See Human Rights Watch, *Decades of Disparity: Drug Arrests and Race in the United States*, 2009; Human Rights Watch, *Targeting Blacks: Drug Law Enforcement and Race in the United States*, 2008; American Civil Liberties Union, *Break the Chains*, and the Brennan Center at New York University School of Law, *Caught in the Net: The Impact of Drug Policies on Women and Families* (New York, 2006).

Introduction: Counting the Costs of the Children's Drug War

Damon Barrett

The drugs law will save our children and young generation . . .
Andi Mattalatta,
Indonesian Law and Human Rights Minister[1]

We are all children of the drug war. While the term was coined by President Richard Nixon in the 1970s, the seeds of the "war on drugs" had been sown many decades earlier. International drug conventions began to be adopted at the turn of the twentieth century, and the bedrock of the international system of drug control, the Single Convention on Narcotic Drugs, is fifty years old in 2011.[2] Certainly, for any of those born in the latter half of the twentieth century, whether they noticed it or not, they were growing up in the midst of the war on drugs.[3] Whether they noticed depends on many things, in particular, where they grew up and under what conditions. For some it depends on who they are. This book is about the impact of the war on drugs on children, young people, and their families today, and the policy questions raised when children are placed at the forefront of the debate.

Whether or not to reform drug laws is not the focal debate of this book. That is a debate that has been widely covered.[4] Indeed, at the time of writing it is high on the agenda in various parts of Europe and Latin America, as well as the United States and Australia.[5] In October 2010, the UN Special Rapporteur on the Right to Health, Anand Grover, submitted a report to the UN General Assembly calling for an overhaul of the international drug control system.[6] At present, more than 17,000 individuals and organizations, including ex-presidents and Nobel laureates, have signed the Vienna Declaration—a global call for a fundamental shift in drug policy in order to tackle HIV/AIDS.[7] And in November 2010, Californians went to the polls to vote on proposition 19 to legalize, tax, and regulate cannabis sales. It lost by a narrow margin, and is expected to be tabled again in 2012, along with similar propositions in multiple states.

It is accepted that change is needed, but how should laws and policies be reformulated if children and young people are, this time, to be at the forefront? What must be avoided? What must be taken into account? What principles would underpin those policies? The chapters in this book deal with these questions in various ways—some directly, others indirectly by looking at specific issues and concerns. Though the book is divided into four thematic sections, three crosscutting questions may assist in guiding the reader through each section and chapter:

- What have been the costs to children of the "war on drugs"?
- Is the protection of children from drugs a solid justification for current policies?
- What kinds of public fears and preconceptions exist in relation to drugs and the drug trade?

In each case, the policy implications of asking and answering these questions should be considered.

Counting the Costs

To begin with there is a basic need to take stock—to count the costs.[8] This necessitates a closer look at what really matters in terms of outcomes.[9] Indeed, it is the way in which "success" has been measured in drug control that has led to some of the strongest criticism. The number of people who use drugs, the amount of kilos of drugs seized, prosecutions secured, and hectares of illicit crops eradicated are some of the key indicators in this regard.[10] But while these indicators can be useful,[11] they are, for the most part, indicators of means, not ends. This is not often recognized, and in the prominence given to such measurements, drug control has, over time, become self-referential and self-perpetuating; a positive feedback loop in which the fight against drugs is an end in itself.[12]

Counting the costs to children is about breaking that loop as the process of investigating the harms of the war on drugs can help to delineate between means and ends and provide an insight into the question of meaningful outcomes. Children's and families' involvement in drug production and trade, for example, is a mix of coercive forces, often driven or even necessitated by poverty and social neglect.[13] These drivers are all but ignored and even exacerbated by current drug policies that focus on eradication and interdiction, as some of the chapters in this book show.[14] Success in dealing with production and trade is for the most part measured in prosecutions, kilos, and hectares. But given such social and economic determinants of involvement in the trade, are these appropriate responses and metrics?

A similar question arises in the context of drug dependence, given contemporary theories about structural and social determinants of dependence and drug-related harm.[15] Are criminal laws an appropriate response? Is the number of people who use drugs an important indicator, or should we be more concerned about drug-related harms such as overdose, crime rates, and blood-borne viruses? These questions pose important challenges to current approaches to drug control, given the international framework and the national systems it has spawned, because they demand that we revisit priorities.[16] In short, counting the costs of the children's drug war both challenges current approaches and contributes to the debate around what goals drug policies should be striving toward. It is no easy task, and requires more qualitative analyses alongside a framework of indicators that relates more closely to quality of life and well-being.

Looking beyond the limits of international drug laws, and refocusing the debate back to what drug control should be achieving, Steve Rolles, in "After the War on Drugs," considers alternative models of control and how such models would better protect children from drugs. The rhetoric of "protecting children" from the "scourge" of drugs is, however, a strong barrier to even beginning these discussions.

The Rhetoric of "Threat"

For many the "war on drugs" is a fitting analogy for the scale of the damage policies have caused, their transnational nature, and the financial and human costs. For some, however, the war is all too real, as some of the chapters in this book illustrate.[17] For critics, the war on drugs is used in the pejorative to draw attention to a disastrous, international error, or to highlight a ruse adopted in the pursuit of hidden agendas.[18] Children often provide a trump card against such criticisms, justification for whatever policies may be employed in the name of tackling addiction and fighting the drug trade. Children, after all, are our future, "our most precious asset."[19] Nothing less than our very way of life is at stake in combating this "evil." This is not an overstatement of the political rhetoric. It is reflected in the core international drug control treaties ratified by almost every state on the planet.[20]

Of course, it is difficult to think of a better goal than the protection of children. But the rhetoric of protecting children from drugs can be unhelpful if it obscures reality. For policymakers and politicians the simple message is useful. It is more easily understood by the general public than some of the more counterintuitive yet evidence-based responses available, such as harm reduction.[21] It makes for engaging press copy. It speaks to our fears (particularly as parents), to our prejudices, and to our ignorance. As such it is misleading. It does not speak to the complex realities of drug use (including culture, peer pressure, sex, pleasure, aspiration, experimentation, and fashion) or to the underlying determinants of dependence and drug-related harm such as social exclusion, mental health, inequality, and poverty. These concerns, while acknowledged in various international declarations, are often mere footnotes in actual responses, overshadowed by the law enforcement–based responses necessitated by the rhetoric of struggle against a perpetual threat.

While the reasons for drug use among young people remain hotly debated,[22] the assumption underpinning most countries' responses to drug use is that it is in all cases aberrant or deviant behavior, and always harmful, always a threat. But while drug use among young people can be an indicator of later problems, experimenting with drugs is becoming increasingly common among young people, and most young people who experiment with drugs or use them recreationally do not develop serious drug problems.[23] While universal prevention measures have little role in preventing drug use among those at most risk of dependence and drug-related harms,[24] measures that focus on the worst-case scenario fail to speak to the lived experiences of recreational users.[25] Accepting this reality and responding to it, however, may require a level of tolerance in policy that the current rhetorical posturing does not readily allow.[26]

Fears, Preconceptions, and Policy

Public support for "get tough" policies is widespread. A 2010 poll, for example, showed that 80 percent of the Mexican public supports the government's militarized confrontation of the drug cartels despite the violence that has ensued.[27] In Thailand, in 2003, a government-sanctioned war on drugs left over 2,000 people dead—many with no connection to the drug trade.[28] Again, this had widespread public support. In Mauritius, during the 2010 elections there was widespread support for reintroducing the death penalty for drug trafficking. The fears and ideas that underlie moral panics relating to drugs and result in instinctive support for crackdowns are understandable. But when unpacked and challenged, they provide important insights into current drug policies. Through the diverse chapters in this book, especially those in which personal perspectives are presented, it is hoped that some of these preconceptions and assumptions around drugs and those involved in the drug trade will be challenged, and discussion of the policy implications of challenging them encouraged.

There is no doubt, for example, that problematic parental drug dependence places children at increased risk of neglect and abuse.[29] But for many it is difficult to accept that not all people who use drugs are bad parents, or that drug use and child neglect is not a straightforward equation. "Ants Facing an Elephant," by Kathleen Kenny and Amy Druker, considers an aspect of this debate, focusing on women who have lost custody of their children to child protection services.

Many see the massive, violent, and destructive drug trade as simply organized crime run by evildoers. Far more troubling is the reality that it is a function of prohibition itself, though this is accepted as fact at high levels.[30] In turn, people involved in the production of illicit crops are frequently equated with drug traffickers, seen as greedy, willful criminals. "In the Shadows of the Insurgency in Afghanistan" is a case study on the scale of poverty in which opium poppy farmers live, while "Real Life on the Frontlines of Colombia's Drug War," based on interviews with children and young people in Colombia, tells a similar story in relation to coca production.

The idea of drug users and dealers as some form of "other" is common.[31] It is easier to accept the shadowy "drug pusher" lurking on the school playground[32] than the reality that most young people experience drug use for the first time via their siblings, sexual partners, or peers.[33] But this is the reality for many and it questions who the "enemy" is in this "war." On this issue, see "Under Cover of Privilege" on college drug dealing by A. Rafik Mohamed and Erik Fritsvold, set against "Getting the Message," Deborah Peterson Small's study of messages about the impacts of the drug war on black and Latino communities told through hip-hop. Through these chapters we get an insight into those young people who experience the drug war, and those for whom it is of no concern.

"Dancing with Despair," "Mothers and Children of the Drug War," and "Between Diego and Mario," meanwhile, focus on the effects of law enforcement and incarceration on families in the United States, Ecuador, and Indonesia. In these personal stories, the users, dealers, mules and prisoners are by no means "other." They are parents, siblings and children.

Structure of the Book

With the exception of one chapter,[34] *Children of the Drug War* consists entirely of original pieces. The chapters are diverse in many ways: geographic origin, discipline, and, of course, subject matter. Each author has his or her own writing style. Some pieces are academic, others are interview-based; still others are more narrative or journalistic. Most of the chapters were included following a call for papers in late 2009. Others were invited, and three are based on interviews specifically commissioned for the book.[35]

There are four thematic sections: production and trade; race, class, and law enforcement; families and drug policy; and children, drug use, and dependence. Many chapters could sit comfortably in a different section; some could straddle three or even all four. They were, however, the best way to group an array of very different contributions in a manner that covered drug control from production to use, and that helped to highlight important policy considerations. The themes are interrelated and should be read as such, bearing in mind the three broad, crosscutting questions raised in this introduction.

Part 1, *Frontlines: Production and Trade*, focuses on production and eradication, trade and interdiction, and the debate around alternative frameworks of legal regulation of drugs. These are well-worn topics, but the chapters presented here offer new insights, focusing entirely on children and young people and the specific risks and harms they face.

The chapters in Part 2, *Targets: Race, Class, and Law Enforcement*, consider the situation of children and young people who are the targets of drug law enforcement, and those who, by virtue of pedigree, race, or economic status, are not. They paint a picture of soft-target law enforcement, disenfranchisement of new generations, and the privilege of race and class in escaping the drug war.

Part 3, *Home Front: Families and Drug Policy*, is central to the drug policy discussion relating to children. The family, after all, is crucial to the child's development and well-being. The chapters in this section consider the effects of polices on families, rather than drug use or the drug trade per se. A main focus is incarceration, while policies relating to child custody, policing, and drug dependence are also touched upon.

The final section, Part 4, *Justification: Children, Drug Use, and Dependence*, contains a collection of essays asking what we know and what we do not know about drug use among young people, and what the answers to these questions mean for policy responses. The chapters tackle three broad areas: recreational use, which makes up the majority of drug use among young people but is largely neglected in policy responses; problematic drug use around which most demand reduction policies and harm reduction interventions are framed; and finally, access to opiates for palliative care, which has suffered due to a range of factors including overly strict narcotics laws and a disproportionate focus on addiction.

Each part begins with a more detailed introduction to present its chapters and the issues raised. It is not intended, however, nor is it possible, to cover all aspects of this enormous debate. The book is clearly not comprehensive. Readers are encouraged to bear in mind not just the problems of the present, but what these questions mean for the policies of the future. As such, each part concludes with questions for further study and debate.

The diversity of the subject matter covered in this book is intentional. Very often issues relating to drugs are considered in isolation. While it is easy to see the connections between drug use, sale, transit and production as a supply chain, the harms associated with these various stages and the policies aimed at dealing with them are not so often connected. HIV related to injecting drug use, for example, is rarely connected to production issues, while drug related violence in Mexico or Brazil is not seen to be related to public health concerns such as the lack of access to controlled medicines for palliative care. But these harms are interconnected. And only when they are seen in this way is the scale of the drug war visible. These connections are not drawn explicitly below, however. It is for the reader to identify them and draw his or her own conclusions.

Endnotes

1. Andi Mattalatta, Indonesian Law and Human Rights minister on the adoption of the country's much criticized narcotics law of 2009. "Indonesia's Parliament Enacts Drugs Law," *Xinhua*, September 14, 2009. One of the many provisions of concern to human rights groups included potential imprisonment of parents for six months for not reporting their children's drug use to the authorities. See *Jakarta Post*, "Drug Addicts Branded as Criminals Under New Law," September 15, 2009.
2. The Single Convention codified numerous international drug conventions dating back to 1912, and extended their scope. Not all of them, however, adopted the approach we see today. The 1931 Opium Convention, for example, created a model of state-controlled supply.
3. "War on drugs" is not used officially by many governments and was recently abandoned by the Obama administration. It is used here to collectively describe the international punitive and prohibitionist approach to drug control, rooted in law enforcement and supply reduction, which has dominated international and national policy for many decades.
4. See, for example, K. Malinowska-Sempruch and Sarah Gallagher, eds., *War on Drugs, HIV/AIDS and Human Rights* (New York and Amsterdam: International Debate Education Association, 2004).
5. For an overview of media coverage of the "decriminalization" debate in the United Kingdom in August 2010, see http://transform-drugs.blogspot.com/2010/08/follow-up-prof-ian-gilmore-for-de.html.
6. UN General Assembly, *Report of the Special Rapporteur on the Right of Everyone to the Enjoyment of the Highest Attainable Standard of Physical and Mental Health*, UN Doc. No. A/65/255, August 6, 2010.
7. See www.viennadeclaration.com.
8. See www.countthecosts.org.
9. See UN General Assembly, *Report of the Special Rapporteur*, para. 71 and 72. See also D. Barrett and M. Nowak, "The United Nations and Drug Policy: Towards a Human Rights-Based Approach," in *The Diversity Of International Law: Essays in Honour of Professor Kalliopi K. Koufa*, ed., Aristotle Constantinides and Nikos Zaikos, 449–77 (Hague: Brill/Martinus Nijhoff, 2009), 468, 469.
10. See the annual *World Drug Report* produced by the UN Office on Drugs and Crime for examples of such figures. In 2009, the report improved on previous years, which contained data weaknesses. It includes a section dedicated to young people. The *World Drug Report*'s summaries of drug-trafficking routes are very useful—though different in character from the indicators referred to here. The annual world drug report is available at www.unodc.org/unodc/en/data-and-analysis/WDR.html?ref=menuside/.
11. For example, those relating to drug use among young people. Early drug use can lead to later negative social and health outcomes, while young people's drug use is also a useful gauge of drug trends. See UN Office on Drugs and Crime, *World Drug Report 2009*, 23.
12. See further in Barrett and Nowak, "The United Nations and Drug Policy"; and D. Barrett, "Security, Development and Human Rights: Legal, Policy and Normative Challenges for the International Drug Control System," *International Journal of Drug Policy* 21 (2010): 140–44.

13. See chapters 1 on Colombia, 3 on Afghanistan, 5 on the United States, 7 on Brazil, and 9 on Ecuador. Materialism, however, and the desire of wealth and status cannot be discounted. See chapter 6 on college drug dealing.
14 See for example chapters 1, 3, and 7.
15. See, for example, B. Alexander, *The Globalisation of Addiction: A Study in Poverty of the Spirit* (Oxford: Oxford University Press, 2008); R. Wilkinson and M. Marmot, *The Social Determinants of Health: The Solid Facts* (Geneva: World Health Organization, 2003), 24–26; T. Rhodes, "Risk Environments and Drug Harms: A Social Science for Harm Reduction Approach," *International Journal of Drug Policy* 20, no. 3 (2009): 196.
16. The 2009 Political Declaration on drug control adopted by the UN Commission on Narcotic Drugs and approved by the General Assembly makes some small progress in this regard due to the efforts of a number of states seeking better-informed and more rights-based policies. See, for example, sections D.3 and D.4 on alternative development. "Political Declaration and Plan of Action on International Cooperation Towards an Integrated and Balanced Strategy to Counter the World Drug Problem," adopted at the High Level Segment of the UN Commission on Narcotic Drugs, March 11–12, 2009.
17. See, for example, chapter 2 on drug-related violence in Mexico, as well as chapter 1 on Colombia and chapter 7 on Brazil.
18. Among these, strengthening foreign positions and scoring easy political points are frequently cited. Indeed, many politicians around the world have run on a "tough on drugs" platform. Recently, the Mauritian prime minister, for example, ran for reelection promising to reinstate the death penalty for drug trafficking. He was duly reelected.
19. "Preamble. Political Declaration and Plan of Action."
20. See the preambles to the 1961 Single Convention on Narcotic Drugs and the 1988 Convention Against the Illicit Traffic in Narcotic Drugs and Psychotropic Substances. The 1961 Convention, for example, recognizes that "addiction to narcotic drugs constitutes a serious evil for the individual and is fraught with social and economic danger to mankind." Single Convention on Narcotic Drugs, 1961, New York, March 30, 1961, United Nations, *Treaty Series*, vol. 520, p. 151 and vol. 557 (corrigendum on vol. 520), p. 280; Convention Against Psychotropic Substances, February 21, 1971, United Nations, *Treaty Series*, vol. 1019, p. 175; Convention Against the Illicit Traffic in Narcotic Drugs and Psychotropic Substances, December 2·. 1988, United Nations, *Treaty Series*, vol. 1582, p. 95.
21. See International Harm Reduction Association, *What Is Harm Reduction?* 2010, www.ihra.net/what-is-harm-reduction/.
22. See, for example, the analysis of the "normalization" debate in F. Measham and M. Shiner, "The Legacy of 'Normalisation': The Role of Classical and Contemporary Criminological Theory in Understanding Young People's Drug Use," *International Journal of Drug Policy* 20, no. 6: 502–8.
23. European Monitoring Centre on Drug and Drug Addiction, "Drug Use Amongst Vulnerable Young People: Prevention Strategies Need to Target Young People Most at Risk," 2003, www.emcdda.europa.eu/publications/drugs-in-focus/vulnerable-young/. See also chapter 12 by Catherine Cook and Adam Fletcher.
24. European Monitoring Centre on Drug and Drug Addiction, *Drug Use Amongst Vulnerable Young People.* See also chapter 14 on random school drug testing.
25. "There is an openness among youth to information, if it is factual and does not contrast too sharply with their personal experience of drugs. Scare tactics used in some information material do not serve the purpose for which they are intended, but rather significantly reduce the trust that youth may have in the advice of adults and in some case even encourage risky behaviours." UN Commission on Narcotic Drugs, *Youth and Drugs: A Global Overview*, Report of the Secretariat, UN Doc. No. E/CN.7/1999/8, para. 65(f).
26. See chapter 13 by Michael Shiner.

27. Pew Research Centre, *Mexicans Continue Support for Drug War*, August 12, 2010, http://pewglobal.org/2010/08/12/mexicans-continue-support-for-drug-war/.
28. Human Rights Watch, "Not Enough Graves: The War on Drugs, HIV/AIDS, and Violations of Human Rights," vol. 16, no. 8(C) (June 2004), www.hrw.org/en/reports/2004/07/07/not-enough-graves/.
29. For more on this, see the introduction to Part 4.
30. See UN Office on Drugs and Crime, *Making Drug Control Fit for Purpose: Building on the UNGASS Decade*, UN Doc. No. E/CN.7/2008/CRP.17, March 7, 2008.
31. On this, see the speech of former executive director of the International AIDS Society, Craig McClure, "Harm Reduction 2009: Harm Reduction and Human Rights," International Human Rights Association's Twentieth International Harm Reduction Conference, Bangkok, April 2009.
32. The 1988 Convention Against the Illicit Traffic in Narcotic Drugs and Psychotropic Substances includes in its list of "particularly serious crimes" the sale of drugs in, or in the immediate vicinity of, schools. Article 3(5)(g).
33. See chapter 15 on the life stories of eight heroin users in Serbia.
34. Chapter 6 is based on a book, and was invited for this collection. A. Rafik Mohamed and Erik Fritsvold, *Dorm Room Dealers: Drugs and the Privileges of Race and Class* (Boulder, CO: Lynne Rienner, 2009).
35 Chapters 1, 3, and 10.

Part I:
Frontlines: Production and Trade

Historically, the main focus of international drug control efforts has been the reduction of supply, and therefore the availability, of drugs on the streets in consumer countries. Supply reduction, as it is known, has taken the form of counternarcotics law enforcement/interdiction as well as forced crop eradication programs, particularly in Latin America, the so-called Golden Triangle in East Asia, and the Golden Crescent in the Middle East. This has long been criticized as developed nations imposing their problems on poorer developing countries. It is difficult to argue with this reasoning given the disproportionate expenditure on supply reduction in producer nations over treatment and harm reduction in those where demand drives the drug trade.[1]

Between all of the regions of production there is shared experience. First, forced crop eradication has not worked. While cultivation and production fluctuate for various reasons,[2] cocaine and heroin are as available on the streets as ever before. The situation has been succinctly described by the high-level Latin American Commission on Drugs and Democracy in its 2009 official statement: "We are farther than ever from the announced goal of eradicating drugs."[3]

Second, forced crop eradication has had severe negative consequences, including for children, contributing to human displacement, violence, food insecurity, and further poverty.[4] School enrollment and child health have also been affected.[5] In Afghanistan, it is accepted at high levels that forced eradication has helped the Taliban to recruit. Richard Holbrook, who was the U.S. Special Envoy to the country, called it "the least effective program ever."[6]

Third, programs to replace such crops with licit alternatives must be properly sequenced (i.e., alternatives in place before illicit crops are removed) to avoid plunging poor farming families further into poverty;[7] basic infrastructure must be developed to assist in production and sale (e.g., roads to transport crops to market, irrigation, and assistance to compete with bigger, better resources companies);[8] "monocropping of plants such as rubber trees and African palm must be avoided; and, to date, such programs, overall, have had limited effect on drug markets. "Alternative development" as such programs are known, is not dealt with in detail here, though chapters 1 and 3 are certainly relevant.[9] It is an important area, however, especially given the strictures of the international legal system for drug control, which do not permit the cultivation of coca, opium poppy, and marijuana outside of narrowly defined exceptions.[10] There are various reports available for further reading.[11]

Transit routes, the avenues by which illicit substances reach the streets in consumer countries, are often areas of extreme violence and corruption, violence that surrounds and often directly involves children.[12] As with forced eradication, however, interdiction measures have not worked. Instead, as transit routes are interrupted by law enforcement, they move, spreading violence, corruption, increased drug use, and drug-related harms, to new countries and territories.[13] West Africa is the most recent victim of this, with Guinea Bissau being one of the countries most affected.[14] Meanwhile, law enforcement in many countries has become ever more draconian and violent, and in some cases militarized, with the army fighting the drug "war."[15]

Part 1 deals with three countries that today represent the frontlines and public face of the war on drugs—Colombia and Afghanistan in relation to production, and Mexico as the most infamous transit country in the world.[16]

Colombia and Afghanistan are the primary sources of global cocaine and heroin supply, respectively, being by far the areas of the greatest production of coca and opium poppy. Both have been the subject of extensive forced eradication campaigns. They are also both mired in conflict, which, while not caused by the drug trade, in both countries is now intertwined with it. In Colombia the drug trade is a key source of funding for illegal armed groups, while in Afghanistan the Taliban benefits significantly from the opium trade.[17] Meanwhile, growers of illicit crops in both countries have two main things in common—poverty and vulnerability to violence and extortion. It is this environment in which the children of these families grow up.

Jess Hunter-Bowman's chapter, "Real Life on the Frontlines of Colombia's Drug War," was commissioned for this book. Along with colleagues from Witness for Peace, Hunter-Bowman interviewed three young people who have all been affected in different ways by the drug trade and drug-fueled conflict. Colombia is currently the only country in the world in which aerial fumigation with chemicals is used as a means to eradicate illicit crops. Javier's interview explains the consequences of fumigation for poor families and the desire of those families to leave the trade in coca, which has brought them only suffering. His outlook is bleak. "I don't think they will ever stop fumigating," he says. The remaining two interviews highlight the scale of drug-related violence in the country, and the involvement of traffickers, police, military, and, indeed, children in that violence.

"Children: The Forgotten Victims in Mexico's Drug War" focuses on the primary transit route for drugs coming from Latin America and destined for the U.S. market. Barely a day goes by without reports of horrific carnage in Mexico since President Felipe Calderón initiated the current war on drugs in the country, deploying tens of thousands of troops onto the streets. Aram Barra and Daniel Joloy work in Mexico focusing on drug policy and human rights and their chapter looks at killings of children and parents in the midst of the drug war; attacks on schools and rehabilitation centers, which have increased since the militarization of the campaign; and the psychological damage of conflict to children based on studies in other conflict zones. According to the authors, next to this collateral damage, the small gains in seizures and arrests are rendered "hollow and irrelevant."

In the context of Afghanistan, Atal Ahmadzai and Christopher Kuonqui, in another piece commissioned for this book, have conducted interviews in Helmand, Kandahar, and Kabul on the practice of child bartering (selling) to pay opium debts when poppy crops fail through disease, natural shocks, or are eradicated in counternarcotics operations. It is an issue not just of drug control, of course, but of culture, tribalism, conflict, and poverty. The result, however, is a fundamental challenge to those who may equate farmers with traffickers, or see them as greedy opportunists, and the often simplistic views of crop eradication as a viable strategy. As noted by one social activist in the country "Opium farmers are the most vulnerable people in the opium cycle, and the uncoordinated war against opium further strengthens their social and economic vulnerabilities." The chapter is an illustration of the depths of poverty in which farming communities live, and the cultural complexities involved in opium production in Afghanistan. "In the Shadows of the Insurgency in Afghanistan: Child Bartering, Opium Debt, and the War on Drugs" shows how children, and especially girls, bear the brunt of Afghanistan's opium culture and counternarcotics strategies.

Finally, the section turns away from specific countries to the legal and policy framework for production and trade itself. Steve Rolles's chapter, "After the War on Drugs: How Legal Regulation of Production and Trade Would Better Protect Children," asks whether a legally regulated model of production and trade, taken out of the hands of criminals and cartels, would better "protect" children from drugs—children who use them, children involved in transporting them, and children who farm them. Set against the harms of the drug war, Rolles's arguments are compelling in their lucidity and underlying morality.

Endnotes

1. Some, however, also see this as a means to pursue other political objectives, such as strengthening foreign strategic positions. Based on these goals, the war on drugs can be seen as a resounding success. The history of the U.S. drug war in Latin America is perhaps the clearest example of this, justifying over many decades U.S. intervention in various sovereign states.
2. In 2009, for example, the Afghan opium poppy crop was badly hit by a blight that greatly affected cultivation.
3. *Drugs and Democracy: Towards a Paradigm Shift*, Statement by the Latin American Commission on Drugs and Democracy, 2009, www.drogasedemocracia. org/Arquivos/declaracao_ingles_site.pdf.
4. International Harm Reduction Association, Human Rights Watch, Open Society Institute, and Canadian HIV/AIDS Legal Network, *Human Rights and Drug Policy Briefing No. 6,* "Crop Eradication," 2010, www.ihra.net/files/2010/11/01/ IHRA_BriefingNew_6.pdf.
5. For example, research conducted in 2002 and 2003 by the UN Office on Drugs and Crime and published in 2005 in the Kokang Special Region 1 in Myanmar (Burma) found that eradication led to a 50 percent drop in school enrolment. Independent Evaluation Unit of the UN Office on Drugs and Crime, *Thematic Evaluation of UNODC's Alternative Development Initiatives*, November 2005, 23–24. In its 2006 report on Colombia, the UN Committee on the Rights of the Child noted it was "concerned about environmental health problems arising from the usage of the substance glyphosate in aerial fumigation campaigns against coca plantations (which form part of Plan Colombia), as these affect the health of vulnerable groups, including children." UN Committee on the Rights of the Child, *Concluding Observations: Colombia*, June 8, 2006, UN Doc. No. CRC/C/ COL/CO/3, para. 72. These concerns were echoed by the UN Special Rapporteur on the Rights to Health in 2007 (P. Hunt, "Oral Remarks to the Press," Friday, September 21, 2007, Bogota, Colombia) and UN Committee on Economic Social and Cultural Rights in 2010 (*Concluding Observations: Colombia*, UN Doc. No. E/C.12/COL/CO/5, May 21, 2010, para. 28).
6. *Christian Science Monitor*, "US Changes Course on Afghan Opium," June 28, 2009.
7. In Burma and Laos, for example, "opium bans" were enforced before alternative sustainable livelihoods were in place, thereby leaving farmers with no source of income. With the additional problem of insufficient development assistance and the insistence on rubber as an alternative crop (which takes years to develop), the policy led to a humanitarian crisis requiring food aid. See Transnational Institute, *Withdrawal Symptoms: Changes in the Southeast Asian Drugs Market*, August 2008, www.tni.org/briefing/withdrawal-symptoms-briefing/.

8. As one nongovernmental organization expert put it, "We are expecting them to produce tons of fruit and vegetables to transport on trucks they do not have, on roads that literally do not exist, to sell in globalized markets against which they cannot compete." Sanho Tree, Institute for Policy Studies, presentation at Bogota University, September 2009.
9. See, for example, Javier's interview in chapter 1, in which he describes farmers' desire for alternative livelihoods in Colombia.
10. Licenses can be obtained to grow opium poppy for medical and scientific purposes (e.g., production of morphine).
11. See, for example, UN Office on Drugs and Crime, *Alternative Development: A Global Thematic Evaluation, Final Synthesis Report* (Vienna, 2005); and Washington Office on Latin America, *Development First: A More Humane and Promising Approach to Reducing Cultivation of Crops for Illicit Markets*, March 2010.
12. On this, see also chapter 7, "Young Soldiers in Brazil's Drug War," by Michelle Gueraldi.
13. Drug-trafficking routes have been shown to have an effect on HIV transmission due to unsafe injecting drug use. See C. Beyrer et al., "Overland Heroin Trafficking Routes and HIV-1 Spread in South and South-East Asia," *AIDS* 14, no. 1 (January 7, 2000): 75–83.
14. See T. McConnell, "The West Africa Connection: How Drug Cartels Found New Routes," *Sunday Times* (UK), February 28, 2009; UN Office on Drugs and Crime, *Cocaine Trafficking in Western Africa: Situation Report*, October 2007; *Time Magazine*, "Guinea-Bissau: The World's First Narco-State," photo essay available at www.time.com/time/photogallery/0,29307,1933291,00.html; UN Office on Drugs and Crime, *The Globalisation of Crime: A Transnational Threat Assessment* (2010), 233–37; Emmanuelle Bernard, "Guinea Bissau: Drug Boom, Lost Hope," *Open Democracy*, October 23, 2008.
15. See chapter 2 on Mexico and chapter 7 on Brazil. See also Human Rights Watch, *Not Enough Graves: War on Drugs, HIV and Violations of Human Rights in Thailand*, 2004, www.hrw.org/en/reports/2004/07/07/not-enough-graves/; P. Gallahue, "Targeted Killing of Drug Lords: Traffickers as Members of Armed Opposition Groups and/or Direct Participants in Hostilities," *International Journal on Human Rights and Drug Policy*, vol. 1 (2010), www.humanrightsanddrugs.org/?p=977/.
16. The Golden Triangle is not covered here, but it is an important region for understanding the global drug trade. For a recent report on this region see Transnational Institute, *Withdrawal Symptoms in the Golden Triangle: A Drugs Market in Disarray*, January 2009, www.tni.org/report/withdrawal-symptoms-golden-triangle-4/.
17. See V. Felbab-Brown, *Shooting Up: Counterinsurgency and the War on Drugs* (Washington, DC: Brookings Institution Press, 2010).

1. Real Life on the Frontlines of Colombia's Drug War

by Jess Hunter-Bowman

At least one fact about Colombia is well known; Colombia exports drugs. Most people know two things and two things only about this South American country; it produces coffee and cocaine. Colombia's love affair with drugs began with marijuana production in the 1970s. In the early 1980s, the Medellin and Cali cartels expanded into cocaine production and trafficking. These two cartels, the Medellin cartel run by Pablo Escobar and the Cali cartel run by the Rodríguez Orejuela brothers, made their fortunes processing coca paste flown from the coca fields of Peru and Bolivia into cocaine, which was exported to markets in the United States and Europe.[1]

Due to multiple factors, coca production shifted from Peru into Colombia during the 1990s, making it the world's leading coca as well as cocaine producer. While a minor player globally, Colombia is also a significant heroin producer. The country's principal drug market is the United States, with a minority share making its way to Europe via West Africa. According to the U.S. Drug Enforcement Administration (DEA), almost 90 percent of the cocaine and 60 percent of the heroin seized in the United States originates in Colombia.[2]

At the same time, Colombia is home to a raging civil war, including the oldest and largest guerrilla group in the Western Hemisphere, the Revolutionary Armed Forces of Colombia (FARC). The multifaceted war pits two leftist guerrilla groups[3] against the Colombian Armed Forces who for more than two decades have worked with paramilitary groups to fight back the insurgency.[4] Many assert that Colombia's war is simply a drug war, suggesting guerrillas and paramilitaries are purely drug traffickers. While both groups are heavily involved in the drug trade, trafficking some drugs themselves and taxing all aspects of the trade, the single goal of the guerrillas is to overthrow the Colombian democracy to install a Marxist government. Solutions to Colombia's stubborn drug production and trafficking problems and its deadly civil war are connected, but distinct.

For four decades, the United States has spent billions of dollars in a failed attempt to disrupt the Andean cocaine trade. At the beginning of the twenty-first century, the United States inserted itself in a new way into fighting Colombia's drug trade and propping up the country's ragtag Armed Forces. Since 2000, the United States has spent $7.3 billion[5] on a fumigation program targeting coca production, spraying 1.2 million hectares;[6] on training and assistance to the Colombian military for counternarcotics and counterinsurgency activities; and on a secondary socioeconomic assistance program.

This assistance has brought with it modest security gains, reducing conflict-related attacks and deaths back to 1990s levels from their peaks in the early years of the twenty-first century. Nevertheless, this drug-fueled conflict killed 32,436 people between 1998 and 2008[7] and displaced an additional 3.4 million. The results are even worse on the counternarcotics front. Policymakers proclaimed that a full frontal assault on coca production through aerial fumigation would reduce production by 50 percent by 2005. Instead Colombian coca production, which appeared to be on the decline as production shifted back to Peru, actually increased by 17 percent over the ten-year period beginning in 1998.[8]

But the human cost of the drug trade and the drug war cannot be accurately measured by statistics. What follows are the stories of three children of the drug war—Colombian children whose lives have been torn apart by drug trafficking, armed groups funded by the drug trade, and punitive counternarcotics policies. These stories, although dramatic, are not unusual in Colombia. They are the untold stories of millions of innocent victims of the drug wars.

Javier

Javier[9] was born and raised in Guaviare province in Colombia's Amazon basin. His was one of an estimated 59,000 households living off of small-scale coca production[10] before his family was displaced and broken apart by the counterdrug aerial spray program. By and large, these families turned to coca production not to get rich, but rather to cross the line from extreme poverty into poverty. The United Nations estimates the annual gross income for a family farming coca in 2009 was US$8,710.[11] As eleven-year-old Javier eloquently explains, coca production is a last resort rather than a dream for Colombian farmers. They know coca production is a magnet for violence associated with Colombia's war as armed groups fight to tax drug production, as well as indiscriminate aerial fumigation, which is purported to target coca fields but in practice destroys any and all crops in the area. Javier offers insights that have escaped many a counternarcotics policymaker; the vast majority of Colombia's coca farmers would jump at a way out, they are just looking for a sustainable alternative.

My name is Javier. I am eleven years old and from a small farming community in Guaviare province. My family farmed coca and food crops. We had a small farm and didn't make much money off of the coca, but the money we made, we used to buy food for the house, seeds for food crops, and more land to raise a cow. The farmers around us did the same. If they had any money, it was because they had some coca. Nothing else makes money.

Most people don't want to grow coca, but they feel like they have no other option. If they were given another option, most would leave coca behind. Where we're from, the people don't get any help. There are no [assistance] programs to support them. People even die of starvation out there. And that's why they grow coca. It's the only way to earn a living. People get scared about the violence and the fumigation that comes with the coca, but they do it because it's the only way to make money.

The planes often sprayed our community. People would get very sad when they saw the fumigation planes. You see the planes coming—four or five of them—from far away with a black cloud of spray behind them. They say they are trying to kill the coca, but they kill everything. I wish the people flying those fumigation planes would realize all the damage they do. I wish they'd at least look at where they're going to spray, rather than just spraying anywhere and everywhere. The fumigation planes sprayed our coca and food crops. All of our crops died. Sometimes even farm animals died as well. After the fumigation, we'd go days without eating. Once the fumigation spray hit my little brother and me. We were outside and didn't make it into the house before the planes flew by. I got sick and had to be taken to the hospital. I got a terrible rash that itched a lot and burned in the sun. The doctor told us the chemical spray was toxic and was very dangerous. I was sick for a long time and my brother was sick even longer.

We were fumigated five times. I don't think they will ever stop fumigating. They'll keep fumigating because there's still coca. They say they won't stop fumigating until all the coca is dead.

CHILDREN OF THE DRUG WAR

Two years ago, after the last round of fumigation, we couldn't take it anymore and we were forced to flee. The farm was abandoned. My parents separated and they put me into an orphanage run by a Catholic priest. I miss my family terribly. When I said goodbye to my mom and dad, I couldn't stop crying.

I really want to go back to our farm, but I am scared because of all of the terrible things that happen there; the fumigation and the armed groups . . . so much violence. The coca brought not only the fumigation planes, but also the war. The guerrillas were around a lot and sometimes even killed people, saying, "They're working with the army." People were also killed by the military. Sometimes people are killed in the fighting between the armed groups.

At first I wasn't so scared by all of this, but now I am terrified by what happens out there. I know if I go back there, I'll see lots of people get killed. I saw two people killed right in front of me; Rebecca and her brother. They lived close by us. The guerrillas had been looking for Rebecca and caught her while she was with her brother. I was standing close by and saw the whole thing. They made them get down on their knees. They shot them many times in the head with machine guns, picked up their dead bodies, put them in chairs, put bags over their heads, and left.

The guerrillas also recruited child soldiers. They would try to seduce us by showing us their machine guns, teaching us how to fire them and to use grenades. My mom told me not to listen to them, that they just wanted to take me. One day I was down by the river with a group of kids and the guerrillas came by, grabbed one kid, and took him off to join them. He screamed, "I don't want to go. I don't want to go." I felt terrible watching him being taken to join the guerrillas by force. I was scared; scared that one day they may come for me, come and kill my mom or take my brother, take me and make me kill someone.

When I was five, my uncle was killed by the paramilitaries. My mom told me that he helped our family and helped pay for me to go to school when I was little. But one day he went to town to buy some chemicals for coca production and paramilitaries pulled up on a motorcycle. They stopped him, tied him up, and tortured him. They asked him questions and if he didn't know the answer, they cut off one of his fingers. They cut off finger after finger until there were none left. While he was still alive, they cut him into pieces with a chainsaw. I remember his funeral. People were crying so much, screaming. I still don't know why they killed him. I wish this violence would end, that the hatred would end.

When I grow up, I want to be a lawyer. But if I end up farming, I think I'll have to farm coca. I know that if I was offered support, a government program that allowed me to farm and survive, I wouldn't go back to coca. There would be no reason to take the risk. But if things remain the same and there is no support, I think I'd have to grow coca. Of course, I'd be scared of the fumigations and all the violence coca production brings with it. I wish we could stop growing coca because it has brought the war to us. I know we can make it, but we'll never make it with coca. I'd like to speak to the president of Colombia; to tell him that he should help farmers like us. If he'd help us, send programs here, people would stop growing coca. And if there was less coca, there'd be less violence.

I'd like to ask people in other parts of the world to help us. People are suffering. People are being killed. People are starving. Please help the people of my community and the other communities all over Colombia.

Alfredo

Alfredo's[12] family knew their uncle's involvement in the drug trade would come back to haunt them, but they never could have imagined the extent to which that would be true. Shady deals put paramilitaries after him and by the time Alfredo was seventeen, paramilitaries had killed his two uncles and his father. A significant and illustrative aspect of Alfredo's story is the role of the Colombian security forces, recipients of billions of dollars in counternarcotics security assistance from the international community, principally the United States. The Colombian security forces have the worst human rights record in the Western Hemisphere and long-standing ties to paramilitary groups (both the United Self-Defense Forces of Colombia and post-demobilization, "next-generation" groups).[13] Alfredo recounts multiple instances in which the Colombian National Police, the principal entity responsible for counternarcotics activities in Colombia, facilitated or turned a blind eye to paramilitary activities.

CHILDREN OF THE DRUG WAR

My family's tragedy started in 2002, when I was seventeen. My uncle was involved in the drug trade. The rest of my family didn't have anything to do with my uncle's business and we told him that he was going to get us into trouble. When he was about twenty years old, barely starting in the trade, he got into trouble. Paramilitaries were after him and he went into hiding. They went to his house looking for him and tied up my grandmother and interrogated her. I don't know what he did, but they looked for him for a long time, many years.

One night at 2 a.m., paramilitaries opened the door and they killed him. They shot him three times and killed him. They also killed the man he worked for, on Christmas Eve. The coroner's report showed that they pulled forty bullets out of his body. That's how the story started, when my uncle, who was the youngest of his three brothers, was killed.

And so my dad and his brother inherited these problems. The paramilitaries who killed my uncle thought his brothers might go to the police or seek revenge. Paramilitaries sometimes showed up at my dad's office to tell him they needed to "fix the problem." They threatened to kill him and his family. He worried about his kids. At times he would cry just thinking about these threats. He told us that if he was ever murdered, we'd know paramilitaries were responsible.

One day my brother and I were coming home from school and there were two men with guns at the house looking for my dad. I asked them why they were looking for him and they said, "So we can take a look at some papers that he's working on." My older brother told my dad that there were some strange guys at the house looking for him. My dad went to the door and they shot him fifteen times right in front of me. The only thing I could do was watch and wait as they pumped bullets into him. I was powerless. The police came and asked what happened. Neighbors pointed out the guys that murdered my dad and said, "Run! You can still catch them! There they go!" But the police just stood around; they themselves were mixed up in this. I grabbed my dad and tried to pick him up, but the police stopped me. They said that he was dead and we had to wait for the coroner's office to deal with the body. But it was so horrible; people were looking at him so I carried him into the house.

And then they killed my last uncle. He was a mechanic and hardly left the house because he knew the paramilitaries were going to kill him. We begged him to leave the city, but he said he didn't want to. One way or the other, he said, they were going to kill him. One morning, as he was feeding breakfast to my eighty-year-old grandfather, they came and they killed him. They left us a message: if any of us talked about these killings, reported them to the police, or sought revenge, we would be killed, just as my dad and uncles were killed.

This has devastated our family. My youngest brother hardly talks anymore. He was about fourteen when my dad was killed. He dropped out of school and locks himself in his room all day. And now my mom works as a street vendor to bring food home for the family. It all makes me sad because you want the best for your family and with this situation, everything is different. Christmas, for example, isn't like it used to be. We now remember Christmas Eve at 5 p.m. as the time they killed my uncle's drug-trafficking partner.

When my mom went to file a report about my father's murder, the lawyer from the Prosecutor General's Office said, "Ma'am, I don't know you but you seem like a nice person. You shouldn't file this report. If you do, they'll kill you and your sons. Let sleeping dogs lie." He was right because the paramilitary leader behind my father's murder later killed a young man and the boy's father filed a police report. The police immediately handed the file over to the paramilitaries with the father's name, address, and what he had reported. The paramilitaries killed him that day. Here we cannot trust the justice system or the security forces. You see paramilitaries driving around on police motorcycles. You see paramilitaries and police playing pool and dominos while drinking beer on street corners. This is normal.

People often ask me, "How do you keep going with everything that has happened to your family? I would have picked up a gun and gone after the people that killed your dad if I were you." And I hope you don't think I am a bad person, but if the guerrillas hadn't lost their ideals, I probably would have joined them. I just want justice so badly and I know that it is never going to come through the justice system. I saw the people kill my dad. I know who they are. Sometimes I pass them on the street. I have this terrible feeling of powerlessness.

But what can I do? There is nothing to do. I have to focus on the rest of my family that is still alive and try to move on.

Yina Paola

Yina Paola[14] was the epitome of a child of the drug war. Now twenty-three, she is also a sign of hope. Yina was born into an opium poppy farming family that treated her more as an employee than a child. At eleven she joined the FARC to escape her family and spent the next three years on the frontlines of Colombia's war. Years later she demobilized and managed to turn her life around. She began working on children's rights with a nonprofit organization and soon founded a new organization to do the same. Thanks to her efforts, she was sent to New York to speak with UN Secretary-General Ban Ki-moon about the plight of child soldiers across the globe. Closer to home, she is breaking the cycle of violence. She took in her fourteen-year-old sister who was recruited to join the FARC and will soon do the same for her young brother.

I lived with my grandparents and started working on the farm as early as I can remember. I had to get up at 4 a.m. most days to start working. My grandparents had a seven-acre opium poppy farm back then. I worked in the fields, weeding and harvesting the sap. On our farm, the sap was processed into morphine bricks and bought by local drug traffickers. The farm was fumigated a couple of times. The planes would fly by, spraying the poison on the crops. We'd run out and try to harvest before the poppies died. The poison was strong and would kill everything. The work was hard; I was treated poorly, especially because I was a girl. The family was sexist and the boys were seen as more important. That is why my aunt and I decided to escape. The only escape we could imagine was the FARC. I was eleven when I joined the FARC.

The FARC was very active in the area. Guerrillas marched by our farm regularly. I was intrigued by the guerrillas. They were the group in charge and having a gun was a quick way to gain respect. One day, when a group of FARC guerrillas passed by the farm, my aunt and I ran up to them and said we wanted to join them. My grandmother came running after us. She yelled at the guerrillas, told them to let us go because we were children. To join the FARC, you had to be fifteen. So, when the FARC commander asked us how old we were, we lied and said fifteen so they would accept us.

My grandfather showed up at the guerrilla camp many times, demanding we be released. Once he came with our birth certificates. He said, "Look, you've taken these girls by mistake. They are under fifteen." The commander asked us about this. We admitted the lie. He yelled at us for lying, but sent us back to work.

The first couple of months we were in training, but the very first day they gave me a revolver. I was very excited. I was soon put on guard duty for an FARC member, a relative of mine who was being punished. He had been tied up for a week awaiting trial. I had to bring him his breakfast and keep him tied up. He had been a member of the paramilitaries and then joined the FARC. One night he got drunk and hit a civilian. That was a big mistake in the eyes of the FARC back then. You were not allowed to mistreat a civilian. He was soon taken before a guerrilla tribunal and tried. The judge asked all the guerrillas in the company to vote on his sentence. He said, "Raise your hand if you think he should be executed by firing squad." Everyone raised their hands. Without understanding what was going on, I raised mine too. Then the judge said, "Raise your hand if you think he shouldn't be killed." No one raised their hand. After everything was done, I asked a guerrilla fighter, "So, is he going to be tied up for another week?" And he said, "No. He's going to be executed by a firing squad." I couldn't believe it. He explained the guerrilla tribunal process to me and said that votes are counted and in this case everyone voted for him to be executed, even me. And in fact he was executed. That is my worst memory from my time in the FARC; naively voting for this person—this relative of mine—to be executed by a firing squad.

When we finished training, my aunt and I were split up. She was sent to a company of guerrillas up north and I was sent south. I soon got word that she was killed fighting the Colombian Army. That set me off. Rage filled me. I hated the Colombian Army and wanted to kill as many of them as I could. That hatred stayed with me for a long time, even after I left the FARC. I was so angry, I always asked my commander to send me to the frontlines to fight. That was my favorite thing, it was like a passion; being on *the frontlines, fighting the army and paramilitaries. There was a lot of fighting as it was a dangerous area, but I was never afraid. My heart had died and I only thought of getting revenge for my aunt's death. Of course, when they killed one of ours, a friend, that hurt.*

I was twelve when I got married to a platoon commander. He was forty-six years old. There are a lot of rules in the FARC about relationships. If you want to date someone, you go to the company commander and tell him or her that you want to be a couple and you are given permission. But you are not allowed to sleep together. If you decide to get married, the commander marries you and then you can sleep together. So, I got married. If you want to get divorced, the commander will divorce you. The FARC is also very careful to make sure no women get pregnant. They put women on birth control and if a woman gets pregnant, she has to get rid of the child.

As I moved up the FARC ranks, I was sent to work with the FARC's financial manager. There we collected FARC taxes. Everyone paid taxes to the FARC—local farmers, drug traffickers, ranchers, businesses, everyone. All opium poppy farmers paid the FARC a share of the money they made selling their products. Coca farmers would also pay a share. The drug traffickers that purchased the morphine brick or the coca paste also paid the FARC.

The FARC also raised funds through kidnapping for ransom. The first time I ever visited the provincial capital of the province where I grew up was to kidnap a wealthy man from the city. We set up a roadblock and stole a couple of SUVs. A small group of us dressed up as civilians, got in the SUVs with our guns and made our way down into the city at night. We broke into the apartment while our victim was watching TV with his kids. We grabbed him and took him away as his family screamed and cried. We spent the whole night marching up into the mountains with him tied up the whole time. At 9 a.m. we arrived at our destination, 10,000 feet above sea level. It may sound strange, but there was no emotion in this, in stealing someone's life. It was just normal. Kidnapping someone was just that: normal. I didn't feel any pain.

I demobilized from the FARC when I was fifteen. I was on an intelligence mission dressed as a civilian and had to go into a small town to get food. That day a woman saw me walking into town and yelled to me from her house, "What are you doing? Who are you?" I said that I was looking for a store. She said she could tell I wasn't from the town and asked again what I was doing. The FARC told us that if we ever ran into any trouble, we should say we were runaways. So I said that I had run away because my parents beat me. She invited me in and offered me a drink and something to eat. While I was there and without me knowing, she called the police, who picked me up and took me to Child Protective Services because I was a minor.

I wanted to escape, get back to the FARC, but they put me under special watch as they thought I was in danger. My family picked me up and took me home. I thought I'd sneak out of the house when the FARC marched by and rejoin. My family pleaded with me not to go back, but I knew what I wanted. So they kept me holed up in a room and when the FARC was in the area, they'd put someone in the room with me so I couldn't yell to them.

My family finally convinced me to go to Bogota, where I entered the Child Protective Services demobilization program. I was in the program until I was eighteen. Like most of the women in the program, we believed we had two options: rejoin an armed group or move in with a man. I moved in with an ex-FARC combatant I met in the program and was soon pregnant. Our relationship didn't last and I ended up on my own with a young son. Then the FARC started recruiting my fourteen-year-old sister, so I brought her to live with us in Bogota. I was twenty, raising a year-old son and my sister without any support and no real income. It was tough. I made US$290 a month and my monthly rent alone cost US$190. There simply wasn't enough money for food and I hardly ate anything. My son would go a whole day eating only an egg. And I'd get a lunch at work and would bring whatever they gave me home to feed my sister. I didn't even have plates to eat off of. That was the most difficult thing I've ever faced. I will never forget it. And if not for my son, I probably wouldn't have overcome that. I would have probably gone back to the FARC.

But, instead, I started a new life. I joined an organization called Taller de Vida that works on children's rights issues with ex-combatants and in local schools. I realized I wanted to dedicate my life to working on human rights and children's rights, and

I dove right in. We worked with children through art and rap, helping them express their feelings about abuse they'd faced and work through it. And last year, two other ex-combatants and I founded a human rights organization called Red Ali Arte. This organization works with ex-combatants on children's rights and women's issues, displaced people, and local community members. Currently, we are working on a play—written by one of our members, an ex-combatant—that will be performed at a theater festival later this year. Because of my work, I was selected by the Coalition to Stop the Use of Child Soldiers to travel to New York in 2009 to speak with UN Secretary-General Ban Ki-moon about the Red Hand Campaign and the use of child soldiers in Colombia and across the world.

For years after leaving the FARC, I had dreams every night about being back with the guerrillas. Sometimes they were nightmares about a commander taking my son away from me. Sometimes they were just dreams about being a guerrilla again. But I had them every single night. Three years ago, when my son was one year old and I started working with Taller de Vida and then Red Ali Arte, the dreams stopped. That life is behind me now and a new one has begun. Today, I am the only person in my family who has a high school diploma. Today I am twenty-three years old, working on children's rights with Red Ali Arte and continuing my studies.

Endnotes

† Diego Benitez, Candice Camargo, and Amanda Hooker assisted with interviews for this project.
1. Winifred Tate, "Colombia's Role in International Drug Industry," *Foreign Policy in Focus*, November 1, 1999.
2. Bureau of International Narcotics and Law Enforcement Affairs, *International Narcotics Control Strategy Report*, U.S. Department of State, March 2010, 201.
3. Colombia is home to two major guerrilla groups, the FARC and the smaller National Liberation Army (ELN), both founded independently in 1964.
4. The consolidated paramilitary group known as the United Self-Defense Forces of Colombia (AUC) demobilized in recent years, leaving behind thousands of loosely organized "next-generation paramilitaries."
5. Adam Isacson, "Don't Call It a Model: On Plan Colombia's Tenth Anniversary, Claims of 'Success' Don't Stand Up to Scrutiny," Just the Facts, www.justf.org.
6. Bureau of International Narcotics and Law Enforcement Affairs, *International Narcotics Control Strategy Report* 2010, U.S. Department of State, www.state.gov/documents/organization/138548.pdf. For the relevant statistics, see p. 217.

7. Comisión Colombiana de Juristas, *Violaciones de Derechos Humanos y Violencia Sociopolítica en Colombia*, Julio de 1996 a junio de 2008, 13 de marzo 2009, http://witnessforpeace.org/downloads/CCJ%20hr%20info%2096-08.pdf.
8. Bureau of International Narcotics and Law Enforcement Affairs, *International Narcotics Control Strategy Report*. For the figure in 1998 see 2009 report, p. 208, and for the 2008 figure, see 2010 report, p. 212.
9. For security reasons, Javier's name has been changed and other identifying details have been excluded.
10. United Nations Office on Drugs and Crime, *Colombia Coca Cultivation Survey 2009* (June 2010): 56, www.unodc.org/documents/crop-monitoring/Colombia_coca_survey_2008.pdf.
11. Ibid., 57.
12. For security reasons, Alfredo's name has been changed and other identifying details have been excluded.
13. United Nations High Commissioner for Human Rights, *Report of the United Nations High Commissioner for Human Rights on the Situation of Human Rights in Colombia,* March 4, 2010, 13; http://daccess-dds-ny.un.org/doc/UNDOC/GEN/G10/118/19/PDF/G1011819.pdf. The information cited is on p. 13.
14. For security reasons, Yina's last name and other identifying details have been excluded.

2. Children: The Forgotten Victims in Mexico's Drug War

by Aram Barra and Daniel Joloy

Introduction

My government is absolutely determined to continue fighting against criminality without quarter until we put a stop to this common enemy and obtain the Mexico we want.

President Felipe Calderón[1]

We live in a state of war and children are left to drift.

Aurelio Paez,
Orphanage director, Ciudad Juárez[2]

The "war on drugs," in most places, is metaphorical. The term is rarely used by governments and was recently abandoned as a rhetorical device by the United States.[3] In Mexico, however, the war on drugs has a very real dimension. It is "declared" government policy, it is militarized, and it is extremely bloody. Shortly after taking power, President Felipe Calderón ordered a military offensive against the country's drug cartels that eventually involved tens of thousands of troops. Keeping drugs away from Mexico's children has been a central justification.[4]

While the consequent violence in Mexico has been well documented, the specific consequences for children are not so often brought to the fore. Despite President Calderón's justification based on the welfare of children, his decision, combined with a zero-tolerance approach to drug use, has contributed to conditions in which children have been killed, orphaned, and neglected. Since the war on drugs began, there have been increased killings of children and parents with thousands dead and tens of thousands orphaned; increased attacks on drug rehabilitation centers, including massacres of young drug users; and increased attacks on schools resulting in a significant drop in school attendance for fear of violence. We consider these effects of the drug war and the long-term psychological damage experienced by children who are surrounded by conflict and violence. Due to space constraints, we cannot analyze all aspects of Mexico's drug problems and policies. The involvement of children in drug trafficking, for example, is not covered, nor is the incarceration of parents. We focus instead on the military intervention against the drug cartels, the related escalation in violence, and the connected zero-tolerance approach to drug use and dependence.

With this focus, it becomes clear that the harms of the drug war not only exist in the present but also will reverberate through many generations due to the specific harms inflicted on children. Next to them, the small gains against the cartels are rendered meaningless. After four years of poor results in frontally combating drug cartels and adopting zero-tolerance approaches to drugs, rethinking government strategies is now unavoidable.

Military Intervention Against the Drug Cartels

Soon after taking power in 2006, President Felipe Calderón directed the Mexican army to wage a battle against drug cartels that, as he himself said, could not be put off any longer. Military operatives soon extended to several Mexican states such as Chihuahua, Sinaloa, and Baja California, and highways and streets were soon filled with armed men. In a matter of days, more than 30,000 soldiers were deployed in different cities in the country in order to avoid, as Calderón explained (somewhat ironically in hindsight) the risk of "being dominated by crime, insecurity and violence resulting from the activities of criminal groups."[5]

Combined with a program to address corruption within the police force, the strategy was intended to shatter the cartels by carrying out arrests of gang leaders, extraditing them to the United States when possible, and seizing drug shipments. According to a report by the Security Cabinet to reflect the achievements made in three years of the drug war, from December 1, 2006, to April 30, 2009, 66,621 criminal suspects were captured.[6] High-profile criminals were extradited for trial in the United States in far greater numbers than in previous administrations,[7] thousands of metric tons of illicit drugs (mainly cannabis) were seized, and hundreds of millions of dollars were frozen.[8]

Initially, this strategy managed to reduce somewhat the presence and visibility of gangs and cartels in the states where they used to operate, such as Sinaloa, Baja California, and Chihuahua. Nevertheless, the so-called cockroach effect soon became evident and cartels moved to new places.[9] In 2007, the presence of cartels was registered in twenty-one of the thirty-two Mexican states. Today they are in all but one.[10]

As a result, violence also spread to an alarming number of states, cities, and municipalities, and the number of casualties of the war has increased with every day that has passed. Although official figures are uncertain, the National Security Center CISEN estimates that there have been more than 28,000 deaths since the war began in 2006.[11] It is a figure that has alarmed many nationally and internationally. Regrettably, all these deaths have been considered simply as "collateral damage."

Cases where civilians have died because of military operations are becoming more and more frequent as the increase in complaints to the National Commission on Human Rights shows. Queries directed against the military rose more than 900 percent in the first three years of the drug war, increasing from 182 cases in 2006 to 1,791 in 2009 at just the federal level. This does not include queries registered at local commissions of human rights.[12] However, in a recent report of the Defense Ministry in response to a request from Congress, it was claimed that only 565 civilian deaths may be linked to military action, a number that includes those suspected of being linked with drug cartels.[13]

Killings of Children and Parents

The death toll among those under the age of seventeen since the war began amounts to over 900, according to the Network for the Rights of Infancy in Mexico. In the first half of 2010, it is estimated that ninety children have lost their lives to drug-related violence.[14] The same nongovernmental organization reported that homicide rates for children under seventeen years of age have increased, especially in the states of Durango, Baja California, Chihuahua, and Sinaloa. During the past three years, child homicide rates have tripled, increasing from 83 per year to 274 per year. Durango itself saw an increase of more than 450 percent in homicide rates for young people in 2006–8.[15]

Those most affected have been young people between the ages of fifteen and seventeen. For example, in Baja California the homicide rate for this age group increased from 8.33 per 100,000 in 2007 to 24.3 per 100,000 in 2008—an increase of almost 300 percent. In

Chihuahua the rate rose from 12.6 to 45.9 per 100,000, an increase of 364 percent.[16] In Ciudad Juárez—now considered the most violent city in the world—from September 2009 to February 2010, three different massacres took place with at least forty-five young people aged between fifteen and nineteen being killed. It is estimated that 30 percent of the 4,500 homicides committed in Juárez from 2007 to 2008 involved young people under the age of nineteen.

But Ciudad Juárez is not the only city where massacres of young people have occurred. In Durango, an armed group in the municipality of Pueblo Nuevo gunned down ten children and young people between the ages of eight and twenty-one after they had received scholarship awards at an official ceremony.[17] In Tijuana, three students (two boys and a girl) all aged sixteen, died on their way back from school when unknown gunmen attacked them with high-powered weapons.[18] In Torreon, five young people between seventeen and nineteen were found stacked in the back of a pickup truck with the engine running. All of them were gagged, had bullet wounds, and signs of torture. According to some neighbors, shots were heard at around five in the morning, though police and military forces did not arrive until almost two hours later.[19]

The killings have included cases where children have died at military checkpoints, such as that of the Almanza boys, killed by army forces on April 3, 2010, on a highway in the state of Tamaulipas. According to statements made by Cynthia Salazar, mother of the two brothers, the family was on their way to the beach to spend the holidays when they passed through a military checkpoint. They reduced their speed and soldiers allowed them through to continue their journey. However, a few meters down the road, soldiers opened fire, killing Bryan and Martin Almanza, aged five and nine.[20]

This case resulted in a recommendation from the National Commission on Human Rights to the military forces. While the official version given by the military and even by the Ministry of Interior argued that the family was caught in crossfire between the military and drug cartels, the National Commission on Human Rights rejected this and concluded that the van in which the two children and eleven other people were traveling was in fact under direct attack from the military.[21] A couple of months later, authorities accepted this version, but no one has yet been charged or indicted for the alleged crimes nor has a full and credible investigation been conducted.

This was not an isolated case. Since 2006, military checkpoints have been widely used in the drug war. In June 2007, two women and three children, aged two, four, and seven, were shot and killed when they failed to stop at a military checkpoint involved in "the permanent campaign against drug trafficking."[22] More recently, a child of fifteen and his father died after being shot by soldiers in the city of Monterrey. The military argued that the vehicle missed a checkpoint, while other relatives who survived the attack declared they were shot at without having been given any indication to stop.[23]

Violence in Mexico has had myriad implications for society and specifically for child development and well-being.[24] It has, for example, eroded adults' capacities to care for, nurture, and protect children. It is important to note that many of the 28,000 who have been killed since the war on drugs began were parents. While neither Mexico's government nor the various nongovernmental organizations working in this area keep track of the number of children who have lost one or both parents in the war, it is estimated that tens of thousands of children are orphaned directly because of the drug war.[25]

Human rights lawyer and investigator for the Chihuaha local commission for human rights, Gustavo de la Rosa Hickerson, has analyzed these numbers and concluded that, based on data that Mexican men aged eighteen to thirty-five have on average 1.7 children, in Ciudad Juárez alone, the war has left more than 8,500 orphans.[26] Extending this figure to the national level, a total of 50,000 drug war orphans is possible.

The growing toll of children left orphaned because of the war is damaging not only to them but also to the country's social network. Government officials at all the different levels have ignored the problem, and failed to take into account the future ramifications. Education and entry into the labor market, for example, may be more difficult for these children. For some this may be an additional factor pushing them toward the drug trade where employment is all but assured. "There is an opportunity cost from these hundreds of thousands of youths in Mexico who are either orphaned or part of criminal gangs," said Eduardo Buscaglia, an expert on armed conflict and Mexico's drug trade. "These are people who are growing up with high levels of deprivation, in dysfunctional families, with sexual abuse, and these risk factors should be addressed."[27]

Young Drug Users: Zero-Tolerance, Stigma, and Violence

Another goal of the Calderón administration's drug war was to prevent the use of drugs, which the government argued had alarmingly increased in recent years.[28] While this argument was on the right track, the government's zero-tolerance response, involving the criminalization of drug users and limited treatment options, has been deeply flawed. Article 4 of the Mexican Constitution provides for universal access to health services, but this is far from the case for people who use drugs. While this should include universal access to treatment options, including access to methadone and buprenorphine as substitution therapy, public funding of syringe exchange programs, and the availability of naloxone for the treatment of opiate overdose, such services are scarce and hampered by a lack of security, criminal laws, and drug-related stigma.

Some years ago, there was only one publicly funded methadone program clinic in the country, located in Ciudad Juárez, and today only two methadone clinics are functioning in all of Mexico—both located in the northern cities of Tijuana and Ciudad Juárez, where use of injectable drugs is more common and heroin dependence has increased in recent years. According to statistics provided by the Health Ministry in 2008 (National Drug Addiction Survey), there were more than 5,000 heroin users in Juárez—where most drug users are between the ages of twelve and seventeen.[29] Despite this, few efforts are being implemented either by the government or by civil society to help fill the gaps in services.

In addition, the criminalization of drug users by the federal government has acted as a significant barrier to health policies, contributing to public stigmatization, and driving them away from services. The National Drug Addiction Survey also states that only 16 percent of problematic drug users seek treatment.[30] Meanwhile, although drug use among young people is a consistent justification for the offensive against the cartels, addiction rates continue to rise, including among elementary and high school students.[31]

Mexican society, however, sees little need to protect the human rights of drug users and people affected by drug use. Recently, widespread stigma and negative public attitudes toward drug users combined with the drug war have made violence against this particular community a valid political statement. Killings of young drug addicts as direct targets started in Ciudad Juárez, but disappearances, *levantones*,[32] kidnappings and killings quickly expanded to the whole country. This is a little-known phenomenon but it is increasingly seen as cartels engaging in a form of "social cleansing."[33] The alarm was raised only recently when nineteen young drug users were gunned down by an armed commando who entered a rehabilitation center in Juárez. Many of the victims were younger than sixteen.[34]

This massacre, however, was in fact the fifth reported attack on rehabilitation centers close to the northern Mexican border since August 2008, when two Alcohol and Drug Addiction Integration Centers were attacked, and ten young drug users were killed. In 2009, two other attacks were reported, one on June 6 at the Doceava Tradición center, where an intern was injured by gunfire and then died at the local hospital; the other one was on May 31, when five men were murdered in the rehabilitation center La vida sin Adicciones.[35] In Ciudad Juárez, there were at least forty-six killings of young people at different treatment centers during 2009.[36]

The government's neglect of drug dependence and treatment is evident in the fact that there is no regulation of rehabilitation clinics. Many now function as "fronts" for criminal gangs, and operate as centers for recruitment or distribution.[37] As explained by Chihuahua's public security minister, "rehab centers have become a nest for criminal groups to recruit young people aged seventeen to twenty-three years, considered 'disposable' because if they are detained or die they can be quickly replaced."[38]

Despite the cruelty of the killings at the centers, the government reaction is to immediately argue that the victims were directly linked to organized crime, overshadowing any due diligence required to protect vulnerable young people from harm. For example, on the same day that ten young people were massacred at a rehab center in Juarez on September 17, 2009, Chihuahua's Governor José Reyes Baeza argued "it is no coincidence, there is a clear motivation: everything is happening in the context of a war between different criminals. Dependent drug users at the clinic belong to one group or another."[39]

Just a few days earlier, at the rehab center El Aliviane, also in Ciudad Juárez, hit men forced twenty-two young drug users to form a row against the wall before shooting with AK-47 rifles, killing eighteen of them, many under age sixteen who had arrived just weeks earlier. After the shooting, the state attorney declared, "the motive for these crimes is extermination between criminal groups."[40]

Human rights defenders have questioned the authorities' responses to these cruel acts. Gustavo de la Rosa, an investigator at the local Commission on Human Rights, criticized the government response for putting the blame on children. He added that "the role of authorities is not to discriminate between good and bad people who die; this only reveals the utter contempt for those who have fallen into drug addiction."[41]

Conflict and Psychological Damage

It is important to take into account the long-term psychological damage to children associated with high levels of violence and the resultant breakdown in family, community, and social structures. That damage is well known and documented from other conflict zones in the world, and some of those countries are still struggling with the harmful effects on children many years after the conflict ended.

Conflict and violence have direct consequences for the individual child, immediate family, and community that can be devastating, but while the long-term corrosive effects of the breakdown of social and political structures may take the severest toll, they are barely spoken of. In addition to understanding the damage to children's developmental processes caused by exposure to ongoing armed violence, it is essential to understand how the maintenance of family and community norms in addition to functioning state structures— such as education and health services—can mitigate the dire situation in which children find themselves when they live in communities exposed to violence.[42]

There is no doubt that exposure to violence, deprivation, fear, and stress affects children's development even before birth.[43] It is well documented that individual development is characterized by the interplay of environmental and biological factors from the outset. For example, evidence from neurological research reveals that, in utero, the wiring of the brain is affected by external factors such as adequate nutrition and levels of maternal stress, which, in pregnancy, may affect the unborn infant's brain development. In essence, exposure to stress hormones before birth can potentially lead to longer term behavioral disorders such as hyperactivity and attention deficit disorder in the young child, which in turn can be precursors of aggressive behavior, making it more likely that cycles of violence are reproduced from one generation to another.

Each child is different, and many variables such as age, cultural norms, gender, and individual temperament will mediate how children experience the threat or reality of violence. Nonetheless, research draws out clusters of typical reactions of children experiencing loss and trauma. When faced with the death or maiming of a family or community member, children's reactions will vary tremendously, and will depend on the ability of the family and community to provide reassurance and explanation. However, reactions to ongoing violence may include increased anxiety, which manifests through emotional and physical withdrawal (e.g., elective mutism or inability to engage in everyday tasks such as washing) or demonstrations of aggression. Children may also find it difficult to separate from family members for fear of what will happen during separation, thereby making attendance at early childhood services or school very difficult. Some children regress to earlier stages and may, for instance, talk or behave like a much younger child. Bed wetting is another common example of regressive behavior. Other children become hypervigilant, feeling it is their responsibility to keep the family safe. Trust in adults and the future can also be eroded, leaving children without hope. This is particularly the case when children witness the helplessness of parents and caregivers to stop violence.

It does not matter to children whether violence is caused by states, militias, rebels, or criminal groups; whatever the cause and whoever is to blame, children experience violation and distress that can have long-term consequences. In the current situation in Mexico, the government must be held accountable for upholding the rights of children and for putting into place measures to reduce the violence children are experiencing, particularly if it emanates from agents of the state, in addition to providing services aimed at mitigating the effects of violence on children.

Attacks on Schools

The constant battles between drug cartels and the military have made it increasingly difficult and dangerous for children in some places to reach school. In its 2010 report *Education Under Attack*, UNESCO documented a significant number of cases in which schools, teachers, and students were attacked and threatened, both by cartels and by police or military forces.

The report found as reasons for these attacks, among others, the desire of irregular groups to undermine confidence in government control of an area or even the functioning of the education system.[44] In November 2008, armed drug gangs threatened teachers in six different schools, stating that they would kidnap students if they were not paid Christmas bonuses. Most of these schools had to evacuate all of their students and close their doors for more than three weeks due to a lack of security that should have been provided by the state.[45] On March 17, 2009, more than twenty high-caliber cartridges were found on the campus of the 83rd Baccalaureate Studies Institute, in the Triqui region of San Juan Copala, Oaxaca, following a raid by armed gangs on a community along its perimeter. Those were days of continued armed attacks attributed to the Union of Social Welfare of the Triqui Region, a paramilitary group that forced primary and secondary high schools to suspend classes during April 2009.[46]

Police and military forces have also been directly involved in cases where accessibility to schools, and even the very security of students, has been compromised. In March 2010, local police burst into a high school in Ciudad Juárez looking for drugs and arms without any previous notification to school authorities. They evicted 2,600 students and took them out for inspection. After a few hours, the police retreated and concluded that the students were not in possession of drugs.[47]

Schools have been a specific target in the government's strategy to reduce the demand for drugs by criminalizing drug use. Thus the program *Mochila segura* (Safe schoolbag) was implemented. It consisted of a series of police-led random search efforts inspecting students' schoolbags to make sure they are not carrying weapons or drugs with them. Different human rights authorities have spoken against this program because it not only pushes students away from schools and damages confidence between pupils and teachers, but also is an invasive measure that violates the right to privacy of children and youth.[48]

In states such as Tamaulipas, Morelos, or Chiapas, students have missed classes because of rumors that heavy shootings will occur around the city. In Reynosa, for example, absence from school extended to 90 percent of all students. Tamaulipas's Education Ministry explained that: "the reason for the large number of absences was primarily email chains that contained phrases such as 'care for your children' and 'don't leave home because it will get worse than Iraq.'"[49]

Experience from other conflict zones has shown the value of reducing the harmful effects of violence on children by ensuring that they have access to safe spaces such as early childhood and community services and schools.[50] If schools are threatened with disruption or targeted as described above, the state must take every action to ensure that they still function. Education has proved its essential role in providing structure, routine, and a focus on the future that is highly beneficial to children and communities affected by violence and conflict. Equally, programs that enable children to explore and come to terms with their experiences in a safe environment through play, music, art, and drama are often sufficient to help most children deal with the extreme effects of exposure to violence. Initiatives such as those in Ciudad Juárez to establish safe spaces for play, supported by the community and World Vision, an international evangelical relief and development agency, will go a long way to lessening the effects of the violence that these children are still experiencing.[51]

Conclusion

Árbol que crece torcido jamás su tronco endereza

Mexican proverb[52]

After four years of poor results in attempts to directly combat drug cartels and to adopt zero-tolerance approaches to drugs, rethinking government strategies is now unavoidable in the face of grotesque violence and rising rates of addiction (both affecting children); increased school absences and the breakdown of educational structures; and the prospect of almost certain long-term psychological damage to children exposed to the drug war.

A radical change in direction is required, for as more and more children fall victim to violence directed at them, their parents, and their schools, and as more and more young people who use drugs are abandoned by the state, the long-term impact of Mexico's violent experiment will become clear. Next to this prognosis, the earlier gains in terms of dollars frozen, criminals extradited, and metric tons of drugs seized, seem all the more hollow and irrelevant.

Former president Vicente Fox has now stated that he is in favor of considering models of legal regulation of currently illicit drugs. President Calderón, while against this proposal, says that the debate is important.[53] Whatever the outcome of such debates, Mexican authorities must refocus and increase actions aimed at promoting young people's comprehensive development, particularly in the areas of education, employment, and leisure. This is possible if it is proactively decided that drugs should be addressed as a public health and development issue, rather than a security issue, and only if children are truly placed at the forefront of more effective drug policies rather than being left to drift in a sea of violence.

Endnotes

† The authors are very grateful to Tina Hyder, senior program manager at the Open Society Foundations' Early Childhood Program, for her important input relating to children in conflict situations.
1. Rory Carroll, "Mexico Drug War: The New Filling Fields," *Guardian*, September 3, 2010.
2. Quoted in *Impresiones Latinas*, "Ciudad Juárez: Familia y niñez son arrebatadas," May 25, 2010.
3. "U.S. Drug Czar Calls for End to 'War on Drugs,'" Reuters, June 8, 2009.
4. Notimex, "Celebra Calderón detención de 'La Reina del Pacífico,'" *Noticieros Televisa*, October 2, 2007; J. Castaneda, "What's Spanish for Quagmire? Five Myths That Caused the Failed War Next Door," *Foreign Policy*, January/February 2011, www.foreignpolicy.com/articles/2010/01/04/whats_spanish_for_quagmire/.
5. Francisco Relea, "Entrevista a Felipe Calderón: La situación en México," *El País*, January 21, 2007.
6. Procuraduría General de la República, *Resultados de la Política Mexicana contra la Delincuencia Organizada*, June 9, 2009.
7. *Milenio*, "Calderón lleva 316 extradiciones; Fox aprobo 219," February 21, 2010.
8. Procuraduría General de la República, *Resultados de la Política Mexicana*.
9. Jorge Chabat, "La respuesta del gobierno de Calderón al desafío del narcotráfico: Entre lo malo y lo peor," Centro de Investigación y Docencia Económica (CIDE), 2010, www.cide.edu/publicaciones/status/dts/DTEI%20196.pdf.
10. Eduardo Guerrero Gutiérrez, "Los hoyos negros de la estrategia contra el narco," *Nexos*, August 1, 2010.
11. Taia Rosas, "Van más de 28,000 muertos, reconoce Cisen," *El Economista*, August 3, 2010.
12. National Commission on Human Rights, *Activities Report 1999–2009*, www.cndh.org.mx.
13. *El Universal*, "Van 565 civiles muertos durante administrción: Sedena," September 24, 2010.
14. Red por los Derechos de la Infancia en México, *Pronunciamiento contra armas*, May 17, 2010, www.derechosinfancia.org.mx/Especiales/Pronunciamiento_contraarmas.html.
15. Ruth Rodríguez, "900 menores han muerto en guerra al narco," *El Universal*, June 8, 2010.
16. Red por los Derechos de la Infancia en México, *Pronunciamiento contra armas*.

17. *La Crónica*, "Investigan asesinato de jóvenes en Durango," March 29, 2010.
18. *El Universal*, "Matan a tres alumnos de bachilleres en Tijuana," January 8, 2010.
19. *El Siglo de Torreón*, "Encuentran a cinco jóvenes asesinados," March 27, 2009.
20. *El Universal*, "Ejército mató a mis hijos: Cynthia Salazar," April 13, 2010.
21. National Commission on Human Rights, *Recommendation 36/2010*, www.cndh. org.mx.
22. *Los Angeles Times*, "19 in Mexican Army Held in Deaths of 5," June 5, 2007.
23. Juan Cedillo, "Fue un error dispararle a familia, admite Sedena," *El Universal*, September 7, 2010.
24. For an overview of the issues and evidence referred to in this article, see T. Hyder, *War, Conflict And Play* (Maidenhead, UK: Open University Press, 2004).
25. Daniela Pastrana, "Mexican Govt Turns a Blind Eye to Orphaned and Disabled Children," Inter Press Service, July 23, 2010. A child who has lost his or her father is considered "orphaned" in Mexico.
26. Catherine Bremer, "Special Report: Mexico's Growing Legion of Narco Orphans," Reuters, October 6, 2010.
27. Ibid.
28. Felipe Calderón's speech at the launch of the program "Limpiemos México," in Monterrey, July 2, 2010.
29. Secretaria de Salud, *Encuesta Nacional de Adicciones*, 2008, 49, www.insp.mx/ encuesta-nacional-de-adicciones-2008.html.
30. Ibid., 52
31. *Milenio*, "Se incrementan índices de niños adictos, dice SSA," May 10, 2010.
32. Popular name given to a kind of kidnapping commonly carried out by criminal gangs to increase their ranks.
33. A similar phenomenon occurs in Colombia, where illegal armed groups have been known to publicly threaten drug users and sex-trade workers. In 2009, a leaflet was dropped in multiple cities by a paramilitary group making such threats. In Santa Fe, a poor area in Bogota, drug users and sex workers were subsequently killed.
34. *La Crónica*, "Nueva matanza en un centro de rehabilitación de Ciudad Juárez," September 17, 2009.
35. Luis Carlos Cano, "Suman 18 muertos en centro de rehabilitación en Juárez," *El Universal*, September 3, 2009.
36. *El Ágora*, "Van 46 ejecutados en centros de rehabilitación," September 17, 2009.
37. *El Economista*, "Gobierno de Chihuahua investigará centros de rehabilitación," September 17, 2009.
38. *El Universal*, "Sicarios fusilan a 17 jóvenes en Ciudad Juárez," September 3, 2009.
39. *Alerta Periodística*, "Actos terroristas, de exterminio entre bandas, justifican autoridades," September 17, 2009.
40. Luis Carlos Cano, "'Exterminio' de narcorrivales: PJE," *El Universal*, September 4, 2009.
41. *El Ágora*, "Van 46 ejecutados en centros de rehabilitación."
42. See United Nations General Assembly, *Impact of Armed Conflict on Children: Report of the Expert of the Secretary-General, Graca Machel*, UN Doc. No. A/51/306, August 26, 1996.
43. On this, see *The Science of Early Childhood Development: Closing the Gap Between What we Know and What We Do*, Center on the Developing Child, Harvard University, 2007.
44. UNESCO, *Education Under Attack*, 2010.
45. *El Siglo de Torreón*, "Evacúan escuelas por amenaza de extorsión," December 17, 2008.
46. Patricia Briseño, "Agresiones y amenazas cierran escuelas Triquis," *Excélsior*, April 1, 2009.
47. Mario Héctor Silva, "Operación Mochila en prepas de Juárez," *El Universal*, March 11, 2010.

48. Claudia Bolaños, "CDHDF se opone a Programa Mochila Segura," *El Universal*, May 28, 2010.
49. *Reforma*, "Pega a Tamaulipas temor por violencia," February 24, 2010.
50. See UNICEF, *Children in Conflict and Emergencies*, www.unicef.org/protection/index_armedconflict.html.
51. See www.worldvisionreport.org/special_report/Children-Affected-by-Violence-in-Juarez.
52. A tree that grows crooked will never become straight again.
53. Reuters, "Former Mexico President Supports Legalizing Drugs," August 10, 2010.

CHILDREN OF THE DRUG WAR

3. In the Shadows of the Insurgency in Afghanistan: Child Bartering, Opium Debt, and the War on Drugs

by Atal Ahmadzai and Christopher Kuonqui

[T]his is a real crisis for the young sisters and daughters of the opium farmers' families in this region.

Khamosh Hezb-u-allah
Freelance Afghan reporter[1]

Introduction

In 2010, Afghanistan produced over 3,600 metric tons of opium. While marking a continual decline over recent years (a 48 percent fall from 2009), this figure represents a tremendous illicit economy, the value of which is on the rise. Farm-gate incomes in 2010 reached an aggregate US$604 million, up from US$438 million in 2009.[2] Many argue that this trade bolsters the Taliban and related networks. Others dispute this. Whatever the security reality, the Afghan opium trade produces an often-ignored face of the global war on drugs: that of the children and families who often pay the steepest human costs of the direct and indirect consequences of national and international policies.

History shows that drug wars and violent wars often travel together. Today's Afghanistan may represent the strongest expression of this pattern. Opium production in the country takes place precisely in those areas where the rule of the gun supersedes the rule of law. As the United Nations Office of Drugs and Crime (UNODC) *Afghan Opium Survey 2010* finds, 98 percent of total cultivation takes place in nine provinces in the southern and western regions, including the least secure areas of the country. The link between opium cultivation and lack of security remains salient despite twists and turns in counterinsurgency and poppy-field eradication strategies, military leadership changes, and national elections, disputed and otherwise.

The war on drugs in Afghanistan pivots on an understanding of the opium trade as a major source of financing terrorism. The UNODC estimated the value of trafficking, lab processing, and the precursor chemical industry in Afghanistan at US$3 billion in 2009, including farmers' and traffickers' incomes.[3] This mirrors roughly one-third of total Afghan gross domestic product in that year.[4] Based on these figures, many argue that the opium trade helps to finance recruitment to the Taliban and other quasi-terrorist groups operating in the largely unregulated Afghan countryside. NATO officials say that insurgents receive 40–60 percent of the income from drugs (though some of this may come from Pakistan's opium fields).[5] Former UNODC head Antonio Maria Costa in turn estimated that the Taliban annually reaps $400 million from the trade.[6] The magnitude of these estimates makes the opium trade a significant concern on many fronts.

But the drug–security dynamic does not exist in a vacuum. Deep, changing cultural practices also provide a backdrop that shapes the war on drugs and its implications in Afghanistan. Driven by shifts in cultivation, market forces put the price advantage of opium over wheat—the main competitor—at three to one in 2009.[7] In 2010, the ratio was more than six to one.[8] Afghan farmers can make far more money growing poppies than pursuing any other alternative. The economic role poppy plays in one of the world's poorest economies influences social perceptions and attitudes, in turn leading to stark practices that include trading in children to resolve opium debts. This double setting of insecurity and profoundly rooted socioeconomic practices informs how the opium trade and the war on drugs affects the children of Afghanistan, a crisis that is otherwise all but invisible in the flight path of the war on terror and global security policies. This chapter sets out some of these more obscure processes.

The war on drugs framework placing poppy-field eradication at the heart of counternarcotics policy[9] in Afghanistan cannot claim victory for the production decline, despite ongoing eradication campaigns. Disease and pests caused the large cultivation drop in 2010. Regardless of cause, however, decreases in opium supply produce two major effects in Afghanistan: as observed in 2010, they sharply edge the price of opium upward; and this is worrisome from the perspective of poverty and livelihoods because it severely stresses farmers who rely on opium for income. Most opium farmers buy their seeds and food for the year on credit from drug lords—a transaction filtered through a debt system called *salaam*. This has potentially significant consequences. When in 2000 the Taliban's Mullah Omar decreed that opium planting was against religious practice, the economic implications were so great that more than 30,000 Afghans fled to Pakistan from Helmand alone to avoid defaulting on *salaam* loans. Some argue that the motivation for the opium ban was to induce a price rise, rather than to prevent use.[10] Since the 2001 invasion, due in part to the onset of eradication practices and, more important for overall reductions in production, disease, and pests, sudden opium income losses can have the result that farmers sell off their children to avoid violent reprisals from drug lords who are unwilling to accept a default.

The crux of the problem is that a drop in opium production leaves farmers with few options to repay *salaam* loans. While abrupt and catastrophic losses of opium crops can be cause for celebration in some circles, the direct consequences for small-scale and poorer farmers' families and livelihoods require deeper caution. Drops in opium can unintentionally harm already vulnerable farmers while not affecting the intended targets—smugglers and terrorists. This suggests that perhaps the most viable means of weaning Afghanistan off opium may be to do so gradually, giving the rural farmer a chance to adapt. Expanding microcredit systems in Afghanistan represents a positive initial step. Another is to implement alternative crop programs that effectively secure livelihoods for farmers, although the record so far is weak.[11] As long as poor decisions remain subsidized, little ground for developing nonopium-based self-sufficiency can form. Either way, the social and economic tragedies wrought by opium production declines complicate this otherwise desirable outcome.

This chapter studies the socioeconomic practices and implications of the *salaam* system, opium cultivation declines, and the consequences for children of the drug wars in Afghanistan. Based on a series of interviews conducted with farmers, villagers, journalists, activists, and policymakers in Helmand, Kandahar, and Kabul, it sets out new evidence that substantiates the links and results. While the scale of the research can only reveal the tip of a large iceberg of consequences, what emerges is how bartered girls, child addicts, and their families suffer the unintended consequences of counternarcotics, counterterrorism, and counterinsurgency stratagems in a society already marred by decades of poverty and violence.

Entrapping Opium Farmers: The Practices of Salaam and "Opium Culture"

The bartering of girls happens more but not exclusively in areas well-known for opium trade such as Naad Ali, Gareshk, Musa

Qala, and Sangeen districts. Recently we got information that in Baba Jee area—walking distance from the provincial capital—a farmer who owed a debt to a drug smuggler gave his daughter to him. One other case that I can remember happened in Musa Qala district. We eradicated a farmer's opium field. The farmer actually took salaam from a drug lord. Eventually, we got to know that the farmer married either his daughter or sister to the salaam provider.[12]

Shafi-u-allah, Head, Department of Counter Narcotics in
Helmand

Farmers form the foundation of the opium economy and culture, planting poppy seeds and setting the stage for one of the most profitable markets in Afghanistan. But despite their role, farmers largely fail to reap the rewards of partaking in the opium industry—earning the least, remaining the most vulnerable, and often suffering the worst consequences affecting their income and family lifestyle when crop or financial shocks take place. Reports in fact suggest that large-scale landowners rarely cultivate opium, leaving the crop to be managed by farmers who lease or mortgage their lands, or else by small-scale landowners. This trend provides wealthier landowners a social and economic buffer from losses due to field eradication or natural disasters, expected or unexpected. As a prominent social activist in Kandahar describes this state of power inequities:

Opium farmers are the most vulnerable people in the opium cycle, and the uncoordinated war against opium further strengthens their social and economic vulnerabilities.[13]

In many if not most cases, farmers cannot afford the upfront capital investment of opium production, from overhead expenses to seeds, fertilizer, and irrigation costs. In these instances a "drug dealer," yet another actor in the opium system, intervenes to offer farmers financial assistance in the form of credit. This special financing mechanism is a conditioned debt called *salaam*—cash money loaned to the borrower. But returns are not paid in cash or with interest (*Rheba*), the latter being strictly prohibited in Islamic jurisprudence. This leaves the *salaam* to be repaid in kind or in goods and products, leaving the distinction between *Rheba* and *salaam* to effectively cloak opium production in a veil of religious legality.

Salaam is generally offered to farmers in cash money equivalents to a specified quantity of processed opium, at market prices at the time of issuing the debt. But the repayment terms obligate the farmer to return the same amount of opium, not cash, to the lender at the time of harvest, usually when opium prices are at their highest. A cycle of financial risk subjects farmers to the full brunt of crop failure or market changes, from expected and unexpected yield losses due to disease, flood, low productivity, or the increasing prevalence of opium-field eradication by the state and war on drugs policies. If any of these crises affect farmers, then they are left with steep debts to *salaam* providers.

Often, farmers do not have alternative means to compensate and release the debt other than to offer their daughters or sisters as repayment, either with bride money[14] or directly to the lender. A civil society activist in southern Afghanistan succinctly captures this tragedy:

Drug lords and sometimes landlords give loans to farmers with cash money and ultimately the farmer is entrapped. For example, at the start of the opium cultivating season, the drug lord gives a specific amount of money and demands a particular amount of opium at harvesting time. Thus, the farmer is under debt from the beginning of the year. The bad times for farmers are when crops fail or are eradicated by police. Subsequently, the farmer does not have any other option except to satisfy the debt using his daughter's bride money or by marrying his daughter directly to the loan provider.[15]

Alongside the promise of higher income rewards of dealing in poppy production, *salaam* is used as an additional tool to encourage farmers to enter opium cultivation rather than other yields such as wheat, maize, and corn.

To be sure, however, the prepaid *salaam* debt does not always prove to be financially damaging to farmers. On the contrary, if opium yields remain immune to natural disasters or field eradication, farmers can stand to benefit. Often, the price of opium at the beginning of the cultivation seasons, when farmers receive *salaam*, is much higher in comparison with the price during the harvesting season. This range of price changes can financially benefit farmers when repaying opium debts at lower prices. Yet, twenty-first-century opium trends have so far provided little consolation with these rewards, more often leaving farmers steeped in financial burdens.

Entrapping Farmers in *Salaam* Debts

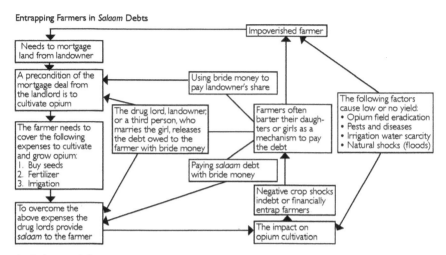

A Culture of Opium

Farmers are the most vulnerable; however, the opium brides
directly suffer from both opium culture and field eradication.
Opium culture instigated the practice of polygamy, and field
eradication mostly and exclusively affects the farmer.

Child Rights Officer, Kandahar[16]

The *salaam* system sets part of the scene for the drug war's
affect on Afghanistan's children. The sociocultural milieu across
Afghanistan sets much of the rest. An "opium culture" practiced by
those high in the narcotics apparatus hierarchy—including dealers,
traffickers, and large-scale landowners—breeds and gives momentum
to polygamy practices. Transformed over generations into a marker of
social status, polygamy is widely practiced among those of this social
faction—with underage girls from poorer rural families having the
least voice in decisions.

The case of Ruzi Mohammad underscores this reality. Ruzi
Mohammad is a farmer living in Alakozo village in the Marja District,
Helmand Province (site of the spring 2010 NATO offensive). Earlier,
in 2008, enjoying relatively good economic standing, Mohammad
mortgaged several *geribs*[17] of farm land from local owners, with
the aim of cultivating opium. That year, however, saw the onset of
a severe drought that dried up traditional irrigation systems such
as springs and *karizes* (underground canals). A local drug dealer
offered help by way of a *salaam* loan, which Mohammad used to
install fuel-run water pumps on a bore well. But then disease hit

the crops. With his investment threatened, the farmer in time found himself under huge financial stress, with a mortgage and *salaam* debt to repay and hardly any means to compensate for his losses. To reconcile his debts, Mohammad married off his sister as a second wife to another villager, an opium dealer. Instead of paying the customary bride money to Mohammad, the dealer secured release of the mortgage and *salaam* debts. At the time of his interview in 2010, Mohammad's family remained in deep poverty and had not heard of his sister since the debt repayment.

The opium culture and the war against drugs levy dual negative effects on farmers and their children in contemporary southern Afghanistan, particularly in the high-producing areas of Helmand. First, children directly participate in opium cultivation through irrigation, harvesting, trade, and, to some extent, addiction. Their involvement in both production and consumption clearly exposes children to high-risk activities and behavior. Second, children, mainly the daughters of poor farmers, are often bartered or "sold" as compensation for their families' financial losses. Instances where drug lords intentionally aim to entrap farmers in order to pave the road to matrimony deals have also been reported from the field. These girls are called "opium brides" in the brief social literature on the practice.

Drug War Impacts

Eradication of opium fields means taking bread away from the farmer's mouth. The farmer who is poor after suffering field eradication does not have any other means to return the debt he owes, mainly to drug dealers. He is disgraced and on the breadline. To save face in society he has to barter his daughter or sister to satisfy the debt.

Abdullah Khan,
Helmand Representative, Independent Human Rights
Commission of Afghanistan[18]

I am not hesitant to state that both opium cultivation and trade and opium eradication are equally endangering the children of farmers' families. You can easily see school-age children who, instead of going to schools, are involved in cultivating, irrigating, and harvesting opium. On the other hand, when

*we eradicate opium fields, we indeed make the farmer and
his family poor and impoverished. In such circumstances the
children of poor families cannot afford to go to school, so they
become means of income for their families.*

Shukran G. Mohammad,
Head, Department of Counternarcotics in Kandahar[19]

Counternarcotics strategies aim to foster alternative livelihoods
and means of diversifying income that encourage farmers to leave the
opium economy. For the most part, these "carrots" include providing
farmers with fertilizer, crop seeds, water pumps, and tractors,
largely *after* the "stick" of field eradication has occurred. The scope of
assistance is rarely (if ever) sufficient to alleviate the financial losses
of the total destruction of a farmer's crops.

The war against drugs initiated by the government of Afghanistan
and the international community appears as a comprehensive
strategy to target cultivation and trafficking, and to support a legal
agriculture-based economy. The practice of antidrug policy presents
a different picture, where farmers and small-scale landowners are
most affected. Opium smugglers and dealers, who have a strong
influence over farmers and small landowners, remain immune.
Moreover, Shafiullah, head of the Department of Counternarcotics
of Helmand Province, notes that, in 2009, existing counternarcotics
practices led to a 33.7 percent drop in opium production. He hastens
to acknowledge that increased child bartering may be a likely
consequence of these practices.[20]

The underlying sociocultural current means that the bartering
of girls is not, of course, exclusively the outcome of field eradication
under drug control policy. Factors such as natural disasters and crop
disease can also devastate yields and leave farmers with high debts.
The perception, however, among those interviewed for this study is
that field eradication plays a dynamic role in financially entrapping
farmers and that the bartering of girls is a means to resolve opium
debt. Yet the generally obscure nature of opium-related culture
similarly prevents gaining access to knowledge of bartering practices,
which remain undiscovered and unreported by civil society and
human rights bodies.

The drug trade also facilitates drug use among Afghan children.
While policies aim to curb Afghanistan's opium exports, the plight
of domestic use goes scarcely noticed, with as many as 1.5 million

CHILDREN OF THE DRUG WAR

Afghans estimated to be dependent on drugs—a substantial share of the 24 million population estimated by national demographic data.[21] According to a recent report by the UNODC, up to half of the drug users surveyed gave their children opium.[22] More than 2,000 drug-dependent children are estimated to live in the western city of Herat alone.[23] These figures point to the need for refined policies able to recognize and better account for child and adult drug dependence.

Obscured Reality

Although the term "opium bride" has emerged to capture the phenomenon of bartering girls to satisfy opium debts,[24] the international and local literatures remain nearly blank on the subject. The fieldwork conducted for this chapter finds that the incidence and practice of bartering girls is more prevalent than this scant coverage suggests. What explains this difference?

The decades-long media focus on war, insurgency, and corruption can serve as a wedge between the actual phenomenon and its media representation. Scarce opportunities for reporters to visit villages and capture local grievances means that the melancholic social character expressed daily by ordinary people is all but ignored. Indeed, as one respondent affirmed:

The reality and concept wrapped in the term "opium bride" exists to a large extent in our society. We accept that "opium brides" exist in the villages.[25]

The Afghan media and civil arenas have altogether failed to report on "opium brides." Several respondents link this paucity of recognition to the social and cultural sensitivities surrounding child-bartering practices, as well as the devastating security situation in areas packed with the opium trade. One journalist describes this situation as follows:

Cases of bartering of girls are not breaking into media to the extent that they actually occur. The reasons are multidimensional, including cultural and social sensitivities and the strong de facto hold on society of drug lords, who obstruct the flow of opium-related information. We receive reports about the bartering of girls but it is difficult to give proper coverage to this phenomenon through firsthand information. The reason is that most of the time drug-related trades including girls are prevalent mainly in unsecured districts and it is not feasible for the media to easily break through.[26]

Strongly acknowledged by nearly all respondents to this study, incidences of "opium brides" are undoubtedly much more numerous than what surfaces in media, human rights, and civil society circles. It represents a social cost whose full magnitude remains unknown. Despite the inadequate literature and discourse, the child-bartering phenomenon is widely acknowledged among average individuals at local levels, from government officials to members of the media and civil society as well as land- and business owners.

In Afghanistan, the quality of life for many children and women is highly compromised in terms of their rights and roles in society. In the southern region, hit hard by active insurgency and counterinsurgency, conditions for women and children exist in even more acute states of crisis. The opium culture and active insurgency pose a double disadvantage to women and children. First, social and political upheaval leaves children and women particularly vulnerable to violation of their rights, such as child bartering. Second, the large focus on these upheavals often leaves children and women neglected, overlooked, and overshadowed by contemporary so-called strategic issues.

Journalists working in southern Afghanistan note the enduring frequency of child and gender discrimination in the shadows of the insurgency:

As a reporter working in Helmand, I know many families have bartered and married their girls to the drug smugglers who gave the farmer money to cultivate opium. Eventually, when there is no yield then they have to get engage in bartering.[27]

Married Lives of Bartered Girls

In our village two families brought brides from farmers' families, yeah I mean opium brides. Now the stories of mistreating and miseries of those brides are spread all around the village. The stories of their suffering are the topic of women in all social gatherings such as weddings, death prayers, and everywhere.[28]

Local shopkeeper
Lashkarga, Helmand

CHILDREN OF THE DRUG WAR

Child bartering as a means of paying opium debt is largely weighted against girls. This fact gives way to two clusters of responses—one driven by values, and the other by consequences—but both are united in their opposition to the practice. The value-driven response consists largely of human and women's rights objections, where the very suggestion of using girls as a legitimate "unit of transaction" to resolve financial debt or to prevent social enmity is a nonstarter. By contrast, the basic thrust of local and village concerns about bartering practices is seen in their actual consequences. Where paying bride money is an embedded cultural value that offers brides some measure of security in married life, the procedure and involvement of money does not figure as a concern. For these, opposition is rooted in what is painted by respondents as a devastatingly bleak post-marriage portrait of bartered girls.

Practical social, cultural, and security constraints to the fieldwork undertaken for this chapter limited firsthand conversation with girls bartered into marriage to resolve opium debts.[29] In addition to other sources, the paternal families of some bartered girls, however, managed to provide some insight into their experience. All respondents reported the suffering of opium brides in their married life. In the local context, a legitimate and plausible reason for suffering was not apparent. But the closer examination made possible by this study highlights the underlying causes of the poor matrimonial living standards and status of the opium brides.

Three structural themes surfaced throughout the interviews. The first involves the implications of a marriage where the bride's family holds a disproportionately inferior social status to the matrimonial husband—and no options are apparent in the matrimonial terms. This widely contradicts the cultural expectations of "normal marriages," where the upper hand usually lies with the would-be bride's father, who has the final choice in weighing suitor options and selecting a husband for his daughter. In opium-debt–induced marriages, the bride's family lacks these freedoms, subsequently severely harming the bride's social status among her in-laws, in turn, initiating a vicious circle that holds the potential to make the bride's married life increasingly difficult.

A second described feature is rooted in the very nature of marriages facilitated by debt. Normally, the paternal family provides the bride with staff to establish the new home; the family in some cases even delivers the bride money directly to the bride to satisfy her household needs. This code of conduct provides the newlywed bride with the desired social status as well as a safety social net. On the contrary, due to the impoverished socioeconomic status of the farmer, the opium bride goes empty-handed to her in-laws' home. This trend deprives opium brides of conventional social status and social security nets. The scenario gets worse when the bride money is already spent by the farmer on expenses required for cultivating opium. A children's rights officer in Kandahar summarizes the result:

These girls have horrible marriage lives. They do not have the same social status and respect as other women do. Mostly they get married to those who already have one or more wives. Second, these girls go empty-handed to their in-laws, which gives them a compromising and disregarded social status among the family.[30]

The third theme recognized in the interviews describing the married life of opium brides involves age gaps and polygamy. In most cases, these brides are underage, not of marriageable age. The rapid and unexpected social change from adolescence and even late childhood into womanhood is an unnatural transformation that is noted to cause immense challenges for the girl. Polygamy, as revealed by all respondents, is one of the principle practices of the opium culture, functioning as what seems a de facto marker of social status among those engaged in opium circles. On the one hand, vulnerable farmers who are deliberately trapped into debt is a means for drug lords to practice polygamy, and on the other hand, the practice serves as a vehicle for the suffering and misery of opium brides. As one respondent notes:

The hallmark of opium marriages is the huge gap in ages. Normally, the girls are much younger and even underage for marriage, while the man is married and overage. The reason for the age gap is the "no option" reality. The farmer does not have another option; in order to overcome the financial and social ordeal originating in opium debt, he must marry the girl to someone who has the upper hand over the farmer.[31]

Mohammad Khan, a farmer in Helmand who married his daughter to an opium trader when she was younger than fifteen years old in return for the debt he owed the trader, describes how he still remains a caretaker of his daughter:

　　　　　　　　　　　　CHILDREN OF THE DRUG WAR

*My daughter has two sons and a daughter. Most of the time, I
purchase medicine for her because her husband does not treat her
like his wife. I take sugar and sweets, and tea to her. My son-in-
law has another wife and he married her with bride money. This
is the difference between my daughter and his other wife.*[32]

The farmer's inferior status, that of his daughter in her marriage
home, and the age gap and polygamous household she is subjected to
each play a role in what Khan describes as the suffering his daughter
experiences as a result of his opium debt.

"Opium Flower"

A web of complexity entangles social attitudes to opium-debt–
induced child bartering. Part of the complexity is due to the significant
social transformations wrought over much of Afghanistan in the past
three decades, rooted in sociopolitical turmoil. These shifts have
led to increasingly incoherent matrimonial practices, such as the
engagement of girls and boys in childhood or even during infancy,
and have served to entrench a patriarchal order in social life across
many villages.

A powerful repercussion of these changes has been weakened social
and cultural practices and the waning importance of traditional
elites, from elders to *Maliks* (tribal leaders), *Khans* (landowners), and
traditional religious figures. These actors have usually functioned as
the mediators of social interactions in conflict, business, and trade,
and played a strong role in marriage negotiations. Today, these elites
are increasingly marginalized, subsequently leaving a social vacuum
to be filled by those with the means to control power—warlords and
drug traffickers often take advantage of these circumstances. The
approaches of the latter to social affairs are undoubtedly different.
While most families still engage in relatively traditional matrimony
practices, early-age marriages, polygamy, age gaps, and exchange
marriages or *Badal*[33] figure more commonly in many villages. What
results is that instances of child bartering are met with silence. The
former gatekeepers of social life largely ignore these cases, as the
traditional elites fail to voice opposition through their respective
platforms in mosques, *Jirgas* (tribal councils), or local community
meetings. Whether the disregard is due to their suppressed social
roles, shifts in their perceived responsibilities, or other factors is

unclear. That drugs and warlords wield their newly evolved influence to their own benefit is less subject to doubt.

Despite these transformations, however, child bartering remains largely an implicitly ill-considered practice. As Khamosh Hezb-u-allah puts it,

> *Culturally, the practice of bartering girls to satisfy opium debts is considered a reprehensible and socially ill practice, and such conduct does not exist in any ethnic or tribal cultural setups. Those involved in practicing "child bartering" are socially stigmatized.*[34]

This strong stigma exists against those involved in bartering girls—on both sides. Farmers who barter their children to fulfill debt suffer subsequent social discrimination and stigma from having done so. Mohammad Khan notes:

> *I am disgraced at home, in the village, and at the mosque. I lost face with my family and my people. I know that I am badly dishonored in the village, though they do not express it verbally.*[35]

He goes on to wish protection for his daughter.

> *May Allah protect even the daughter of Kafir*[36] *from the suffering that my daughter is having. She has been teased by other women of her in-laws and she is called "the opium flower." They tell her that wherever the opium flower grows it destroys everything, and eventually you will destroy our home.*[37]

While the practice of bartering girls to resolve opium-induced debt remains obscure and in the shadows of better-known crises in Afghanistan, there may exist no clearer representation of suffering among the children of Afghanistan's terror and drug wars.

Endnotes

† We would like to thank the individuals interviewed for this chapter for agreeing to discuss a sensitive topic, and at times putting their lives at risk. Atal especially thanks Safatullah Zahidi, Internews reporter in Helmand Province, for his efforts in assisting data collection. Our hearts go out to the children adversely affected by the consequences—intended or unintended—and we hope this essay in some small way helps to shed light on their conditions.

1. Khamosh Hezb-u-allah, freelance Afghan reporter in Helmand Province, August 16, 2010.
2. All estimates are from United Nations Office of Drugs and Crime, *Afghanistan*

Opium Survey 2010, www.unodc.org/documents/crop-monitoring/Afghanistan/
Afg_opium_survey_2010_exsum_web.pdf.

3. Gretchen Peters, *Seeds of Terror: How Heroin Is Bankrolling the Taliban and Al Qaeda* (New York: St. Martin's Press, 2009).

4. UNODC, *Afghanistan Opium Survey 2009*.

5. George Gavrilis, "The Good and Bad News About Afghan Opium," Council on Foreign Relations, February 10, 2010, http://rebecca.cfr.org/afghanistan/good-bad-news-afghan-opium/p21372/.

6. Colum Lynch, "U.N. Finds Afghan Opium Trade Rising, *Washington Post*, June 27, 2008.

7. UNODC, *Afghanistan Opium Survey 2010*.

8. Ibid.

9. [It should be borne in mind that the eradication of opium poppy is a specific obligation of the 1961 Single Convention on Narcotic Drugs and the 1988 Convention Against the Illicit Traffic in Narcotic Drugs and Psychotropic Substances.—Ed.]

10. Edith M. Lederer, "U.N. Panel Accuses Taliban of Selling Drugs to Finance War and Train Terrorists," Associated Press, May 25, 2001; Peters, *Seeds of Terror*.

11. Pierre-Arnaud Chouvy, *Opium: Uncovering the Politics of the Poppy* (Boston: Harvard University Press, 2010), 184–85.

12 Shafi-u-allah, Department of Counternarcotics, Helmand Province, August 15, 2010.

13. Mohammad Omer, social activist, is the managing director of both Hewad TV and Azad Afghan Radio, stationed in Kandahar, March 5, 2010.

14. In contrast to other societies, across much of Afghanistan, the groom's family provides a mutually agreed sum of money to the bride's family, which is called "bride money."

15. Ghulam Nabi Popal (not real name), civil society activist in the southern region, Kabul, August 22, 2010.

16. Shams-u-Din Tanveer, children's rights officer, Afghanistan Independent Human Rights Commission, Kandahar Regional Office, February 26, 2010.

17. A *gerib* is a local unit of land measurement equivalent to 2,000 square meters (0.2 hectare) or 21,528 square feet (0.49 acre) of land.

18. Abdullah Khan, representative, Afghanistan Independent Human Rights Commission in Helmand Province, Lashkarga, August 16, 2010.

19. Shukran G. Mohammad, head of the Department of Counternarcotics, Kandahar Province, March 3, 2010.

20. Ibid.

21. Dan Williams, "Child Addicts Find Succour in a Corner of Kabul," Reuters, June 15, 2010.

22. Aunohita Mojumdar, "In Afghanistan, Drug Rehab for Children," *Christian Science Monitor*, July 14, 2010.

23. Sadeq Behnam and Sudabah Afzali, freelance journalists in Herat reporting for the Institute for War and Peace Reporting. In 2010, the Central Statistics Organization estimated a total of 410,700 people living in Herat City, the province capital.

24. Sami Yousafzai and Ron Moreau, "The Opium Brides of Afghanistan," *Newsweek*, April 7, 2008.

25. Shafi-u-allh, head of the Department of Counternarcotics of Helmand Province, Lashkarga, March 3, 2010.

26. Meenapal Dawa Khan, southern region correspondent, Radio Liberty, March 3, 2010.

27. Khamosh Hezb-u-allah, freelance reporter in Helmand Province, August 16, 2010.

28. A local shopkeeper in Lashkarga city, August 17, 2010.

29. Security constraints were not primarily tied to the well-known active insurgency and counterinsurgency in Helmand. Rather, the acute insecurity felt in the field

is driven by the desire of participants in the drug culture to remain hidden and undercover—in fact using the violent insurgency as a veil for their activities.

30. Tanveer.Shams-u-Din, children's rights officer, Afghanistan Independent Human Rights Commission, Kandahar Regional Office, February 26, 2010.
31. Meenapal Dawa Khan, southern region correspondent, Radio Liberty, March 3, 2010.
32. Mohammad Khan, farmer in Nawa District, Helmand Province, August 18, 2010.
33. *Badal* literally means "exchange" and in matrimony practices it refers to a traditional bilateral conduct in which two families marry girls. In these circumstances, the families do not pay bride money.
34. Khamosh Hezb-u-allah, freelance Afghan reporter in Helmand Province, August 16, 2010.
35. Mohammad Khan, farmer in Nawa District of Helmand Province, August 18, 2010.
36. Literally means "infidel," though in common usage tends to refer to a "vicious person."
37. Mohammad Khan, farmer in Nawa District of Helmand Province, August 18, 2010.

4. After the War on Drugs: How Legal Regulation of Production and Trade Would Better Protect Children

by Steve Rolles

Children in the Political Narrative of the Drug War

The emergence of the "war on drugs"—shorthand for a broader punitive and prohibitionist paradigm—has been predicated on the concept of drugs as an existential "threat" rather than a more conventionally conceived health or social policy issue.[1] Prohibitionist rhetoric frames drugs as menacing not only to health but also to national security (our borders), and not infrequently, to the moral fabric of society itself, using the "drug threat" to children as the specific rhetorical vehicle.

Emotive plays on the threat to our children have a long history in political propaganda (particularly in times of war), exploiting the potency of the parents' greatest fear. Drug-war rhetoric presents the threat to youth both as the drugs themselves (although significantly only the illegal ones) and the sinister drug dealers who prey on the young and vulnerable (lurking at the school gates, etc.). While there are, of course, very real risks for children and young people associated with both drug use and illegal drug markets, perception of these risks has been dramatically distorted by the populist fearmongering of politicians (who can then position themselves as "tough" on the drug threat), aided and abetted by a sensation-hungry mainstream media.

The prohibition paradigm is very much framed as a response to such threats, and its popular narrative has cast itself as a moral crusade against an "evil" that threatens mankind itself. The preamble to the 1961 UN Single Convention on Narcotic Drugs, for example, establishes the context of the legal framework it has enshrined in these terms:

- Concerned with the health and welfare of mankind.
- Recognizing that addiction to narcotic drugs constitutes a serious evil for the individual and is fraught with social and economic danger to mankind.
- Conscious of their duty to prevent and combat this evil.

Given this rhetorical context, it is easy to see how supporters of prohibition understand any kind of moves toward legal regulation of drug production and supply as being immoral, a form of surrender, or a descent into anarchy in which our children will be the first and most obvious victims.

Criticisms of less punitive drug policies are, in fact, often framed in these terms. Critics define one or more worst-case scenarios, often extrapolated from "what if?" thinking built on an immediate and total absence of all drug control legislation, and then argue from the basis that such scenarios will be the norm. The popular public discourse on alternatives to prohibition is thus frequently characterized by the "imperiled child" narrative, with apocalyptic visions of stoned school bus drivers, heroin in candy stores, and armies of child drug-zombies. As advocates of legal regulation of drug markets have made abundantly clear (see below), this is a grotesque misrepresentation of what is actually being proposed.

Supporters of prohibition also frequently present any steps toward legal regulation of drug markets as "radical," and therefore innately confrontational and dangerous. However, the historical evidence demonstrates that, in fact, it is prohibition that is the radical policy. Legal regulation of drug production, supply and use is far more in line with currently accepted ways of managing health and social risks in almost all other spheres of life. Yet prohibition has become so entrenched and institutionalized that many in the drugs field, even those from the more critical progressive end of the spectrum, view it as immutable, an assumed reality of the legal and policy landscape to be worked within or around, rather than as a policy choice.

Given that the war on drugs is predicated on "eradication" of the "evil" drug threat as a way of achieving an (entirely fantastical) "drug-free world," it has effectively established a permanent state of war. A curiously self-justifying logic now prevails in which harms that are a direct result of drug prohibition—such as children killed in drug gang drive-by shootings, drug-fueled conflict, environmental damage, corruption or deaths from contaminated street drugs—are confused and conflated with harms related to drug use. These policy-related harms then bolster the "drug menace" rhetoric and justify the continuation, or intensification of prohibition.

This has contributed to a high level policy environment that routinely ignores critical scientific thinking, and health and social policy norms. Fighting the threat—defending the vulnerable from the evil of drugs—becomes an end in itself, one that is seen as intrinsically righteous, and as such it creates a largely self-referential and self-justifying rhetoric that makes meaningful evaluation, review, and debate difficult, if not impossible. Indeed, while the drug-related victimhood of the child is a key part of prohibition narrative, furnished with emotive anecdotes of wasted youth and bereaved parents, prohibition's effect generally, and its influence on children specifically, remains largely immunized from meaningful scrutiny and evaluation.

Practical and Intellectual Challenges to the Prohibitionist Status Quo

Despite this hostile ideological environment, two distinct policy trends have emerged in recent decades—harm reduction and decriminalization of personal possession and use. While both nominally permitted within existing international legal frameworks, they pose serious practical and intellectual challenges to the overarching status quo. Both have been driven by pragmatic necessity; harm reduction emerging in the mid-1980s in response to the epidemic of HIV among injecting drug users, and decriminalization in response to resource pressures on overburdened criminal justice systems (and to a lesser extent, concerns over the rights of users).

Both policies have succeeded in demonstrating effectiveness to the extent that harm reduction is now used in policy or practice in ninety-three countries,[2] while decriminalization (in various forms) has spread across mainland Europe, Central America, and Latin America, with cannabis-only decriminalization more widespread still—including states in Australia and the United States.

Decriminalization has demonstrated that less punitive approaches do not necessarily lead to increased use, most notably in Portugal, where even though drug use more generally has risen in line with its European neighbors, use among young people has actually fallen since the 2001 decriminalization of personal possession of all drugs (now dealt with via civil/administrative interventions).[3] While we should not assume a causal link between this positive development and the decriminalization itself—there being many other policy and wider environmental variables at play (not least the substantive investment in public health programs)—the fact that the apocalypse predicted by many doomsayers has failed to materialize remains significant.

More broadly an extensive World Health Organization study concluded:

> Globally, drug use is not distributed evenly and is not simply related to drug policy, since countries with stringent user-level illegal drug policies did not have lower levels of use than countries with liberal ones.[4]

Similarly, cannabis decriminalization states in the United States do not have higher levels of use than those without, and more significantly, the Netherlands, with its de facto legally regulated cannabis availability (for adults), does not have higher levels than its prohibitionist neighbors (for all age groups).[5] If there is a deterrent effect from increasingly punitive responses to drug use, the evidence base for it is strikingly weak. The near universal research aversion of governments to this question, despite the central role of punitive deterrence in the drug war narrative, is a particularly telling indicator of the paradigms roots in populist polemic, rather than science.

Without diminishing the importance and effect of these emerging policy trends, they can, however, be seen primarily as symptomatic responses mitigating against harms created by the prohibitionist policy environment. Neither directly addresses the public health or wider social harms created or exacerbated by the illegal production and supply of drugs.

The logic of both, however, ultimately leads to confronting the inevitable choice: nonmedical drug markets can remain in the hands of unregulated criminal profiteers or they can be controlled and regulated by appropriate government authorities. There is no third option under which there are no drugs in society. There is a need to make this choice based on a rational objective evaluation of which option may deliver the best outcomes in terms of minimizing harms, both domestic and international, associated with drug production, supply, and use. The impact on different policy regimes on vulnerable populations will naturally be one of the priority indicators of any policy's success or failure.

Exploring legal regulatory approaches does not preclude demand reduction as a legitimate long-term policy goal, indeed it is argued that it may facilitate it among vulnerable groups. Acknowledging the need for regulation does, however, accept that policy must also deal with the reality of high levels of demand as they exist now. However, a historical stumbling block in this debate has been that the eloquent and detailed critiques of the drug war have not been matched by a vision for its replacement. Unless a credible public health-led model of drug market regulation is proposed, the myths and misrepresentations will inevitably fill the void. So what would such a model look like?

A "Blueprint for Regulation"

Transform Drug Policy Foundation's 2009 *After the War on Drugs: Blueprint for Regulation* attempts to answer this question by offering a menu of options for controls over all aspects of production, supply/availability, and use. This includes controls over products (dosage, preparation, price, and packaging); vendors (licensing, vetting and training requirements, marketing, and promotions); outlets (location, outlet density, appearance); where and when drugs can be consumed; and, crucially for this discussion, who has access to the legally regulated availability including age controls, along with explorations of licensed buyer and club membership access models.[6]

Blueprint then rationally explores options for different drugs and different using populations to suggest the regulatory models that may deliver the best outcomes. Lessons are drawn from successes and failings with alcohol and tobacco regulation in the UK and beyond, as well as controls over pharmaceutical drugs and other risky products and activities that are regulated by government. Such regulated models occupy a space on the continuum of policy options between the poles of the absolute prohibitions of a war on drugs and entirely unregulated free market models (such as the online sales of "legal highs" such as mephedrone).

Moves toward legal regulation of drug markets would naturally need to be phased in cautiously over a number of years, with close evaluation and monitoring of results and any unintended negative consequences being essential elements of any roll out—not least the negative effects on the most vulnerable. Where problems emerge controls could be adapted with alternative approaches or increased levels of regulation.

Clearly, there are particularly important lessons to be learned from alcohol and tobacco policy, most significantly the corrosive effects on public health of unregulated commercial promotion aimed at children and young people. These experiences and the variety of responses to them over the past century do, however, mean that we now at least have a clear idea of how to effectively regulate these products to reduce the harm they cause to society. This understanding—while far from universally adopted—is clearly outlined in guidelines produced by the World Health Organization, in documents such as the *Framework for Alcohol Policy in the WHO European Region*, and the *Framework Convention on Tobacco Control*, that in many respects embody precisely the kind of rational public health-based regulatory approaches to drug control being advocated by the drug law reform movement.

There is, of course, no universal regulatory model. A flexible range of regulatory tools would be available and applied differentially across the spectrum of products and production/supply/using environments. Naturally, the more restrictive controls would be deployed for more risky products, and, correspondingly, less restrictive controls for lower-risk products. This potential for differential application of regulatory controls according to risk could additionally help create a "risk-availability gradient." This holds the potential not only to reduce harms associated with illicit supply and patterns of consumption as they currently exist but also, in the longer term, to progressively encourage or "nudge" patterns of use to move toward safer products, behaviors, and using environments.

An understanding of such processes is emerging from both the literature on alcohol control (for example, progressive tax increases according to alcohol content) and the emerging understanding of *route transition interventions*[7] aimed at encouraging injecting drug users to move to lower risk noninjecting modes of administration via, for example, providing foil for smoking heroin. This process is the precise opposite of what has happened under prohibition, where an unregulated profit-driven dynamic has tended to tilt the market toward ever more potent (but profitable) drugs and drug preparations, as well as encouraging riskier behaviors in high-risk settings.

The oversight and enforcement of new regulatory regimes would fall to a range of public health, regulatory, and enforcement agencies—including established health and safety and policing infrastructure. Activities that take place outside of the regulatory framework would naturally remain prohibited and subject to civil or criminal sanctions, or appropriate nonpunitive interventions for nonadults as deemed appropriate and established to be effective.

Children in a Post-Prohibition Model?

Restricting or preventing access to drugs by nonadults is a key element of any existing or future regulatory models. Any rights of access to psychoactive drugs and freedom of choice over drug-taking decisions should only be granted to consenting adults. This is partly because of the more general concerns regarding child vs. adult rights and responsibilities. More important, however, in line with a risk-based regulatory logic, the specific short- and long-term health risks associated with drug use are significantly higher for children, and, of course, the younger they are, the greater the risks.

This combination of legal principle and public health management legitimizes a strict age-control policy. In practical terms, it should also be noted that stringent restrictions on young people's access to drugs—while inevitably imperfect—are more feasible and easier to police than population-wide prohibitions. Generally speaking, children are subject to a range of social and state controls to which adults are not. More specifically, drug restrictions for minors command near universal adult support—making them a more practical proposition than the widely flouted laws criminalizing adult drug use.

Combined with this is the fact that while markets created by any prohibition will always attract criminal interest, the nonadult market for drugs is a small fraction of the total adult market. Thus, enforcement could be brought to bear on it with far more efficiency, and correspondingly greater chances of success.

It is also worth pointing out that one ironic and unintended side effect of prohibition can potentially make illegal drug markets, that have no age thresholds, easier for young people to access than legally regulated markets for (say) alcohol or tobacco. According to the U.S. drug use surveillance systems funded by the U.S. National Institutes on Drug Abuse, over the past thirty years of cannabis prohibition, the drug has remained "almost universally available to American 12th graders," with 80–90 percent over this period saying the drug is "very easy" or "fairly easy" to obtain.[8]

Of course, there is an important debate around what age constitutes an acceptable age/access threshold. Different countries have adopted different thresholds for tobacco and alcohol, generally ranging from fourteen to twenty-one for purchase or access to licensed premises. Where this threshold should lie for a given drug product will depend on a range of pragmatic choices. These should be informed by objective risk assessments, evaluated by individual states or local licensing authorities, and balanced in accordance with their own priorities.

As with all areas of regulatory policy there needs to be some flexibility allowed in response to changing circumstances or emerging evidence. In the UK, for example, the age of access for tobacco purchase has recently been raised from sixteen to eighteen, while in the United States there is a growing debate over whether the alcohol age threshold of twenty-one is too high. The Amethyst Initiative (supported by 135 chancellors and presidents of U.S. universities and colleges) argues, for example, that the age twenty-one limit has created "a culture of dangerous, clandestine 'binge-drinking'— often conducted off-campus" and that "by choosing to use fake IDs, students make ethical compromises that erode respect for the law."[9] Even within a legal regulatory framework, inappropriate prohibitions evidently have the potential to create unintended consequences. They can undermine, rather than augment, the development of social controls and responsible norms regarding drugs and drug use. It is clear that age limits need to be realistic and, crucially, properly enforced to be effective.

In the UK, for example—where "binge-drinking" among young people has been a growing problem—there has been a widespread lack of age restriction enforcement, with Alcohol Concern reporting that: "10–15% of licensed premises are found to persistently sell alcohol to the under-aged yet only 0.5% licensed premises are called up for review."[10] Secondary supply of legitimately obtained drugs to nonadults will also require appropriate enforcement and sanction, perhaps with a graded severity depending on distance in age from the legal threshold.

Legal age controls can, of course, only ever be part of the solution to reducing drug-related harms among young people. Effective regulation and access controls must be supported by concerted prevention efforts. These should include evidence-based, targeted drug education that balances the need to encourage healthy lifestyles

CHILDREN OF THE DRUG WAR

(including abstinence) while not ignoring the need to reduce the related risks. Funding for such programs could be easily met by the inevitable savings in criminal justice and enforcement expenditure as a program of reform is rolled out.

Drug Policy: Trying to See the Bigger Picture

Perhaps more important is longer-term investment in social capital. Young people—particularly those most at risk in marginal/vulnerable populations—need and should be given meaningful alternatives to drug use, and there is a strong evidence base to support the effectiveness of such interventions. The SMART program in the United States, for example, which works on public housing estates, has found that providing youth clubs has a real influence on reducing drug use, dealing, and overall criminal activity in both young people and adults.[11] It is also worth noting that the Netherlands and Sweden regularly top the United Nations Children's Fund (UNICEF) child well-being table and have relatively low levels of drug misuse (despite markedly different drug policies), while the United States and the United Kingdom invariably sit at or near the bottom and have relatively high levels of misuse and a lower age of misusers.[12]

It is increasingly clear that levels of problematic drug use (among all age groups) primarily reflect a complex interplay of social, economic, and cultural variables. Key drivers include social deprivation, inequality, and broader measures of personal and social well-being. The corollary of this is that the results of drug policy as traditionally conceived (prevention, treatment, and enforcement) should not be overestimated, may be marginal, and, in many cases, irrelevant, relative to the underlying social determinants of drug-using behaviors.

This analysis—that problematic use is essentially a barometer of a social well-being (or its lack)—has obvious implications for longer-term prevention and harm reduction strategies. It suggests that success is likely to flow more from investing in social capital and addressing multiple deprivation and inequality issues, particularly as they affect young people, rather than from pouring ever more money into more conventional interventions that are poorly supported by evidence. This naturally points to a much broader program of social policy reform and investment, and notably highlights the need for drug policy to emerge from its drug war bunker mentality, adopt a more holistic worldview, and integrate far more effectively with parallel disciplines and institutions involved with social and public health policy.

While conventional drug policy may only be able to achieve, at best, fairly marginal effects with respect to the prevalence of problematic use, the overarching prohibitionist legal framework can clearly have a dramatic influence on levels of harm associated with drug use, both by increasing health risks associated with use, and through the wider social harms created or exacerbated by the illegal drug market.

While it is specifically not envisaged that legal availability of drugs would be extended to children, it remains the case that illegal production and supply serves to maximize the risk associated with use itself for all age groups. As already discussed, an unregulated market serving the interests of criminal profiteers will tend to shift toward the most concentrated products—for example, why you can buy crack on the streets of London, but not coca. Furthermore, illegal products are of unknown strength and purity, often cut or contaminated, and without packaging information about dosage, safety, or risks. Legally regulated products—even if sold or passed on in an informal secondary marketplace or via peer networks—would be intrinsically less risky than their illicit counterparts. Furthermore, barriers and distrust between youth and authority figures perpetuated by punitive prohibitions—be they educators or law enforcers—would be progressively reduced, facilitating more effective communication and dialogue about drug risks and healthy lifestyles.

Arguably much more significant would be the reduction in harms to children and young people that would follow the progressive contraction of the illegal drug market as the trade shifted into the legally regulated models. As has been so eloquently described elsewhere in this collection, the harms to children from the war on drugs and its unintended consequences—quite aside from drug use— are profound and terrifying in scale. Even a small reduction in the extent of these harms, which include the brutality of the markets whose frontline children live on, the conflict fueled by illicit drug profits, and the destabilization of social infrastructure by illicit drug market-related corruption and violence, would be a huge social positive.

Prohibitions on commodities for which there is high demand

inevitably create criminal opportunities, pushing production, supply, and consumption into an illicit parallel economy. Such illicit activity is flexible and opportunistic, naturally exploiting the most vulnerable workforce and seeking out locations where it can operate with minimum cost and interference, hence the attraction of geographically marginal regions and fragile, failing or failed states. As a result, many countries or regions involved in drug production and transit have weak or chaotic governance and state infrastructure.

The illegal drug trade can be seen as providing a vital income stream for a range of insurgents, militias, and terrorist groups. The cocaine trade, for example, directly fuels the long-running civil wars in Colombia, and now undermines emerging transit states in West Africa, such as Guinea Bissau. The opiate trade similarly contributes to wider regional conflicts in Central Asia—prominently in Afghanistan, now spilling over into Pakistan, in which the Taliban and various rival political factions and warlords are substantially funded via their control of the opium/heroin trade.

At the same time, Mexico has witnessed a horrifying explosion of violence, with estimates of as many as 28,000 deaths in the past four years, as the government has tried and failed to use military force to crush the drug cartels (sustained by an impoverished population providing a ready supply of young foot soldiers), which are now powerful and rich enough to outgun state enforcement efforts. A similar, although largely unreported, level of violence has unfolded in Venezuela, which is also fighting its own very real, but equally futile, war on drugs.

Large-scale illicit activity can thus undermine governance and social infrastructure at local regional and even national levels, feeding into a downward development spiral. In such a spiral, existing social problems are exacerbated and governance further undermined through endemic corruption at all levels of government, judiciary, and policing, another inevitable feature of illicit drug markets entirely controlled by organized criminal profiteers.

As with all wars, in the drug war it is the young, poor, and marginalized who are most vulnerable to the violence and wider social harms that conflict creates.

Clearly, any high-value natural resources, whether legal or illegal, can potentially fuel conflict. Legal examples include oil, diamonds, and coltan. But for these legal products high value is intrinsic and relatively consistent, regardless of international legal frameworks. By contrast, drug crops such as opium poppy and coca are essentially low-value agricultural commodities. They have only become high value as a result of a prohibitionist legal framework (a combination of unregulated profiteering and the high risk to producers/traffickers is passed on to the consumer), which in turn encourages expanded criminal control of the trade. By the time they reach developed world users, the alchemy of prohibition is such that they have become literally worth more than their weight in gold.

Progressive shifts toward legal regulation of these products would naturally undermine the markets, remove the extraordinary profits on offer, and choke off a key a source of funding for so much of the conflict and corruption. About half of the world's opium production is entirely legal and regulated—that is, for the medical market. This legal production of opium (and indeed coca—albeit on a smaller scale) is associated with few, if any, of the problems highlighted above.[13] In this legal context, they essentially function as regular agricultural commodities—much like coffee, tea, or other plant-based pharmaceutical precursors.

Under a legal production regime, drug crops would become part of the wider development discourse (and drug products more resemble conventionally controlled pharmaceuticals). While such agricultural activities still present a raft of serious and urgent challenges to both the local and international communities—for example, coping with the whims of global capitalist markets and the general lack of a fair trade infrastructure—dealing with such issues within a legally regulated market framework means they are not additionally impeded by the negative consequences of prohibition and the criminal empires it has created.

Similar effects would be seen in the reduction of all specifically drug war-related harms: increased regulation of production would reduce the environmental impacts of the unregulated parallel trade; a key driver of urban gang violence would be reduced; family breakups related to incarceration of parents and caregivers would be reduced; and so on.

We should be careful not to imagine such reform as a silver bullet solution or panacea for the people or regions of the world blighted by the unintended fallout of prohibition, or that change could happen overnight. Instead it should be realistically considered more as a gradual, probably generational, process of removing a key driver of personal and social harms, and an obstacle to longer-term social and economic development.

There can, however, be hope that reform would help facilitate more positive change, albeit indirectly, via the potential for the billions, *even trillions*, of dollars still being poured into failed, futile, and actively counterproductive enforcement efforts—to be redirected toward more socially beneficial ends, be it housing, food security, education, public health, environmental protection, or any number of worthwhile social programs. This holds enormous promise for the children and young people negatively affected by the war on drugs—and indeed, the poor and marginalized in society more broadly.

Different social environments will require different approaches in response to the specific challenges they face. Transform's *Blueprint* does not seek to provide all the answers—but rather seeks to move the debate beyond "should we end the war on drugs?" to "what could the world look like after the war on drugs?"

Endnotes

1. D. Kushlick, *International Security and the Global War on Drugs: The Tragic Irony of Drug Securitisation* (Bristol, Transform Drug Policy Foundation, 2011), www.tdpf.org.uk/Security%20and%20drugs%20paper%20Feb%20final%20for%20 website.pdf.
2. C. Cook, ed., *The Global State of Harm Reduction 2010: Key Issues for Broadening the Response* (London: International Harm Reduction Association, 2010).
3. C. Hughes and A. Stevens, "What Can We Learn from the Portuguese Decriminalisation of Illicit Drugs?" *British Journal of Criminology* (July 2010), http://bjc.oxfordjournals.org/content/early/2010/07/21/bjc.azq038.full.
4. L. Degenhardt, W-T. Chiu, N. Sampson, R.C. Kessler, J.C. Anthony, M. Angermeyer et al. "Toward a Global View of Alcohol, Tobacco, Cannabis, and Cocaine Use: Findings from the WHO World Mental Health Surveys," *PLoS Med* 5, no. 7 (2008): e141.
5. R. Room, W. Hall, P. Reuter, B. Fischer, and S. Lenton, *Global Cannabis Commission Report* (Oxford: Beckley Foundation, 2009).
6. S. Rolles, *After the War on Drugs: Blueprint for Regulation* (Bristol: Transform Drug Policy Foundation, 2009), www.tdpf.org.uk.
7. J. Bridge, "Route Transition Interventions: Potential Public Health Gains from Reducing or Preventing Injecting," *International Journal of Drug Policy* 21 (2010): 125–28.
8. L.D. Johnston, P.M. O'Malley, J.G. Bachman, and J.E. Schulenberg, *Monitoring the Future: National Survey Results on Drug Use, 1975–2005. Volume I: Secondary School Students.* (Bethesda, MD: National Institute on Drug Abuse, 2006), NIH publication no. 06-5883.

9. See www.amethystinitiative.org.
10. Alcohol Concern, *Unequal Partners: A Report into the Limitations of the Alcohol Regulatory Regime* (2008), 19, www.alcoholconcern.org.uk/assets/files/Publications/Unequal%20partners.pdf.
11. Steven P. Schinke et al., *The Effects of Boys & Girls Clubs on Alcohol and Other Drug Use and Related Problems in Public Housing. Final Research Report* (New York: Education Resource Information Center, 1991).
12. UNICEF, *Child Poverty in Perspective: An Overview of Child Well-being in Rich Countries, Innocenti Report Card 7,* 2007, 4, www.unicef-irc.org/publications/pdf/rc7_eng.pdf.
13. See Rolles *After the War on Drugs*, Appendix 2.

Discussion Questions

1. What is the connection between poverty and illicit crop production? What are the specific issues facing children? What are the policy implications of this?

2. The drug trade is a global security threat requiring a military response. Discuss, considering the impact of war and conflict on children.

3. Barra and Joloy claim that the gains in Mexico's drug war, measured in seizures, frozen assets, and arrests, are not worth the price that has been paid. Eighty percent of the Mexican public appears to disagree.[1] What is your view?

4. Do you agree that alternative regulatory frameworks may better protect children from drugs? What are the risks to children of this approach? How can they be addressed?

---

1. Richard Wike, "Mexicans Continue Support for Drug War," Pew Research Centre, August 12, 2010; http://pewresearch.org/pubs/1698/mexico-support-drug-war-less-supportive-of-american-involvement/.

Part 2:
Targets: Race, Class, and Law Enforcement

Thirty-two states retain the death penalty for drug offences in violation of international human rights commitments.[1] In Georgia, drug crackdowns in 2007 resulted in 4 percent of the country's male population being tested for drugs, many under forced conditions. Thirty-five percent of these went on to be imprisoned on a drug-related charge.[2] Military and police have been responsible for hundreds of killings in Mexico's drug war since 2006.[3] Singapore applies long-term imprisonment and corporal punishment (caning) for drug dependence.[4] In China, hundreds of thousands have been detained without trial in drug detention centers and subjected to forced labor under the guise of drug treatment,[5] while punitive laws and abusive policing practices have impeded the response to HIV among injecting drug users in country after country around the world.[6]

The excesses of law enforcement in the war on drugs are clear. What is hidden by the top line facts and figures above, however, is the fact that, by and large, it is poorer people, those from ethnic minorities, and those at the margins of society who feel the brunt of these excesses. While law enforcement-based policies have dominated drug control for many decades, their focus has been far from equally distributed. In Ecuador, for example, women drug mules, often driven to the trade by poverty are now disproportionately represented in the country's prisons.[7] In Ukraine, people who are drug dependent are often seen as "soft targets," particularly when arrest quotas place quantity of arrests over the severity of crimes.[8] In the United States, approximately half a million people are incarcerated for drug offenses. But African Americans are ten times more likely than whites to be incarcerated for such crimes.[9]

The first two chapters in this section deal with this last statistic from the perspective of young people. These chapters, which focus on racial and class disparities in the war on drugs in the United States, hone in on preconceptions about drug users and drug dealers—who they are, and what their motivations may be. Deborah Peterson Small's chapter, "Getting the Message: Hip-Hop Reports on the Drug War," is a fascinating and colloquial insight into the effects of the war on drugs on young black and Latino American men. She documents messages about drugs, prison, and law enforcement in hip-hop music, which has, through the years, been the "newsstand" for young people, where information about the realities of life for black and Latino communities is passed on. As Peterson Small says, "Anyone seeking to understand the effects of decades of drug law enforcement on poor black and Latino youth should listen to the lyrics and music of the generations of young people who have lived on the frontlines of the U.S. 'war on drugs.'"

A. Rafik Mohamed and Erik Fritsvold complement these insights with a study of drug dealing among fifty affluent, mostly white, male college students. Their chapter, "Under Cover of Privilege: College Drug Dealing in the United States," shows that despite what the authors called "collective bungling" and the students' utter lack of risk-aversion strategies, few of these dealers were ever the focus of law enforcement efforts, nor had they any fear of the drug war. Only one was convicted for drug offenses and none were incarcerated for their crimes. All but one eventually transitioned out of drug dealing and into licit occupations, leaving drugs and the drug war behind. The disparity with "open market" dealers in poor, black, and Latino neighborhoods, and the experiences of those represented in Peterson Small's chapter, could not be greater.[10]

From the United States, the next chapter moves south to Brazil, where the war on drugs has been described as "organised armed violence."[11] Indeed, "Young Soldiers in Brazil's Drug War," by Michelle Gueraldi, could be included in part 1, alongside Mexico. It has been included here, however, due to the author's focus on young, poor, black boys as targets of the drug war. Gueraldi, a human rights lawyer, questions why a more holistic children's rights-based approach, already reflected in Brazilian law, has not been adopted given the socioeconomic forces driving involvement in the drug trade for many of these children. Her chapter portrays a childhood for many of those living in the *favelas* that is brutal and short—in which involvement in the drug trade is a rational choice set against a vacuum of realistic options. At the root of Gueraldi's analysis is the impact of public attitudes toward poor, marginalized young people. In her words, public opinion has become "cynical to the point of supporting or turning a blind eye to the systematic killing of children."

Endnotes

1. See R. Lines, "A Most Serious Crime? The Death Penalty for Drug Offences in International Human Rights Law," *Amicus Journal*, no. 21 (2010): 21–28.
2. D. Otiashvili, "Georgian Drug War—Ignoring Evidences, Neglecting Human Rights," paper presented at the International Harm Reduction Association's Nineteenth Annual Conference, Barcelona, Spain, May 14, 2008.
3. See chapter 2.
4. Central Narcotics Bureau, *Annual Bulletin* (2007), 19.
5. Human Rights Watch, *Where Darkness Knows no Limits: Incarceration, Ill-treatment and Forced Labor as Drug Rehabilitation in China*, January 2010, www.hrw.org/en/reports/2010/01/07/where-darkness-knows-no-limits-0/.
6. See *The Vienna Declaration: A Global Call to Action for Science-based Drug Policy*, July 2010, www.viennadeclaration.com.
7. See chapter 9.
8. See, for example, Human Rights Watch, *Rhetoric and Risk Human Rights Abuses Impeding Ukraine's Fight Against HIV/AIDS*, May 2006, www.hrw.org/en/reports/2006/03/01/rhetoric-and-risk. See also chapter 10 on Indonesia.
9. Human Rights Watch, *Targeting Blacks: Drug Law Enforcement and Race in the United States*, May 2008, www.hrw.org/en/node/62236/section/1/.
10. See also D. Simon and R. Burns, *The Corner: A Year in the Life of an Inner City Neighborhood* (New York: Broadway, 1997).
11. See L. Dowdney, *Children of the Drug Trade: A Case Study of Children in Organised Armed Violence in Rio De Janeiro* (Rio De Janeiro: 7 Letras, 2003).

5. Getting the Message: Hip-Hop Reports on the Drug War

by Deborah Peterson Small

Hip-Hop and the Drug War

Music and drugs are fellow travelers. Music is a universal medium of expression. Drugs have been used throughout human history by people of all ages. Both stir emotion and moods, and can alter one's state of mind in minutes. Music is a particularly favored medium of youth. Throughout modern history music has provided a means for young people to express their concerns and angst. Illicit drug use is also a common experience of youth, particularly in the United States. According to the most recent Monitoring the Future (MTF) survey more than 45 percent of all high school seniors reported using an illicit drug in their lifetime. Consequently, it is no exaggeration to say that music, drugs, and youth travel in the same circles.

Hip-hop began as an urban movement encompassing rap music, break dancing, graffiti art, and fashion. Created in New York City during the late 1970s, it reflected the hopes and aspirations as well as the many challenges facing inner-city youth. Its dominant feature is "rap" (performed by MCs—aka "masters of ceremonies")—a discursive oral art form that traces its roots to the griots of West Africa.[1] In its purest form, known as "freestyling," rap is about creating extemporaneous poetry delivered to rhythmic beats. A rapper is distinguished by verbal agility, demonstrated in competitive "battles." DJs (disc jockeys) create the soundtrack of hip-hop by sampling parts of existing songs, looping them, and adding new sounds to create music to rap to. Break-dancing is competitive street dancing consisting of elements that demonstrate physical agility and strength. Graffiti is a popular method used by young urban artists to communicate identity, expression, and ideas through drawings, markings, and messages painted, written, or scratched on a wall or surface (in New York City, the surface was often subway trains).

The advent of hip-hop coincided with the escalation of the "war on drugs" in the United States in the early 1980s. In response to concern over growth of the illicit drug trade and increasing use of smokable cocaine (known as "crack" or "rocks") in inner-city communities,

Congress passed new laws that intensified the war on drugs, and in a short time, state legislators followed suit. At both the federal and state levels, lawmakers adopted expansive definitions of "drug-related crimes" and required the imposition of harsh sentences aimed at keeping individuals with any connection to drugs behind bars for longer periods of time. Despite the reality of problematic drug use among every socioeconomic and demographic group, these new laws would be enforced most vigorously in poor black and Latino communities—with devastating effects on multiple generations of men, women, and children.

A frequent justification given by U.S. officials for enacting such "get tough" approaches is the need to protect vulnerable youth from drugs, drug sellers, and drug-related crime. Ironically, the expanding definition of "drug-related crimes" increasingly ensnared juveniles who were charged and prosecuted as adults for drug offenses. Not surprisingly, black youth are disproportionately represented among youth arrested and charged with drug offenses and among juveniles prosecuted as adults for drug offenses, despite consistent evidence that black youth have a lower rate of illicit drug use than their white counterparts. According to the most recent MTF survey:

> *Among the most dramatic and interesting subgroup differences are those found among the three largest racial/ethnic groups— Whites, African Americans, and Hispanics.* **Contrary to popular assumption, at all three grade levels African-American students have substantially lower rates of use of most licit and illicit drugs than do Whites.** *These include any illicit drug use, most of the specific illicit drugs, alcohol, and cigarettes.*[2] [emphasis added]

Over the past three decades, legislators throughout the United States have adopted a variety of policies that send more minority youth to criminal court. These measures include: lowering the age at which juveniles can be prosecuted as adults; expanding the categories of crimes for which youth are automatically prosecuted in criminal court; giving prosecutors the exclusive authority to decide which juveniles are charged as adults; and limiting the discretion of judges to overturn decisions by prosecutors and law-enforcement officials. The impact of these policies has been dramatic, nowhere more so than in New York (the first state to adopt long mandatory drug sentencing) and California, which have the distinction of sending more young black and Latino men to prison each year than graduate from their state colleges and universities. Not surprisingly, New York and California have been at the center of major developments in the history of hip-hop.

Much has been written regarding the dramatic growth in the U.S. prison population; the role of punitive drug policies in fueling this growth; and the racially disparate consequences of drug-law enforcement on poor black communities. In addition to the numerous books, articles, reports, and research studies chronicling these developments, stories of the drug war and its influence pervade hip-hop music. Anyone seeking to understand the effects of decades of drug-law enforcement on poor minority youth should listen to the lyrics and music of the generations of young people who have lived on the frontlines of the U.S. "war on drugs."

Delivering the Message: News from the Streets to the Ears of the World ...

Hip-hop was created by alienated and marginalized youth seeking to tell their stories. In the 1980s, rappers used hip-hop to express their disillusionment, despair, anger, and impatience about what was happening to them and their communities. Hip-hop music revealed the not-so-hidden consequences of growing income inequality.

One of the first consciously political hip-hop recordings was "The Message" by Grandmaster Flash and the Furious Five. Released in 1983, it is a musical exhortation against complacency in the face of growing poverty and desperation. Its opening lines paint a bleak but honest picture of daily life in many ghettoized communities:

Broken glass everywhere
People pissing on the stairs, you know they just don't care
I can't take the smell, I can't take the noise
Got no money to move out, I guess I got no choice
Rats in the front room, roaches in the back
Junkies in the alley with the baseball bat

A later verse explains how childhood deprivation, *living second rate,* often leads to involvement in the criminal justice system. The lack of options for such children is acutely observed—their environment mirroring their future—*one great big alleyway.*

You'll admire all the number book takers
Thugs, pimps, pushers and the big money makers
Driving big cars, spending twenties and tens
And you wanna grow up to be just like them

The attraction of criminality set against such a bleak outlook is clear. The song, however, is a warning. It predicts education loss, violence, and inevitable incarceration. It predicts the loss of youth. Its chorus could not be more explicit or poetic in describing the artists' feelings about this: *Don't push me cause I'm close to the edge.*

The issues addressed in "The Message": poor living conditions; dearth of positive male role models; nonengagement with education; chronic unemployment; the lure of criminality; police brutality; and incarceration are recurring themes in hip-hop music and culture.

Crack Game: Dealing Drugs, Employment Opportunity for the Discarded

Hip-hop developed during a period of extraordinary economic transition—the flight of manufacturing and other traditional businesses from urban areas left a significant portion of young men with minimal employment prospects. Black and Latino males with poor grades and especially those who dropped out of school, faced a hostile and competitive labor market—long periods of unemployment soon became the norm. Into this vacuum stepped drug cartels that saw in these young men a ready labor pool with direct ties to new, lucrative markets, and considerable drive to make enough money to get out of their ghetto neighborhoods. The economic pressures that compel many young black and Latino men to enter the illicit drug market are described repeatedly in hip-hop music.

In "Love's Gonna Get' Cha/Material Love" (1990) KRS-One tells a compelling story of coming of age into the drug business, rapping about growing up poor and being lured by the opportunity to make money to help his family. *Every day I see my mother struggling, now it's time I've got to do something,* says the narrator, describing then the embarrassment of rejection from work and the degradation of menial jobs. Easy money comes in the form of a *quick delivery* for a local dealer—*I do it once, I do it twice, now there's steak with the beans and rice . . . my family's happy everything is new, now tell me what the fuck am I supposed to do?* The narrator soon becomes a moderately successful drug dealer able to provide for his family and enjoy some of the finer things in life for a while, but a beef with a rival dealer results in the shooting of his brother leading to a gun battle that results in the police killing two of his friends.

Most politicians, community leaders, and media portrayed young minority men involved in the street drug trade as lazy, irresponsible parasites. As the drug war raged on through the 1980s and 1990s, hip-hop artists responded to the demonization of drug dealers by pointing to the hypocrisy of a system that rewarded wealth and power regardless of the method by which it was acquired and yet penalized black men who sought the same by utilizing the few economic options available to them.

In "I Want to Talk to You" (1999), Nas—considered by music critics one of the most lyrically gifted hip-hop artists—challenges the prevailing condemnation of drug dealing, asserting that for many it is a means of survival amid a desert of other options—*Niggaz gotta go create his own job.* He asks the nation's political leaders what they would do in the same situation: *Mr. Mayor imagine this was your backyard/Mr. Governor imagine it's your kids that starved.* And he implicates them in the situation facing young black men, explaining in so few words how racism, capitalism, and class make involvement in criminality all but unavoidable: *all I got is what you left me with, I'm gonna get it.*

In "Manifesto" (1998), Talib Kweli tells the truth succinctly:
Supply and the demand it's all capitalism
People don't sell crack cause they like to see blacks smoke
People sell crack cause they broke

The rise of hip-hop came at a time when the U.S. music industry was in transition. New technologies brought unanticipated changes— affecting record sales and profits. Hip-hop provided a much needed boost to an ailing industry with its new sounds, creativity, and energy. The commercial success of hip-hop correspondingly provided economic opportunities for marginalized black men at a time when other employment options were becoming scarce. One group well positioned to seize the opportunities hip-hop provided for financial reward was ghetto entrepreneurs (aka drug dealers). Ironically, some of the most successful and well-known hip-hop moguls were involved in the illicit drug economy early in life. Many leveraged the proceeds from illegal drugs to finance their start in the music industry. This path, followed by Russell Simmons, Jay-Z, Master P, Nas, Notorious B.I.G., Eazy-E, Suge Knight, 50 Cent, Lil Wayne, and countless others, has led generations of hip-hop fans throughout America to believe that if you are smart and lucky, selling drugs can be a step toward establishing a successful music career.

In "Drug Dealer" (1992), KRS-One makes the point that historically profits from crime have eased the path for many upwardly mobile Americans:

Drug dealer, understand historical fact
Every race got ahead from selling drugs except Black
We are under attack here's another cold fact
In the 30s and 40s the drug dealer wasn't Black
They were Jewish, Italian, Irish, Polish etc., etcetera
Now in the 90s their lives are a lot better

Thugs with Drugs: The Rise of Gangster Rap

We treat this rap shit just like handlin weight.
JAY-Z, "Rap Game/Crack Game" (1997)

Given the relationship between hip-hop music and street drug culture it is not surprising that rap lyrics reference the many similarities between the music and drug businesses.

The economic success of hip-hop music and culture created a new path to escape ghetto life. While many inner-city youth dreamed of a career in professional sports, achieving it required extraordinary physical attributes and gifts that few are born with. Hip-hop provided the promise of fame and fortune to the verbally gifted who did not sing or dance. Anyone with the ability to write and deliver rhymes or create new beats could ostensibly become a star. As hip-hop continued to grow in popularity and influence, the numbers of young black men and women who sought to ride the hip-hop train to fame grew exponentially. However, as is true in many markets, the proliferation of hip-hop talent made it easy for the industry to exploit new and unsophisticated artists. Many artists were unaware that the *commercial* success of hip-hop culture was built on appealing to a demographic different from the group the music was initially created for. Record companies discovered a highly lucrative market for hip-hop in alienated suburban white youth who reveled in the violence, misogyny, and criminality expressed in some hip-hop music, which they adopted as the authentic experience of inner-city youth. By some estimates, 80 percent of hip-hop music is bought by white youth.

The genre of hip-hop music most appealing to alienated white youth is "gangster rap," celebrating the lifestyle commonly associated with gamblers, gangsters, pimps, hustlers, and drug traffickers. Its essence is selfish, misogynistic, violent, materialistic, and amoral. Gangster rap first developed in Los Angeles and is directly related to the growing involvement of LA gangs (primarily the Crips and Bloods) in the drug trade. The group that put gangster rap on the map was N.W.A. (Niggaz with Attitude). By taking on the hated "N word" (nigger) and the negative characteristics associated with it, the group was declaring itself outside contemporary society—both white and black. By adding the description "with Attitude," they were serving notice that, like gangsters, they were dangerous and not to be messed with. One of the founding members, Eazy-E, initially conceived of the group and the record label they started as a way to launder the money he made selling drugs. As gangster rap grew in notoriety and profits, many hip-hop artists promoting themselves as "gangster rappers" conspicuously took the names and aliases of well-known mafia and drug cartel leaders (e.g., Junior Mafia, Noriega, Gambino, Escobar) to establish their affinity with those choosing to live by the "Code of the Streets" (1994) as described by Gang Starr:

I'll organize some brothers and get some crazy loot
Selling d-r-u-g-s and clocking dollars, troop
Cause the phat dough, yo, that suits me fine
I gotta have it so I can leave behind
The mad poverty, never having always needing
If a sucker steps up, then I leave him bleeding
. . .
You gotta be a pro, do what you know
When you're dealing with the code of the streets

The Wu-Tang Clan succinctly summed up the prevailing value in the United States, when they proclaimed in their mega-hit "C.R.E.A.M." (1994), "Cash Rules Everything Around Me, Get the Money, Dollar, Dollar Bills Y'all." Gangster rap celebrates this lifestyle with its promise of quick financial gain and easy sexual conquests. However, it is worth noting that aside from the prevalence of guns, the sentiments and attitudes reflected in gangster rap are very similar to the values and behavior that have prevailed on Wall

Street over the past three decades. "Greed is good," has been the dominant ethos of mainstream financiers who made billions selling toxic products to unwitting customers who became addicted to the financial "high" of increasing profits and cheap borrowed money, no matter how risky. Unlike the titans of Wall Street who were rescued from the consequences of their follies by the federal government and successfully avoided prosecution, today's rappers are increasingly caught in a trap partly of their own making. Establishing one's criminal bona fides has become a prerequisite for legitimacy as a gangster rapper, and artists vie to exceed each other in verbal boasts of flouting the law. Prosecutors have become creative at using the lyrics of gangster rappers as evidence of criminal activity, leading to several high-profile prosecutions.

In reality, the life of the average street drug dealer is often harsh, dangerous, and financially unrewarding. This is well-described in "Last Dayz," by Onyx (1995). Beginning with a line borrowed from the 1993 film *Menace II Society*—*I'm America's nightmare, young black and just don't give a fuck*—the track describes a life of zero options, crime, and violence. There are messages of suicide—*thinking of taking my own life, might as well*—and violent ends—*and I'll probably bite the bullet cause I live by the gun*. Perhaps most striking, however, is the sense of resignation. The chorus sums it up:

It's life on the edge, a dangerous
way of livin, never givin a shit
cause we livin in it—we never givin a shit
cause we living in it

The opportunity to earn big money as a street-level drug dealer is almost as elusive for most black and Latino men as making it into professional sports. Several studies suggest the average street drug dealer earns slightly more than minimum wage and receives no extras for the safety hazards associated with the job (e.g., gunshots, beat-downs, theft), or compensation if hurt or arrested.[3] Guns are not a vicarious thrill but a fact of life—the number-one cause of death for young black men, especially those involved in drug-related activities. Nor is going to prison just tough-guy talk but a general eventuality, since one in four black men will do time at some point in their lives, usually while young.

"Sound of Da Police": Hip-Hop on Law Enforcement

The rise of hip-hop paralleled the exponential growth of imprisonment fueled by drug law enforcement. Hip-hop expresses the sentiments of minority inner-city youth who profoundly distrust the criminal justice system. This distrust begins with law enforcement. The police are viewed by many as a legal gang with which minority youth are perpetually at war.

In "Sound of da Police" (1993), KRS-One expands the critique of police harassment suggested at the end of "The Message" with a direct attack that connects modern-day police practices with the behavior of plantation overseers during chattel slavery:

> *Take the word "overseer," like a sample*
> *Repeat it very quickly in a crew for example*
> *Overseer, Overseer, Overseer, Overseer!*
> *Officer, Officer, Officer, Officer!*
> *Yeah, officer from overseer*
> *You need a little clarity?*
> *Check the similarity!*
> *. . .*
> *The overseer had the right to get ill*
> *And if you fought back, the overseer had the right to kill*
> *The officer has the right to arrest*
> *And if you fight back they put a hole in your chest!*

N.W.A. (Niggaz with Attitude) gained fame and notoriety for expressing the absolute contempt many young black Angelenos had for the Los Angeles Police Department, which was considered to be brutal and corrupt. In "Fuck tha Police" (1988) the group holds a mock trial where they find the police guilty of multiple crimes against young black men from Compton. They describe harassment:

> *Fuckin with me cuz I'm a teenager*
> *With a little bit of gold and a pager*
> *Searchin my car, lookin for the product*
> *Thinkin every nigga is sellin narcotics*

and racially motivated violence, accusing the police of claiming *the authority to kill a minority.*

Bass, How Low Can You Go? Hip-Hop on Drug Addiction

Bass, How Low Can You Go? is the famous double entendre opening to "Bring in the Noise," the opening track to Public Enemy's 1988 album *It Takes a Nation of Millions to Hold Us Back*. Bass, of course, refers to a male vocal range, the bass guitar, the bass drum, a bass line. Base, on the other hand, refers to freebase. "White Lines" (1983) by Grandmaster Flash and the Furious Five, however, was one of the first hip-hop songs to address the problem of drug addiction—in particular, the growing menace posed by cocaine, specifically freebasing.

Ticket to ride, white line highway
Tell all your friends, they can go my way
Pay your toll, sell your soul
Pound for pound costs more than gold
The longer you stay, the more you pay
My white lines go a long way
Either up your nose or through your vein
With nothin to gain except killin' your brain

While drinking and cannabis smoking are often glorified in gangster rap (e.g., the entire *Doggystyle* album by Snoop Doggy Dogg, 1993), this is not reflective of hip-hop more broadly. "I Need Drugs" (2000) is an amusingly ironic ode to crack cocaine addiction by Necro. While funny in places, it glorifies nothing. If anything, the core message is a sense of shame:

I ain't got no pride, While buying the shit
I'm lying to myself telling the runner I'm trying to quit
It's all make believe, I pretend that I'm true
When you give me credit, I'll dodge you every chance that I get to
Even if it's good, I'll sniff it up in a minute
Beep you back and complain that you put too much cut in it

What We Seeing Is . . . : Hip-Hop on Prison

Public Enemy's "Bring the Noise," quoted above, relates not only to addiction but also to the drug trade and prisons. *Bass, how low can you go?* is the question. *Death row, what a brother know* is the answer. In just twelve words, Chuck D had drawn the connection between drugs, addiction, the consequences of involvement in the drug trade, and the violence that surrounds it for young black men. Throughout the many genres of hip-hop music, there are messages about prison and prison life. While gangster rap is best known for its glorification of drug dealing, gang banging, and lifestyles of hedonistic criminality, many of the same groups that made gangster rap popular also rap about prison life, much based on personal experience. Hip-hop artists who have been through the criminal justice system are too numerous to count, a reflection of the prevalence of incarceration among young black men. Since "The Message," hip-hop music has included tales of incarceration.

In "Locked in Spofford" (1993) Mobb Deep describes juvenile detention and violent necessities of getting by—*Here, it takes a lot of heart to live . . . Niggaz got me fightin for my life, cause shit is real.* DMX, meanwhile, describes the revolving door of the criminal justice system and lock-down in maximum security in 2001's "Who We Be":

The release, the warning, "Try not to get in trouble"
The snitches, the odds, probation, parole
The new charge, the bail, the warrant, the hole
. . .
The twenty-three hours that's locked, the one hour that's not
The silence, the dark, the mind, so fragile

Ludacris's "Do Your Time" (2006) develops this theme. The track is a call to those incarcerated to endure:

I'd dream that I could tell Martin Luther we made it
But half of my black brothers are still incarcerated
. . .
If you doin 25 to life—stay up homie
I got your money on ice so—stay up homie
If you locked in the box keep makin it through
Do your time (do your time) don't let your time do you

In an imaginative take on the subject Nas, "Last Words" (1999), writes from the perspective of the prison, describing its relationship with the inmates who inhabit its world. The approach amplifies the experience for the listener, and brings home the reality of prison, in particular, the utter lack of privacy:

Convicts think they alone but if they listen close
They can hear me groan touch the wall feel my pulse
All the pictures you put up is stuck to my skin

I hear ya prayers (even when ya whisperin)

. . .

And the erosion of dignity:

I saw too many inmates fallin apart
Call for the guards to let them out at night when it's dark
. . .
No remorse for your tears I seen em too often
When you cry I make you feel alive inside a coffin

Conclusion

It is difficult to fully appreciate the influence of hip-hop culture on generations of young men of color growing up in the era of the modern "war on drugs" in the United States. Rather than attempting to encapsulate it, I leave it to the eloquent words contained in the following quotation from Aneraé "X-Raided" Brown, a California inmate:

I am the fabled crack baby. A boy who became a teen during what some argue was one of the roughest, most dangerous periods in U.S. history. I turned 14 in 1988, a black boy, a fledgling member of the notorious Crip gang, trying to learn how to fly, in the wrong direction, unknowingly, with lead wings. Pistols, cocaine, HIV/AIDS, the Cold War; how those things became the concerns of a 14 year old . . . God only knows. A boy who learned by what he decried, I was an impressionable teen absorbing the teachings that emanated from the conditions I saw on a daily basis, which included police brutality, the devastation of the gang and crack epidemics on the black community, and an overall fear and disdain of both white people and law enforcement, issues which were largely ignored by the mainstream media. The only journalistic reports being published that addressed these matters to reach my eyes and ears were coming to me in the form of hip-hop music, videos, movies and magazines . . . and the strongest voices of all, which came from a few little groups you may have heard of that went by the names of Public Enemy, NWA, and the Geto Boys. They were, to the streets, what The Beatles were to white folk. What James Brown, Curtis Mayfield and Marvin Gaye were to older black folk. They were the voices of our generation. Chuck D *and Ice Cube's voices are as recognizable to us as Paul McCartney and John Lennon's are to, say, a Baby Boomer, for perspective. "Fight the Power," "Fu*k the Police"—You know Chuck D and Ice Cube's voices and the sounds of Dr. Dre and The Bomb Squad, even if you do not know their names and faces.*[4]

Endnotes

1. A griot is an African poet, musician, and oral historian.
2. L.D. Johnston, P.M. O'Malley, J.G. Bachman, and J.E. Schulenberg, *Monitoring the Future National Results on Adolescent Drug Use: Overview of Key Findings, 2010* (Ann Arbor: Institute for Social Research, University of Michigan, 2011), 50. (emphasis added).
3. [For an accessible take on this see Steven D. Levitt and Stephen J. Dubner, "Why Do Drug Dealers Still Live with Their Moms?" in their *Freakonomics: A Rogue Economist Explores the Hidden Side of Everything* (London: Penguin, 2007).—Ed.]
4. Aneraé "'X-Raided' Brown, Black History Month: A Convict's Perspective," www.amoeba.com/blog/2009/02/jamoeblog/black-history-month-a-convict-s-perspective-pt-1-longtime-incarcerated-california-rap-artist-x-raided-offers-his-perspective-.html.

6. Under Cover of Privilege: College Drug Dealing in the United States

by A. Rafik Mohamed and Erik D. Fritsvold

For nearly forty years, the United States has been the driving force behind the international drug-eradication effort commonly referred to as the "war on drugs."[1] Most of the United States' partners in this "war" share an interest in reducing the harms associated with illicit drug use; however, the drug-war approach taken by United States differs in significant ways from the tactics preferred by most of its partner nations. While the majority of Western industrialized nations have responded to the global drug crisis by adopting harm-reduction, therapeutic, and public-health models in their efforts to curtail illegal drug use, and others have considered the decriminalization of drug use for personal possession, drug policies in the United States have been distinguished by strict prohibitionist "get tough" policies and a heavy dependence upon the criminal justice system. The direct result of this approach, discussed in greater detail in this chapter's next section, has been a quadrupling of the jail and prison population in the United States and the disenfranchisement of millions of U.S. citizens.

However, as our research on college drug dealers reveals, the war on drugs in the United States has not been waged with an even hand. Instead, despite the unyielding "zero-tolerance" zealotry accompanying U.S. drug policy, the illicit drug-using and drug-dealing behaviors of the most vulnerable and marginalized members of U.S. society have been more heavily scrutinized by the drug war hawks than similarly illicit behaviors of those with more social, political, and economic capital.

What follows in this chapter is a short synopsis of the effect of the U.S. war on drugs on incarceration and its disproportionate focus on African Americans; and a summary of a six-year ethnography in which we observed and interviewed approximately fifty affluent drug dealers, all of whom were current or former college students and nearly all of whom were white males. Despite operating significant and frequently conspicuous drug-dealing enterprises, and despite their collective bungling and a dearth of risk-aversion tactics, few of these *dorm-room dealers* were ever entangled in the drug war web. While a handful of the dealers serving as our informants had brushes with the law for their illicit drug activities, only one was convicted for drug law violations and none were incarcerated for their crimes. Unlike their street-corner peers, likely in part due to the fact they were never formally stigmatized for their drug-dealing activities, all but one of our study's subjects ultimately transitioned out of their statuses as drug dealers and into the licit workforce. Ultimately, the drug-dealing network we uncovered challenges the archetypical "shadowy figure" portrayal of drug dealers in the United States and calls into question some of the foundational elements of contemporary U.S. drug policy, particularly in light of seemingly more successful strategies employed by other members of the international community in their efforts to curtail drug abuse.

The War on Drugs

In 2005, while reflecting upon the state of international drug control efforts, then executive director of the United Nations Office on Drugs and Crime (UNODC), Antonio Maria Costa, remarked, "This is not a small enemy against which we struggle. It is a monster. With such an enormous amount of capital at its disposal, it is bound to be an extremely tenacious one."[2] At the time of Costa's assessment, the UNODC estimated the worldwide retail market for illegal drugs at US$320 billion,[3] larger than the gross domestic product of 88 percent of the world's nations.

The U.S. demand for illicit drugs is perhaps the most substantial catalyst behind this "monster" global drug trade. An estimated 44 percent of the retail sales of illegal drugs worldwide are in North America.[4] According to the U.S. Department of Health and Human Services 2008 National Survey on Drug Use and Health, more than 20 million Americans aged twelve or older were current illicit drug users, meaning they had used an illegal drug at least once in the past month. U.S. Americans are the world's largest consumers of cocaine and, according to the 2009 UNODC *World Drug Report*, about 6 million of the estimated 16–21 million individuals who used cocaine one or more times in 2007 were in the United States.[5] Further, Americans rank among the top consumers of other drugs like heroin, marijuana, and methamphetamine,[6] prompting the U.S. Drug Enforcement Agency

(DEA) to conclude that "The illegal drug market in the United States is one of the most profitable in the world."[7]

In response to drug use and drug trafficking, the United States has pursued a zero-tolerance, law-enforcement-focused prohibitionist policy since the mid-1970s. While quite literally millions of primarily minor drug offenders have been arrested over the course of the U.S. war on drugs and hundreds of thousands have been incarcerated in U.S. prisons for drug law violations, little has been accomplished in reducing either supply of or demand for illicit drugs in the United States. On the contrary, after forty years of criminal justice-centered drug-eradication efforts, in the United States, illicit drugs are "more accessible, more widely utilized, and more potent than ever before."[8]

What the United States has succeeded in doing during its drug war is to amass the largest jail and prison populations in the world. Inhabitants of the United States comprise approximately 5 percent of the world's population, but inhabitants of U.S. jails and prisons make up about 25 percent of the world's incarcerated population,[9] giving "the land of the free" the contradictory distinction of having the highest incarceration rate of any country on the planet.[10] While these figures are startling in and of themselves, they only tell part of the U.S. criminal justice story in the new millennium. These data fail to show the extent to which the present-day girth of the U.S. criminal justice system has been fed by excessively punitive drug policies, enacted primarily during the Ronald Reagan and George H. W. Bush administrations and enhanced during the subsequent continuation of the war on drugs by the Bill Clinton and George W. Bush administrations. Over the course of these four administrations, the number of incarcerated drug offenders rose by more than 1,000 percent, primarily as a result of increased law-enforcement scrutiny and not as a result of increased rates of offending.[11] Currently in the United States, approximately 20 percent of state prisoners and more than 50 percent of federal prisoners are incarcerated for drug-law violations as their most serious offense.[12] In the pre–drug-war context, in 1980, only 6.5 percent of state and 25 percent of federal prison inmates were sentenced to prison for drug-law violations.[13]

Perhaps the most widely commented upon and ethically problematic outcome of the war on drugs has been the disparate and negative effects of these policies on poor and minority communities in the

United States, the brunt of which has been felt in particular by African Americans. While constituting only 13 percent of the U.S. population, African Americans make up nearly one-half of all people behind bars in the United States, approximately 35 percent of all people arrested for drug-abuse violations,[14] and 45 percent of state prison inmates serving time for drug offenses.[15] This is despite the fact that federal government drug-use surveys indicate that African Americans make up about 15 percent of the total drug-user population while white Americans comprise over 70 percent of all drug users.[16]

In contrast to this overrepresentation of the poor and minorities, relatively well-off and white Americans have been conspicuously underrepresented among those arrested, prosecuted, and incarcerated for drug offenses. In the particular context of our study, affluent college students have been nearly invisible in the criminal justice data. This is in spite of this population's seemingly disproportionate embrace of recreational drug use and high levels of conspicuous drug-trafficking activity organized around supplying collegiate drug-use demands.

The College Drug Scene

> Stopper (college drug dealer): *Where I'm from, stoners were kids who wore hemp. We have a kind of granola culture. But these kids [at this university], you weren't looking at the 4.0 students,[17] but they were normal, they were involved, good majors—business majors—they didn't fit the stereotype of what a drug user would look like. These kids were pretty upstanding kids to most people. They just smoked a lot of weed.*

In the midst of the sweeping international drug-control efforts and the draconian drug-control policies adopted by the federal and various state governments in the United States, just a short distance north of the U.S. southern border with Mexico, a drug market thrives, ostensibly immune to the force of the drug war. Over a six-year period, we had access to this market and observed, interviewed, and otherwise interacted with approximately fifty drug dealers and user-dealers, all of whom were prosperous students at Southern California colleges and universities.[18] We initially gained entrée to this drug-dealing network through key informants whom we knew beforehand. From this point of access, we were able to establish trust and rapport with some of the network's other drug dealers, ultimately culminating in hundreds of hours of observation and dozens of formal interviews with current and former dealers and their clients conducted by us and our research assistants. When we began this research, we anticipated that we would find low-level college drug use and only modest drug dealing. However, rather early in the research process, we were genuinely surprised by the scope and extent of criminality engaged in by the affluent college drug dealers who served as the network's nucleus.

These dealers ranged in age from eighteen to twenty-four. With the exception of three women, all of the dealers we formally interviewed or observed were men and all but six were Caucasian. Disproportionately, the subjects' chosen course of study was business administration, economics, and accounting, and the overwhelmingly majority of the dealers in the network were from upper-middle- to upper-class families. In fact, most of our dealers' parents held prestigious social and professional positions that ranged from high level business executives, business owners, medical doctors, and accounting executives, to political figures.

The illicit market in which our dealers sold their goods functioned as a "closed" drug market with dealers only selling to other college students, friends, acquaintances, and people who could be directly vouched for by other known buyers. While closed markets are quite common in the United States, they deviate significantly from the "open" drug markets that have come to characterize the urban drug scene. These open markets typically operate around known "drug spots" and dealers actively solicit strangers as customers.

Our network's members sold and consumed various types of drugs, but most of the network's drug activity revolved around the sale and consumption of marijuana. That understood, some of our dealers did traffic in modest quantities of cocaine, and others sold party drugs, with ecstasy being the most common. While not entirely mutually exclusive, of our fifty subjects, roughly thirty focused primarily on marijuana and other "street drugs." The remaining twenty subjects typified the "user-dealer" model and focused their transactions around the nonmedical use of prescription drugs including stimulants (Adderall, Ritalin), opioids (OxyContin, Percocet, Vicodin), and central nervous-system depressants (Valium, Xanax, Librium).

Our dealer-subjects ranged from those who sold drugs solely to support their own drug habit (sometimes unsuccessfully) to those who provided relatively large quantities of drugs that were then distributed to a significant number of drug consumers and smaller distributors at area colleges. The half-dozen largest dealers in our sample sold between one and two pounds of high-quality, high-potency marijuana per week.[19] These dealers would typically buy their wholesale marijuana in multipound bundles costing between $4,000 and $4,400 per pound. They would then break the marijuana down into market-standard one-eighth or one-quarter pound increments for retail sale. Diamond, the largest dealer in our sample, eventually became one of the region's foremost marijuana dealers, moving anywhere from five to ten pounds of marijuana per week and earning gross profits of $80,000 to $160,000 per month. Despite the significance of their criminality, even the largest dealers in our sample haphazardly approached their drug transactions in a manner that suggested a genuine lack of concern for law enforcement.

In striking contrast to the drug-dealing networks commonly described in the criminological literature, this affluent college network did not employ even rudimentary risk-minimization strategies. Ounces or pounds of marijuana were often thrown into school backpacks or Styrofoam coolers, or simply stuffed into pockets. Sophisticated packaging was rare and most transportation techniques could be characterized as reckless. Primarily, these college drug dealers operated out of the same rented apartments or on-campus housing in which they resided. With few exceptions, most of their illegal business was on full display upon walking through their front door. Incriminating evidence was rarely hidden in backrooms; legitimate houseguests, neighbors, and solicitors regularly had a full view of these ongoing drug operations. By way of example, upon arriving at a dealer's home for an interview and observation session, ounces of marijuana, a scale, and large amounts of cash and paraphernalia were clearly visible from a relatively busy street. On another occasion, one of our subjects reported forgetting four ounces of marijuana (with a street value between $1,200 and $1,600) in a university classroom. He returned a few hours later to find left behind only the sweatshirt in which he had casually "concealed" the drugs. Most interestingly, especially among college-educated criminal entrepreneurs, there was virtually no discussion about or apparent awareness of core U.S. constitutional protections, the Fourth Amendment, probable cause, and other presumably obvious matters that would seem valuable in minimizing police detection and prosecution. These dealers' pervasive lack of basic security precautions reflected the fact that law enforcement was not perceived as a substantial threat within this network.

By virtue of their social location and their status as college students, all of the dealers we interviewed and observed were poised to live successful and materially comfortable lives after college. Unlike many of their street-corner counterparts, they were not driven to illicit drug sales out of desperation or bleak economic and educational opportunities. Thus, these affluent college drug dealers were making a seemingly irrational choice to sell drugs, one that caused us to wonder why they would place their near-certain positive futures in jeopardy. We ultimately found that these college dealers were motivated by a series of material and nonmaterial rewards. Further, because of their heeling and the lack of law enforcement scrutiny of their activities, they were largely oblivious to the criminal justice consequences that could befall them if the drug war were to be waged in a less discriminatory fashion.

Regarding their particular motivations, we found that many of the dealers began selling drugs to their college peers as a means to underwrite the costs of their personal drug use and other incidental and entertainment expenses associated with the college lifestyle. In addition, many dealers were inspired by the spirit of capitalism; recognizing an opportunity in the marketplace fueled by unyielding demand, drug dealing offered them a practical business opportunity to earn a relatively low-risk return on an investment. And since these dealers had their basic living expenses and tuition paid for by their parents, their drug profits were directly parlayed into entertainment monies, international vacations, accessories for their already expensive vehicles, and other impulsive expenditures.

Beyond these and other tangible and material rewards of being a dorm-room dealer, we also found a host of nonmaterial identity-based rewards that served as enticements for some of our subjects' beginnings in the drug trade. Among the relatively elite collegiate set, some degree of ego gratification and elevation in social status could be achieved by becoming a campus drug dealer and challenging society's conventional norms. More precisely, a significant number of the nonprescription-drug dealers in our sample seemed motivated by the simple thrill of deviant behavior, the excitement of getting away with activities they knew to be criminal, and otherwise displaying the ornaments of pseudo "gangstaism." As Jack Katz contends in his book, *Seductions of Crime*, "It is not the taste for the pizza that leads to the crime; the crime makes the pizza tasty."[20] Therefore, for some of our dealers, it seemed that the "sneaky thrills"[21] associated with antiauthoritarianism and attempting to outwit formal agents of social control served as an enticement into criminality. Indeed, the pseudo-gangster airs exuded and often internalized by some of our dealers seemed somewhat conspicuous attempts to combat the appearance of being a coddled child of privilege and to stand out among equally affluent peers. Interestingly, in spite of these outwardly displayed rejections of legal conventions, a core finding of our research was that these apparent risks were somewhat artificial. Paradoxically, the very privilege many of these dealers seemed to be rebelling against is the same privilege that ultimately provided them sanctuary from law enforcement scrutiny and the ire of the drug war.

In fact, despite the collective bungling of dealers in our network, there were noticeably few interactions with law enforcement. Moreover, even when suspected of drug activity (or, in the very rare case, caught for drug activity) the symbolic,[22] political, and actual capital possessed by our dealers and their families mitigated the formal consequences of their criminality. Throughout the course of the entire study, there were only a handful of arrests of any of our dorm-room dealers or their associates. Relatively early in the study, Beefy, a twenty-one year-old white middle-class college drug dealer with a 3.1 grade point average, had been apprehended by campus police and cited for possession of drug paraphernalia. While clearly in violation of campus drug policies as well as state laws, Beefy's transgressions were never brought to the attention of local or state police. Instead, Beefy's case remained internal to his university, he received a small fine, and he continued on as a relatively significant campus marijuana dealer. As Beefy said of his final disposition:

You were supposed to pay a $150 fine and go to like two drug classes and some kind of shit. I never called. They never did anything. There's no block on my account so . . . Pop's probably paid for it. [laughs] Who knows? I never checked any receipts so I don't have any idea of what happened to it. But they've never contacted me to take any of the classes and I've never contacted them so . . .

LaCoste was perhaps our study's most colorful character. He was a blonde-haired, blue-eyed, freshman from the midwestern United States who, by his own declaration, was "untouchably wealthy" and, in our assessment, worked hard to portray a "gangsta" persona. He dealt marijuana, cocaine, and ecstasy out of his dorm room and routinely took his operation mobile in the $50,000 Cadillac Escalade SUV purchased for him by his parents. He was also one of the very few dealers in our study to have significant prior encounters with the criminal justice system.

> LaCoste: *Yeah, for like ah . . . I don't know, I got real good lawyers [laughs]. Like real good lawyers . . . and I got a concealed gun charge and a possession over an ounce charge and they were trying to give me some intent to distribute. But I just got a possession ticket that's all and then the weapon and everything else disappeared.*

> Interviewer: *How did you pay for these lawyers?*

> LaCoste: *Na, that's not me . . . I'm not gonna claim to have paid for those. Turn that off [points to the tape recorder], I don't want to say that [laughs]. No, but that would have to be my dad. Or my parents . . . I can't pay for fucking like six lawyers.*

In what proved to be a signature moment, our initial point person into this particular drug market, Brice, was arrested on federal felony drug cultivation and distribution charges that carried a six-year prison sentence if he were to be convicted. After raiding his two-bedroom apartment (with a garage that he used exclusively for marijuana cultivation), federal and local authorities seized roughly $30,000 of Brice's cultivation equipment and over 100 marijuana plants at various stages of maturation. Brice immediately turned to his parents, admitted to them his involvement in marijuana dealing, and they, in turn, paid a prominent attorney to defend Brice in federal court. As Brice's case unfolded, it vividly illustrated many of the theoretical and substantive critiques of bias in the U.S. criminal justice system and drug war, and his case also put a tangible face on the concepts of symbolic capital and privilege. In an email he sent the day after his final hearing in federal court, Brice wrote:

> *Just signed a deal yesterday! . . . Basically, they dropped the big charge, and the other will not be on my record within 18 months. I have to do 100 hours community service, lose my 4th Amendment, get drug tested, and have to remain in therapy for at least 6 months. However, once it's all over I can answer that I've*

never been arrested, and nothing will ever be on my record. Even now, it's not recorded anywhere since they never made a judgment against me. Kind of like the diversion program, but better, because I have no parole or probation counselor. I am free to leave the state any time I want, I just cannot get any misdemeanor offenses otherwise I break the terms of the deal.

Conclusions

While perhaps not as expansively as Brice, every college drug dealer we encountered over the course of this research routinely sold large enough quantities of marijuana and other drugs to be prosecuted under the harsh laws that have come to characterize the U.S.-led war on drugs. Yet, all but one of the fifty dorm-room dealers we encountered over the course of our six-year study emerged unscathed from their forays as drug dealers. Around the same time that we were bringing our research on this network to a close, we were informed that LaCoste had been academically disqualified from college, had returned to his home in the midwestern United States, and was facing several unknown felony charges. With that sole exception, all of our dealers completed their respective college degrees and transitioned into conventionally productive lives in the legitimate economy.

Perhaps most important, all of our dealers were fully aware that they benefited from a luxury that their street-corner peers did not; they all knew that the war on drugs was not a war waged in their direction, and, consequently, in spite of their flagrantly illegal behaviors, they were a relatively low priority on the law-enforcement totem pole. When asked why they felt that was the case, our dealers acknowledged that physical and social location, socioeconomic status, and race influenced the way their activities were perceived by police and other officials. As Ann, one of the few female dealers in our study said:

I mean if someone really wanted to bust us they could, all they would have to do was get someone to sit on our house to get some evidence against us to be able to go in there. No one cares that much. I think a lot of it has to do with the people we are, we don't live in the ghetto. We don't make noise, we don't have parties, we don't bring attention to ourselves, we are quiet, we pay everything on time. In the beach environment you can get away with a lot more.

While the particular characteristics that defined our network might have been specific to this drug market, it is reasonable to assume that drug networks like ours exist and thrive at and around universities across the United States. In February 2002, police made six arrests on the American University campus in Washington, DC, seizing ecstasy, marijuana, and $15,000. In the months following the conclusion of this study, a significant drug bust at Southern California's San Diego State University resulted in 125 arrests, the seizure of $60,000, fifty pounds of marijuana, four pounds of cocaine, and an assortment of other illicit drugs. In April 2010, fourteen Illinois State University students and two others faced felony drug charges after a drug sweep by state and local police. In December 2010, five Columbia University students were arrested for the alleged sale of LSD, cocaine, and ecstasy on their Ivy League campus. And, as Colin Diver, president of Reed College, remarked of his university in early 2010, "When you say Reed, two words often come to mind. One is brains. One is drugs."[23]

Nonetheless, in spite of these well-publicized drug busts and public acknowledgments of illegal drug activity on college campuses, the actors in these networks remain largely unpoliced and conspicuously off the radar of the American drug war. As criminologist William J. Chambliss concluded in his classic study of societal responses to delinquency, "Selective perception and labeling—finding, processing and punishing some kinds of criminality and not others—means that visible, poor, non-mobile, outspoken, undiplomatic 'tough' kids will be noticed, whether their actions are seriously delinquent or not."[24] Extending Chambliss's conclusions, the deliberately invisible people of relative privilege in our society who fundamentally exist behind veils of immunity, like those people who made up the majority of dealers in our study, will continue to be largely unnoticed whether their actions are law-abiding or not.

Rather clearly, the "get tough" drug-war strategies employed by the United States have been misguided, ineffective, and rife with bias. After spending hundreds of billions of dollars fighting this metaphorical war, little has changed with regard to drug use in the United States or U.S. dependence upon the illicit international underground to supply these needs. What has changed substantially is the vastness of the U.S. criminal justice system, an expansion largely attributable to the policing and prosecution of poor and minority members of our society, often for relatively minor drug-abuse violations.

However, there are signs suggesting that the United States might be poised to turn a corner in its approach toward drugs and drug crimes, and that the nation that has been attempting to navigate the course of the drug war for the better part of a century might begin to tack back in a direction more in step with its European drug war partners. In the United States, several states have enacted laws decriminalizing marijuana possession, creating a medicinal marijuana backdoor through which people can lawfully obtain marijuana with a doctor's permission, and in one case proposing legislation to legalize and tax marijuana as a source of state revenue. Perhaps as the most encouraging statement in the rethinking of U.S. drug policy, Barack Obama, shortly after taking office as president of the United States, ordered the Department of Justice to discontinue raids on state-licensed medicinal marijuana dispensaries. It is hoped that these trends, along with research shedding light on the disparities and hypocrisy of the U.S. drug war, will continue to spark conversation about a more reasonable, equitable, and balanced set of international and domestic drug policies as we move forward in the new millennium.

Endnotes

1. As early as 1911, well before the contemporary drug war, the United States pressed for international control of cannabis and other drugs. The outcome was the Hague Opium Convention of 1912 and, in the 1930s, attempts at international treaties requiring the control of certain drugs. However, these proposals were met with a "cool reception" by an international community less preoccupied with drug control. See David Musto, "The History of the Marijuana Tax Act of 1937," *Archives of General Psychiatry* 26 (February 1972): 101–8.
2. United Nations Office on Drugs and Crime (UNODC), *World Drug Report, 2005* (Vienna: United Nations Publications, V, 2005), 2.
3. Other estimates place the size of the global drug market at closer to $400 billion.
4. UNODC, *World Drug Report 2005*, 2.
5. UNODC, *World Drug Report 2009*, 63 (estimates of worldwide cocaine use in 2007); 80 (estimates of U.S. cocaine consumption in 2007).
6. Central Intelligence Agency, *World Factbook: Field Listing—Illicit Drugs*, 2006, www.cia.gov/library/publications/the-world-factbook/fields/2086.html.
7. U.S. Drug Enforcement Administration, *Briefs & Background: Drugs and Drug Abuse, Drug Descriptions, Drug Trafficking in the United States*, www.cia.gov/library/publications/the-world-factbook/fields/2086.html.
8. See www.justice.gov/dea/concern/drug_trafficking.html, 4.
9. U.S. Department of Justice, Bureau of Justice Statistics, *Key Facts at a Glance, Correctional Populations. 2008*, http://bjs.ojp.usdoj.gov/content/glance/tables/corr2tab.cfm/.
10. U.S. Department of Justice, Bureau of Justice, "Statistics Number and Rate (per 100,000 U.S. Residents) of Persons in State and Federal Prisons and Local Jails," in *Sourcebook of Criminal Justice Statistics* (2006).

11. Human Rights Watch, *Punishment and Prejudice: Racial Disparities in the War on Drugs*, 2000, www.hrw.org/legacy/reports/2000/usa/.
12. U.S. Department of Justice, Federal Bureau of Prisons, *Quick Facts About the Bureau of Prisons*, www.bop.gov/about/facts.jsp#4/.
13. Human Rights Watch, *Punishment and Prejudice*.
14. U.S. Department of Justice, Federal Bureau of Investigation, *Crime in the United States, 2008* (September 2009), www2.fbi.gov/ucr/cius2008/data/table_43.html.
15. U.S. Department of Justice, Bureau of Justice Statistics, *Prisoners in 2008*, Bulletin NCJ 228417, December 2009, 37, Appendix Tables 15 and 16, http://bjs.ojp.usdoj.gov/index.cfm?ty=pbdetail&iid=1763/.
16. United States Sentencing Commission, *Cocaine and Federal Sentencing Policy*, May 2007. A link to the report is available at www.ussc.gov/Publications/Reports_to_Congress/index.cfm.
17. This refers to the traditional grade point average (GPA) scale used in the United States; 4.0 is typically the maximum possible GPA produced by earning an A grade in every course.
18. Geographically speaking, Southern California is roughly defined as that part of California south of Santa Barbara (approximately 100 miles north of Los Angeles) encompassing the major metropolitan areas of Los Angeles, San Diego, San Bernardino, and Riverside. Collectively, this region has a known population of approximately 25 million people and is home to well over sixty colleges and universities.
19. [One pound is approximately 450 grams. One ounce is approximately 28 grams.—Ed.]
20. Jack Katz, *Seductions of Crime: Moral and Sensual Attractions in Doing Evil* (New York: Basic Books, 1988), 52.
21. Ibid.
22. Pierre Bourdieu, "The Forms of Capital," in *The Handbook of Theory and Research for the Sociology of Education*, ed. J. Richardson (New York: Greenwood, 1986), 241–58.
23. Tamar Lewin, "Reed College's President Is Told to Crack Down on Campus Drug Use," *New York Times*, April 26, 2010.
24. William Chambliss, "The Saints and the Roughnecks," *Society* 11, no. 1 (1973): 24–31.

7. Young Soldiers in Brazil's Drug War

by Michelle Gueraldi

Introduction

In recent decades, Brazil has become an increasingly important transit route for illicit drugs.[1] This is partly because traffickers are avoiding traditional routes as these have become more heavily targeted by law enforcement. The expansion of drug trafficking in the country has been combined with both a strong militarization of the gangs and an increase in the participation of children.[2] These children are mostly poor, black boys—*favela* (slum) residents fighting for their lives in a country of deep socioeconomic inequality. Meanwhile, repressive drug control policies turn the *favelas* and adjacent areas into battlefields.

Young people, especially black males, constitute a high proportion of homicides in Brazil, a situation that is aggravated by the war on drugs. These children, whose lives are short, are a very sad picture of abandonment, discrimination, poverty, and rights violations in Brazil. Set against the backdrop of the moral stigmatization and demonization of *favela* children, this chapter looks at the underlying conditions of poverty and social neglect driving children's involvement in the drug trade, and the impact of activities and drug-related violence on children's rights.

Public Attitudes to Marginalized Children

Brazil was one of the first countries to ratify the UN Convention on the Rights of the Child (CRC) in 1990. The new civilian government announced to the nation that children would be the absolute priority in the country. The president publicly recognized the tragic picture of abandonment and marginalization in which Brazilian children lived and died. At the time, Brazil had around 65 million children below the age of nineteen. Of those, annually: 250,000 died before completing their first year; one in four suffered from malnutrition; 61 percent of children aged one to four lived without basic sanitation; and more than 4 million children from seven to fourteen years of age were out of school. In the same year, the Statute of the Child and Adolescent (SCA) was adopted, incorporating the CRC into national legislation.

The new legal regime, rooted in the rights of the child, required fundamental changes in social policy toward children in the country. Unfortunately, today inequality and poor socioeconomic conditions continue to pose significant barriers to the full realization of the rights of the child in the country.[3] In addition, negative public attitudes toward marginalized children contribute to their vulnerability.

Prior to the adoption of the 1990 act, the Minors' Code of 1979 was the primary legislation relating to children. By this doctrine, there were two kinds of children: those in "regular" and "irregular" situations. The Minors' Code was aimed at the latter—those in need of special protection such as children without parental care, without a home, or at risk of violence, or children who have infringed the law. It adopted a punitive and corrective approach and viewed such "irregular" situations as pathological.[4] The powers available to police and judges were extensive, including imprisonment without a judicial order and without a crime being committed. The status of being a minor was sufficient. This is reflected in article 1 of the code, which refers to "vigilance" relating to minors.[5] In contrast to this, the SCA (considered by many to be one of the most advanced pieces of child rights legislation in the world) applied to all, and focused on the holistic protection of children rather than on disciplinary intervention. The law, in keeping with the CRC, saw the child as a rights bearer, and an active participant in seeing those rights fulfilled. There was no distinction or discrimination between classes or groups of children. It was a major shift, but one that has yet to take root in public opinion.

The Minors' Code was a reflection of a time when children who did not belong to the middle or upper classes, or who were orphans, and in need of state protection, were referred to as "minors." They were not "children," as such, but a different breed—so-called minors who collided with the existing and generally approved social order. The Minors' Code reinforced this view. While intended to protect vulnerable children, it perpetuated a culture of stigmatization and discrimination that can still be felt by street children today, despite the changes brought in following the adoption of the SCA. This culture contaminates the state institutional apparatus and the mentality of a great part of the population—and even the children themselves. The dominant ideology in society is one that criminalizes poverty and blames victims of inequality for the situations in which they find themselves. Punishment is presented as the most effective measure against violence and crime. Rather than these being understood as social phenomena, generated by society, they are considered to be generated by an individual will for delinquency.

Current debates relating to the age of criminal responsibility highlight this view, which is held by many. At present those under eighteen cannot be responsible for their criminal acts. The Penal Code is applied to adults and the SCA to crimes committed by children. The maximum penalty for adults in Brazil is thirty years of imprisonment while the penalties applied by the SCA are "social-educative measures," adequate to the incomplete development of children. The most severe measure applied to children is detention in state shelters for a maximum period of three years. However, congress members in the National House of Representatives strongly campaign for a shift in the legislation in order to lower the age of criminal responsibility. As one congressman, Jair Bolsonaro, stated, "We deny the arguments of those who are against reducing the legal age for criminal responsibility, for we choose to overcrowd prisons with marginalized minors rather than fill cemeteries with innocents."[6]

Such statements show just how far from reality the vision of the SCA is, the abiding view of marginalized children as separate from the mainstream, and the culture of blame contributing to the targeting of these children in the drug war.

Violence and Rights Violations Against Children in the Drug War

The children most likely to suffer violations of their fundamental rights due to the drug war are those living in the slums where drug dealers assemble their armies and build their factories. Some are engaged in the drug trade, working for criminal organizations, while others coexist with them without direct involvement. Their vulnerability has many sources. Apart from their age, most are black and poor. They live in conditions of poverty and in a situation of "organized armed violence."[7] While the state has specific obligations under the Convention on the Rights of the Child to protect these children, according to testimony from children themselves, the state not only enables violence but generates it.

In 2008, several nongovernmental organizations, coordinated by the Brazilian Association of Child's Defense Centers and Terre des Hommes Foundation, prepared a civil society report about child rights in Brazil. The report was prepared focusing on Article 12 of the CRC, which recognizes the right of children to be heard and have their views taken into account. Four hundred children were listened to throughout Brazil, and included many vulnerable groups including children raised in landless movement camps, sheltered girls, physically challenged children, and those of African descent. While the report was broader in focus, several lived in situations of armed violence.[8] The reports[9] convey the children's opinions on many issues and also the positive experiences and views they had about their lives and about the country. Answering the question "What is it like to be a child in Brazil?" a seventeen-year-old boy from Rio de Janeiro responded:

Good and difficult. Good, because I feel free. Bad because there is much evil . . . police, trafficking, and drugs.[10]

The children's views reveal deep concerns about their basic rights, such as access to education and health care, their families' well-being, and how the state fails to provide for them. The children criticize politicians and identify the police and drug dealers as violent and guilty of committing terrible crimes. They also explain that robbery and crime are their only choice in order to make money for survival due to state abandonment. Asked about the most serious problems facing the country, one boy, also seventeen years old from Rio de Janeiro, said:

I agree with them, but disagree when they say that Brazil's problem is the violence. Do you know why I disagree? Because violence is a consequence of what they (the politicians) make out of politics. [W]ith that division in social classes, the person that lives in a community and needs money, the way to get it quick is stealing, selling drugs.

Other children provided accounts of more specific problems:

I was with my cousins. The police stopped us and said many things: "Pull up your shirt." I said: "I'm no bandit." And so he said: "Go." (Iago, nine years old)

The police beat the boy, slap in the head. The bandit said that, when police arrive, I must let him know. If I don't, I'll get hurt. The police job is to protect criminals. (Matheus, eight years old)

Thieves walk by us holding guns in order to make us fear them.

My father's wife's son got shot only because the man did not like
him. He's a paralytic now. (Kilvia, thirteen years old)

From the statements above, a number of themes come through: the
assumption of guilt toward children from the slums; the involvement
of the police with drug dealers and their disrespect for the rights of
the child; and the violence surrounding the children on a daily basis.

Invasive Searches and the Presumption of Guilt

Iago's testimony above refers to a time when police officers
attempted to search him, looking for guns. Iago lives in Vicente de
Carvalho community in Rio de Janeiro, an area rife with armed
violence. In these communities, police searches of children's backpacks
and clothes are common and frequently result in abuses. In Morro
do Alemão, for example, during a major confrontation between police
and the drug traffickers in 2007, police were publicly denounced for
searching under young girls' skirts.

Police searches, according to Brazilian penal law, can occur
only when there is strong evidence that the person is suspected of
involvement in criminal acts. In addition, the CRC and the SCA
recognize both that the best interests of the child must be a primary
consideration and that the child has rights to freedom from unlawful
interference with his or her privacy. Due to these ongoing searches,
however, families have sought the assistance of human rights groups.
In 2007, a child rights nongovernmental organization from Rio de
Janeiro, Projeto Legal, filed a habeas corpus petition on behalf of
children living in the *favela* of Vigário Geral who were subjected to
embarrassing invasions of their privacy during police searches. The
petition focused on Patrick (age four), Bruna (age eleven), and Brenda
(age fifteen), and was filed against the order given by Rio de Janeiro's
Public Security secretary to search Vigário Geral residents, including
children, for drugs. Projecto Legal, in its petition, stated:

Yesterday morning, 15th of March 2007, at about 8 a.m.,
a police operation coordinated by the Explosives and Guns
Repression Precinct took place in Vigário Geral Community,
with the participation of around 100 policemen. . . . In daytime,
in a residential area, due to Rio de Janeiro's political strategy
of state enforcement through direct armed conflict, there was a
long shootout between the police and members of a drug dealing

organization. During the operation, a significant number of school children were searched by policemen, due to an alleged suspicion of drugs and guns inside children's backpacks. . . . It is all about the old and well known public security project, based on the idea of militarization of social crises and criminalization of Rio de Janeiro's subordinated population . . . violating the principles established in the Constitution of the Republic and the Statute of the Child and Adolescent.[11]

The organization alleged that the searches violated the constitutionally recognized rights of the child to freedom and privacy and claimed that it was not part of public security authorities' powers to create and implement policies aimed at children, especially those in a situation of great vulnerability, as in this case. Initially, a judicial order to stop child searches was given, but afterward it was adapted, sparing only children under twelve years of age. According to the Brazilian legislation, "child" means someone up to the age of twelve and an "adolescent" is someone aged twelve to eighteen. The final decision was based on the assumption that, for the most part, children under twelve are not involved with drug dealers. It was an arbitrary distinction, and those over twelve years of age, though guaranteed in law the same rights as those under twelve, continued to be targets of the police searches and to be considered natural suspects as working for drug dealers, simply because they live in the *favela*.

Child Homicide: A Growing, Selective Crisis

Brazil has one of the highest homicide rates in the world, with over 48,000 people killed each year. Murders by gangs, inmates, police, death squads, and hired killers regularly make headlines around Brazil and the world. Extrajudicial executions and vigilante justice are supported by a sizable proportion of the population who fear high crime rates, and who perceive that the criminal justice system is too slow to effectively prosecute criminals. Many politicians, keen to curry favour with a fearful electorate, have failed to demonstrate the political will necessary to curb executions by police.

UN Special Rapporteur on extrajudicial, summary, or arbitrary executions, Philip Alston, 2008[12]

Young people are overrepresented in homicide[13] statistics in

Brazil. This is reflected in several UNESCO reports, known as *Maps of Violence*. Published since 1998, the most recent one in 2010 reflects the "anatomy of child homicides in Brazil."[14] The *Maps of Violence* recognize Brazil as a violent place for young people to live. According to the third map of violence published in 2002, in the 1990s the number of youth homicides rose by 77 percent, against a 50.2 percent rise among the entire population. According to the report, 4.7 percent of deaths in the entire population are caused by homicide, while that figure is 39.2 percent among youth. In some cities, such as Rio de Janeiro, Vitória, and São Paulo, it can be as high as 50 percent.[15]

The 2010 *Map of Violence* showed that until 2003, the overall rates of homicide were growing more than 5 percent per year. After 2003, those rates decreased. Among children, however, they stayed the same, and among adolescents the number of homicides has been growing drastically. From 1997 to 2007, homicides rose 24 percent among those aged twelve to eighteen. Although youth represented only 18.6 percent of the Brazilian population in 2007, the rate of homicide affecting them was of 36 percent.

A 2001 study carried out by CLAVES/Fiocruz, a renowned Brazilian research center, affirmed that one of the most serious issues facing Brazil was the scale of death, injury, and trauma among children and young people due to violence. CLAVES, using public data on the mortality of young people aged fifteen to twenty-four from 1990 to 1998, indicated an endemic situation and an increase in homicides among this group.[16] According to data assembled by CLAVES, in 1998, throughout Brazil, 65 percent of youth homicides involved guns, which is corroborated by the UNESCO *Maps of Violence*. In addition, and of particular concern is that the CLAVES study indicated a sort of *specie selection* due the victims' common profile: young, male, resident in poor peripheral areas of major cities, and of African descent.

But who is responsible for the youth homicides? During the 1980s, death squads, formed by urban vigilantes, and groups of policemen played a large role in the killings; a form of "social cleansing" as indicated by several case studies and promoted by Justiça Global, a Rio de Janeiro-based nongovernmental organization.[17] However, the profile of the death squads changed during the 1990s as they began working for drug traffickers. With the absence of the state in the slums, traffickers are becoming better equipped in terms of weapons and technology, and the employment of children and killings of young people in the context of the drug trade has escalated.

In a report submitted to the UN Committee on the Rights of the Child in 2004, the Brazilian Association of Child's Defense Centers identified three kinds of exterminators in the 1990s: those who gave the orders; the killers themselves; and the advocates of extermination, people who occupy prominent positions and status in the community. Among them were drug traffickers and police. Philip Alston, UN Special Rapporteur on extrajudicial, summary, or arbitrary executions, following his mission to Brazil in 2008 explained that:

Members of the police forces too often contribute to the problem of extrajudicial executions rather than to its solution. In part, there is a significant problem with on-duty police using excessive force and committing extrajudicial executions in illegal and counterproductive efforts to combat crime. But there is also a problem with off-duty police themselves forming criminal organizations which also engage in killings.[18]

According to Amnesty International, cases of battering, shootings (at hands or feet), and executions performed by the drug traffickers are common. These are directed not only at rivals but also at alleged offenders and criminals inside the areas in which they operate.[19] Again, this is a form of "social cleansing," ridding their area of undesirables and rivals. Due to the absence of any official state presence in those areas, criminal activities thrive. It is estimated in the Amnesty International report that approximately 10,000 armed drug dealers, including 6,000 children, are directly involved with drug dealing in Rio de Janeiro.

Children Employed in the Drug Trade

Luke Dowdney, following an in-depth study of children involved in the drug trade in Rio de Janeiro, attributes the increased involvement of children during the 1980s to the greater need for the gangs to defend themselves and the use of light guns by the dealers. Dowdney identified a number of aspects characterizing their employment, such as: voluntary recruitment;[20] an average age of first employment at thirteen, and of becoming a soldier (i.e., to be allowed to carry guns) at fifteen to seventeen; a strong hierarchy, enforced by punishment, rules, and orders; regular payment; and active and progressive involvement in armed conflict.[21]

An independent documentary made in 2006, *Falcão: meninos do tráfico* (Falcons: Boys of the Drug Trade)[22] portraits the lives of seventeen boys working in the drug trade in slums throughout Brazil. Their stories reveal the reasons that led them into crime as well as the violence perpetrated and suffered by them due to their activities. Several testimonials point to the absence of a father figure, the absence of a family, the discrimination that prevents them from finding a job, the desire to help their mothers, inadequate education, and the dream of leaving crime behind. One of the boys told how his work in the drug trade pays him 500 reais per month (about US$300). "I deal for my mother," he said. According to another boy:

I'm no outlaw . . . I don't want to see my mother suffering.

The testimonials also lucidly demonstrate the awareness of danger, the reasons for getting involved in crime, related drug addiction, and social exclusion.

I do not get sad about anything. I'm always drugging myself. I am a thief. I rob because no one gives me anything . . . I have to rob. I rob to live.

If the men arrive, we'll be treated like outlaws, they kill everyone.

Reporter: *What do you want to be when you grow up?*

Outlaw. Because it makes money and helps. Hell is where we are. . . . Here we live the reality, where there are bullets everywhere and the law is the worst possible. My mother already has three dead children.

Bribery and corruption are also recurring themes:

If ending crime, the police must end too, as we give money to the police. We pay them so we can work. If not for the drug dealing, the police would only "take" their wages. They take more. . . . So, drug dealing will not be over any time soon.

Reporter: *Tell me about your day.*

Not my day, my night. Because I sleep during the day and stay awake during the night. During the day (there are) lots of policeman in the slum. At night there's bribery.

The boys were under no illusions about their bleak futures.

Reporter: *And if you die?*

If I die another one like me will be born. . . . If I die I will rest. It is too much bashing in this life. My future is three ways: wheelchair, death, or prison.

By the end of the research all but one of these young boys was dead, having never reached their eighteenth birthday.

Accompanying the film was a diary written by the filmmakers.[23] In one section, one of the producers explains how he wanted to film the children playing in order to show that the children of these communities were not born to be criminals. When he approached a group of children they were pretending to be traffickers, playing out the violence.

Conclusion

Long before becoming adults, young soldiers in Brazil's drug war have given up their dreams. They grow up learning to accept that an education is not a reasonable goal; that there is no medicine at the public hospitals they have access to; that their parents have died or are missing; that politicians are corrupt and not to be trusted; and that the police are discriminatory, violent, and on the take. In this scenario, many see joining the drug traffickers as their only option, despite knowing that in doing so they may cut their own lives short.

The many violations of the rights of the child associated with this situation are exacerbated by indiscriminate repressive drug-control policies. While being ineffective, given that the traffickers are now stronger than ever, the *favelas* have been turned into battlefields. In the midst of the violence, boy soldiers end up being killed by the police, while those who are not involved in the drug trade are caught in the crossfire. Added to this, violent and corrupt police are the only state presence in these areas, transforming traffickers into local authorities who own the land and dictate the laws applied to it.

Of the thousands of Brazilians who die each year from gunfire, it is accepted that they have a common profile: poor, black, and young. Those in this group are regarded as potential enemies rather than human beings—a prejudice held by many in Brazilian society and a legacy of past policies relating to "minors." A human rights perspective seems to be the only way to reaffirm the values of humanity in a society that has become cynical to the point of supporting or turning a blind eye to the systematic killing of children.

Endnotes

1. See UN Office on Drugs and Crime, *World Drug Report 2010* (Vienna, 2010).
2. In Rio de Janeiro, for example, a city where the traffickers are extremely numerous and organized, in 1991, 7.7 percent of criminal offenses committed by children were associated with drugs. In 1998 the figure had risen to 53 percent. Data provided by the 2ª Vara da Infância e da Adolescência at the Rio de Janeiro State Court.
3. In 2006, according to the Instituto Brasileiro de Geografia e Estatística (*Pesquisa Nacional por Amostra Domiciliar*, 2006), 56 percent of children aged six and younger lived in families whose income was less than half the minimum wage. According to UNICEF, children in Brazil whose per capita family income is less than half the minimum wage are three times more likely to die before their fifth birthday, twenty-one times more likely to be illiterate, and thirty times more likely to live in a home without an adequate water supply. UNICEF, *State of the World's Children 2005: Childhood Under Threat*, 27, www.unicef.org/publications/files/SOWC_2005_%28English%29.pdf.
4. M. Garcia and C. Fernandez, "The Care and Shelter of Children and Adolescents in Brazil: Expressions of Social Issues," *Social Work and Society* 7 (2009), no. 2, www.socwork.net/2009/1/special_issue/garciafernandez/.
5. The Minors' Code is available at www.glin.gov/view.action?glinID=10802/.
6. "Convoca Plebiscito nos termos do art. 49, XV da Constituição Federal para os fins que especifica," www.camara.gov.br/sileg/integras/522766.pdf,2.
7. L. Dowdney, *Crianças do Tráfico: um Estudo de Caso de Crianças em Violência Armada Organizada no Rio de Janeiro* (Rio de Janeiro: Editora Sete Letras, 2003).
8. Terre des Hommes, *Vozes de Crianças e Adolescentes no Monitoramento da Convenção Internacional sobre os Direitos da Criança* 9, Rio de Janeiro, 2009, 83–85.
9. Two separate reports were prepared by the nongovernmental organizations.
10. The testimony that follows is contained in the report of the Association of Child's Defense Centers, which was presented to the public in March 2009, but has not yet been published or sent to the UN Committee on the Rights of the Child.
11. Carlos Nicodemos, *Advogando pelos Direitos Humanos dos Adolescentes no Sistema Socioeducativo: Dez Casos Exemplares de Enfrentamento às Violações de Direitos Humanos dos Adolescentes Autores de Ato Infracional* (Rio de Janeiro: Secretaria Especial de Direitos Humanos, 2007), 85.
12. Human Rights Council, *Promotion and Protection of All Human Rights, Civil, Political, Economical, Social and Cultural Rights Including the Right to Development*. Report of the Special Rapporteur on Extrajudicial, Summary, or Arbitrary Executions, Philip Alston, Addendum, Mission to Brazil, August 29, 2008, UN Doc. No. A/HRC/11/2/Add.2, Summary.
13. Understood as death caused by intentional assaults.
14. UNESCO, *Map of Violence 2010: Anatomy of Homicides in Brazil*, www.institutosangari.org.br/mapadaviolencia/.
15. UNESCO, *Map of Violence 2002*, www.sociologiadajuventude.hpg.ig.com.br/mapadaviolenciaiii.htm.

16. Fiocruz, Boletim do CLAVES (Centro Latino-Americano sobre Violência e Saúde), *Padrão de mortalidade por homicídios no Brasil 1980 a 2000*, Ano II, no. 7 (2002).
17. Justiça Global Report, *Os Muros nas favelas e o processo de criminalização, 2009*, http://global.org.br/wp-content/uploads/2009/12/Relat%C3%B3rio-Os-Muros-nas-Favelas-e-o-Processo-de-Criminaliza%C3%A7%C3%A3o.pdf.
18. Human Rights Council, *Promotion and Protection of All Human Rights*, para. 5.
19. Amnesty International AI Index: AMR 19/015/2003 (Rio de Janeiro, 2003), *Candelária eand Vigário Geral–10 years on*, 22, www.amnesty.org/en/library/asset/AMR19/015/2003/en/a7e85b79-d6aa-11dd-ab95-a13b602c0642/amr190152003en.pdf.
20. [Compare the story of Yina Paola in chapter 1.—Ed.]
21. Dowdney, *Crianças do Tráfico*, 124–32.
22. The "falcons" are night watchmen. There are also "steam," children who sell small quantities of drugs and the "fireworks guy," who is responsible for lighting fireworks to warn drug dealers about the police or rivals.
23. Celso Athayde and M.V. Bill, *Falcão:meninos do tráfico* (Rio de Janeiro: Objetiva, 2006).

Discussion Questions

1. How important is public opinion in drug policy? What is the role of popular culture in this regard?

2. Are criminal laws an appropriate basis for drug control? What are the limitations of the law in dealing with drugs and children's involvement in the drug trade?

3. Peterson Small, and Mohamed and Fritsvold show that drug laws are not equally applied in the United States. Why? How may this be resolved?

4. Gueraldi's article suggests that the root of Brazil's problems with drug-related violence is not the drug trade itself, but socioeconomic and racial disparities in Brazilian society. Do you agree?

Part 3:
Home Front: Families and Drug Policy

The family[1] is at the core of the social, emotional, and psychological development of the child. It therefore has a special place in the UN Convention on the Rights of the Child, in which the family is seen as key to the full realization of the rights contained within the treaty.[2] No book about children in the context of the war on drugs would be complete if the effects on families were omitted. Drug dependence within a family, for example, can have a massive devastating influence. This is particularly the case when it comes to children of drug dependent parents.[3] This section, however, is not about drug use and drug-related harms. It is about how *policies* affect families— policies relating to drug dependence, law enforcement, prisons, and child protection.

The section begins with "Dancing with Despair: A Mother's Perspective," a personal account by Gretchen Burns Bergman, executive director of A New PATH (Parents for Addiction Treatment and Healing) of her experiences as a mother of two sons who are both heroin dependent. Both have been involved in the criminal justice system. She tells of her own feelings of despair, fear, and guilt, the effects on her family, and the conclusions she has reached about drug policies based on her experiences. For Bergman, the war on drugs only served to further harm her sons. While many parents who have lost children to drug dependence or overdose call for tougher law-enforcement measures with the intention of protecting others from such tragedy,[4] Bergman calls for harm reduction and legal regulation of drugs with the exact same intention.

The following two pieces deal more closely with the effects of incarceration for drug offenses on women, children, and families. Jennifer Fleetwood and Andreina Torres show how women, intentional targets of the war on drugs, are overrepresented for minor offenses (the chapter may be read in conjunction with Part 2). "Mothers and Children of the Drug War: A View from a Women's Prison in Quito, Ecuador" shows how the proportion of women—many of whom are primary caregivers to children—in prisons for drug offenses has risen, due to a focus on drug mules in order to meet arrest and prosecution quotas. Through ethnographic research at a women's prison, the effects of incarceration on these women and their attempts to continue being active mothers despite their imprisonment (sometimes far from home) are discussed. For some, their only option is to have their children imprisoned with them in the same poor, overcrowded conditions.

Not all harms are headline catching. Some are smaller, more personal, yet of great importance for the individuals affected. Focusing on the effects of incarceration of parents and/or siblings, Asmin Fransiska, Ajeng Larasati, and Ricky Gunawan, consider two case studies in Jakarta, Indonesia: Diego, a young boy whose mother (who is drug dependent) has been both incarcerated for drug offenses and placed in compulsory residential treatment; and Mario, the eldest child of a poor family entrapped for a minor possession charge, and imprisoned. "Between Diego and Mario: Children, Families, and the Drug War in Indonesia" discusses the economic, emotional, and psychological harms associated with incarceration and experienced by the whole family. For many, imprisonment of a family member will plunge the whole family further into poverty. The authors ask whether it is defensible, from a children's rights perspective, that the best interests of dependent children are not currently a consideration in sentencing for nonviolent drug offenses.

A recent report from the UK charity ChildLine highlighted the neglect, abuse, and distress experienced by children of drug- and alcohol-dependent parents through direct quotes from callers to the charity's helpline:

"My dad is beating me and my younger brother. Dad injects something into his arm and shouts at me and beats me. My brother and I have bruises. My teachers see this and when they ask, I tell them I had a fall." (Tyrone, age twelve)

"My mom hit me and pushed me into a wall. Every weekend she gets drunk and has a go at me. Mom leaves me in the house until 11 pm. I have to make my own food. My dad died when I was five." (Michelle, age nine)

"My mom is taking drugs and stealing my things, which is upsetting me. I live alone with mom. My brother died when he was two years old and my dad committed suicide." (Angie, age thirteen)[5]

It is important to note, of course, that all of these children were calling a helpline because they were already in distress, so this is not to suggest that these experiences are indicative of every child living in a household with drug- or alcohol-dependent parents. But there are nonetheless too many children experiencing these kinds of problems, as a range of qualitative research studies show.[6] Such potential for harm justifies increased, close attention to parental drug use. In turn, policies relating to parental drug use demand scrutiny.

Part 3 concludes with " 'Ants Facing an Elephant': Mothers' Grief, Loss, and Work for Change Following the Placement of Children in the Care of Child Protection Authorities," by Kathleen Kenny and Amy Druker of Canada, which considers the aftermath of removing a child from custody of mothers with drug and/or alcohol problems. It is not disputed (by the authors or the mothers represented in the chapter) that the best interests of the child must come first and that removal of a child from an unsafe environment may be necessary. In some cases it is requested by the mothers involved. However, the authors, through a description of their work with mothers who have lost custody of their child(ren), challenge the widely held view that mothers who use drugs are always or necessarily bad parents. They also challenge the presumption that removal from custody is always in the child's best interests, and they detail the women's recommendations for improved child protection policies[7] and parental support.[8]

Endnotes

1. There is no universally accepted definition of family. For the purposes of Part 3, "family" is not limited to the nuclear or traditional family, but includes extended families, single-parent families, and so on.
2. See Preamble, UN Convention on the Rights of the Child, G.A. res. 44/25, annex, 44 U.N. GAOR Supp. (No. 49) at 167, UN Doc. A/44/49 (1989), entered into force September 2, 1990.
3. As an example of the intensity of feeling surrounding this issue, there have been calls in recent years for people who use drugs to be sterilized in order to protect their unborn children from future abuse. See, for example, Jenny Kleeman, "Should Drug Addicts Be Sterilised?" *Guardian*, June 12, 2010.
4. The case of the formerly "legal high" mephedrone in the United Kingdom serves as an example. See BBC News, "Scunthorpe Parents Call for Mephedrone Ban," March 17, 2010.
5. ChildLine Casenotes, *Children Talking to ChildLine About Parental Alcohol and Drug Misuse*, ChildLine and NSPCC, August 2010, www.nspcc.org.uk/ inform/publications/casenotes/clcasenoteparentalalcoholdrugabuse_wdf78112. pdf. See also D. Olszewski et al., *Children's Voices: Experiences and Perceptions of European Children of Drug and Alcohol Issues* (Lisbon: European Monitoring Centre on Drugs and Drug Addiction, 2010), 5–13.
6. From the UK, see, for example: Joseph Rowntree Foundation, *The Effect of Parental Substance Abuse on Young People* (2004), www.jrf.org.uk/publications/ effect-parental-substance-abuse-young-people/; Advisory Council on the Misuse

of Drugs, *Hidden Harm: Responding to the Needs of Children of Problem Drug Users, Report of an Inquiry* (London: Home Office, 2003); D. Forrester and J. Harwin, "Parental Substance Misuse and Child Care Social Work: Findings from the First Stage of a Study of 100 Families," *Child and Family Social Work* 11, no. 4 (November 2006): 325–35; A. Wales et al., *Untold Damage: Children's Accounts of Living with Harmful Parental Drinking* (Edinburgh: Scottish Health Action on Alcohol Problems, 2009); M. Barnard and J. Barlow, "Discovering Parental Drug Dependence: Silence and Disclosure," *Children and Society* 17, no. 1 (2003): 45–56.

7. A recent story from the United States highlights the need for such improvements. In the summer of 2010 a mother in the state of Florida was arrested for child neglect because her baby tested positive for cocaine through breastfeeding. The woman had called the Department of Children and Family Services as she was concerned that her drug use might be harming her child. The baby was screened and tested positive for traces of cocaine and oxycodone. Despite the mother's proactive decision to seek assistance, she was arrested for child neglect, jailed, and the baby placed in foster care. While the mother and baby are now reunited, under the court-ordered supervision of a drug treatment center, the case raises important questions on the way in which authorities deal with mothers who are drug dependent, and how they can encourage them to come forward for help. NBC Miami, "Drug Addicted Mom Abuses Child by Breastfeeding," September 23, 2010; *Palm Beach Post*, "Tequesta Woman Charged with Child Neglect After Drugs Found in Baby's Blood," September 23, 2010.

8. See D. Forrester et al., *Happiness Project Working with Resistance in Families Experiencing Violence: Option 2—Cardiff and Vale—Evaluation Report 2008*, report prepared for the Welsh Assembly Government, UK, 2009. "Option 2" is a service funded by the Welsh Assembly that works with families in which parents have drug or alcohol problems and there are children at risk of harm. A particular focus of the service is reducing the need for children to come into public care. The intervention is short (four to six weeks) and intensive (workers are available 24 hours a day). Workers use a combination of motivational interviewing and solution-focused counseling styles, as well as a range of other therapeutic and practical interventions.

8. Dancing with Despair: A Mother's Perspective

by Gretchen Burns Bergman

The world of addiction is like a never-ending dance, twisting, turning, and weaving a web of disaster. For people with addictive illness, the twirling and whirling engagement with drugs continues to escalate until an outside force restrains them or they die. For the family members, it is an intricate, partially choreographed and partly improvisational pattern. You exhaust yourself with hope, and then release yourself to frustration. You manipulate for change, only to abandon yourself to abusive victimization.

Long before I became a social advocate, and way before I was a mother—in fact from the time I was five years old—I have been a dancer. I taught dance for more than twenty-five years and seem to see the universe in terms of dance movement. I chose the label of "dancer" for myself, because it identified how I felt, and I believe that the quest for self-knowledge is one of life's most important journeys. I have become very aware of labels over the years, as they can often be punitive and discriminatory, particularly when society places them on you. "Codependent," "addict," "dysfunctional family," "ex-convict," "enabler" . . . these are all societal assignations.

Of all the roles I have played in my life, motherhood is the most treasured. I delivered my babies by natural childbirth because my pregnancies gave me a real sense of the central core of myself, and I just knew that returning to the natural rhythms of life was right. I mean, who were these doctors to take away a woman's right to be in charge of the delivery of her own child and be guided by her own maternal instincts! The fear of blundering when it comes to something so deeply important drove many women to turn the process over to a medical professional, and the fear of pain made it easier to numb the experience with drugs.

I loved being a mother and nursing my babies. It was a time of pure give and take, simple supply and demand. It felt natural and organic. It gave me a chance to breathe in the sweet sweaty smells of my infants' heads and to rock in harmony with them and the universe. I enjoyed being a mother to young boys who were full of life and mischief. I can still conjure up the smell of dirty socks after a little league game, the sound of laughter at "bathroom humor," and wet kisses from an exuberantly affectionate eight-year-old.

I remember other parents having such tension-laden concerns about their children being smarter than others, as if it were a competition. My two sons were bright and beautiful. One had big brown eyes, brunet curls, and a thoughtful nature, and the other was a sunny freckle-faced blond with a carefree attitude. Both were clearly intelligent, so my greatest hope was that they become happy and healthy adults.

Sadly, happiness, for the most part, has eluded them, and their health has been severely affected by the insidious disease of drug addiction. Both began experimenting with drugs in their early teens, and drugs became the sludge that seeped through all the layers of our lives. Now, in their thirties, both are heroin addicts, one in long-term recovery and one still struggling to find a way to leave the tenacious and demanding grip of narcotics. They will grapple with the challenges of this chronic illness throughout their lives, and our family will continue to work to denounce stigma-induced guilt, and to walk the never-ending tightrope of when to help our loved ones and when helping is hurting.

My story of lives being derailed by addiction has an even darker chapter and a deeper emotional wound, as my older son spent eleven years of his young life in the criminal justice system cycling in and out of prison for nonviolent drug offenses and relapses. It took him longer to stop seeing himself as an ex-convict who did not deserve to have an enriched and fulfilling life, than to stop seeing himself as a hopeless addict.

People who do not have addictive illness cannot understand why an addict does not just stop the destruction of their disease. What we do not understand, we fear, and what we fear, we hate. This is how prejudice is nurtured, and why the war on drugs became such a lethal plague to our society, a constant and continuing battle that does worse damage to children and their families than the drug abuse.

When I was riding the emotional waves of my first son's active addiction and incarceration I wrote a piece of prose called "Strangulation Tango" to describe the enmeshed interaction and relationship between mother and son. I described the incomprehensible irony of my son's drug use as choosing only neon sparklers in a sea of gray, instead of the vibrant and constant colors of life.

The pain that families endure is almost unbearable, but what is more intolerable is that they must also deal with the anger, blame, and shame of a fearful and ignorant society. The spider web of the criminal justice system and the punitive policies of mass incarceration that are unleashed by the drug war throw acid on open wounds. Nonviolent drug users are thrown into a violent prison atmosphere that is a breeding ground for their transformation into criminals and drug dealers.

Like a floodgate, images come back to me of the frail bodies and hollowed eyes of my eldest son and his girlfriend during their heroin heydays; of trashed apartments filled with the stench of stained mattresses, week-old garbage, dog feces, and piles of dirty clothes. I remember searching for him at night on the streets, days after vowing to let him go, but unable to rest until I found him alive. I piercingly remember earlier days and the hatred in his eyes when I tried to step between him and his drugs, and I choke over the memory of him being led down the courthouse hall, drug-sick in manacles, attached to a line of other young men. I clearly recall visiting him in prison when he appeared behind glass in an orange jumpsuit, and I could not reach out and touch my own son, whom I had nursed and nurtured; and I screamed at the cruelty of a system that would not allow a mother to hug her own sick child. Then he started the prison swagger and clipped convict conversation, and I watched his expression disappear behind a blank facial facade.

I re-experienced the survivor's guilt after each weekly prison visit, having endured the process of going into the prison and being made to feel like a criminal myself; the depression provoked by the cold, cruel atmosphere seeping into my bones; the relief of freedom when the outside gate clicked behind me, and the immediate feeling of a mother's guilt that I was leaving my son behind in this violent cement jungle.

It is impressive to see how each parental fear led to forced acceptance, only to be replaced by a greater trepidation. The first fear was about drug use—then expulsion from high school—then homelessness—then arrest—then overdose—then prison—then overdose again. A close friend and social worker says that mothers of drug addicts have a high tolerance for aberrant behavior. She is right, and most of us have tried and would again try anything to save the lives of our children. When people tell us to let them "hit bottom," we know that after witnessing so many overdoses, their "bottom" could mean death, so we continue to try to keep them "alive for the cure."

It is generally accepted that drug addiction is our number-one public-health problem, yet despite decades of research showing that addiction treatment is successful at reducing drug use and arrests, we continue to employ "tough on crime" tactics, rather than providing treatment programs. We allow addiction to be handled by a criminal justice system that is totally incapable of understanding the intricacies of the disease, and is highly motivated to incarcerate its way out of the problem.

My experiences have led me to advocate against this failed policy. Our children are at the forefront of the war on drugs, and our families are the collateral damage. Instead of working in partnership with health care providers and criminal justice to intervene and usher a sick individual into proper services, families are stranded in our collective frustration and grief. There are an estimated 2.3 million people behind bars in the United States today (one in a hundred adults).[1] Approximately one-quarter of those people held in U.S. prisons or jails have been convicted of a drug offense.[2] Half a million people are incarcerated for drug crimes, more than the European Union incarcerates for all crimes, and they have 100 million more people. The United States represents 5 percent of the world's population, but 25 percent of the world's prison population.[3] Now California has a $10 billion prison budget, largely because of drug offenses and drug-related parole violations. California spends approximately $49,000 per year to house an inmate.[4] Two-thirds of people admitted to prison in California are parole violators,[5] which I find to be the absolute definition of "revolving door" insanity.

The increasing incarceration numbers are a direct response to our failed policies. Now it is estimated that one in four U.S. families struggles with a loved one's addiction to drugs or alcohol,[6] so in addition to coping with the painful process of addictive illness, more and more families are also experiencing the devastation of having a loved one behind bars. In many neighborhoods of color and/or poverty, it has become the norm to have a parent locked away in prison for drug use or drug-related behavior. The consequences of a drug conviction may include permanent loss of educational and employment opportunities, as well as public housing, food stamps, and in many states, the right to vote.

My younger son has recently been arrested on drug possession charges, so once again our family is trying to navigate the cumbersome and challenging criminal justice system. In the year 2000 I served as California state chair of Proposition 36, which mandates treatment instead of incarceration for nonviolent drug offenders. It was passed by 61 percent of state voters, proving that the people were ahead of the politicians in understanding this problem and the need for alternative sentencing. Every year since 2001, more than 30,000 individuals have been sent to this court-mandated treatment, and half of them had never received treatment before.[7] At the time Proposition 36 was passed, my older son was in prison, and although I knew that he would not be helped by this measure, I felt that it would help so many others for years to come, and would be instrumental in changing public opinion about the true nature of addictive illness as well as the addicted individual's right to services and recovery. How ironic that my second son just received alternative sentencing under Proposition 36 a decade later. It would seem that we have come full circle.

But now funding for this life-saving law has been slashed, while the war on drugs costs U.S. taxpayers roughly $40 billion annually in direct costs and tens of billions in indirect costs.[8] And yet, after four decades of the drug war, it seems that drugs are cheaper, purer, and more easily obtained than ever before, while our prisons are filled with drugs, drug users, and drug dealing. We will never eradicate drugs from our society, so we had better figure out how to more conscientiously reduce the harm.

A dancer is both an artist and an athlete . . . a risk-taker with a safety net. You must be a daredevil in order to explore freedom of expression, while at the same time remaining grounded and controlled while practicing and strengthening the body. With a dancer's spirit I understand the hunger to get high, to experience more, and to enhance emotion. What is hard to fathom is watching a beautiful and bright individual lose his freedom and soul by not being able to stop the drug demons from destroying his life. But what is even more difficult to accept is the calamitous devastation of the drug war.

As I get older I am less free as a dancer. I can no longer fling myself into the universe with the same spirit of abandon. Thoughts of protecting bones and joints caution me to be more careful, just as

I try to avoid the emotional turbulence of an addicted offspring. My experience warns me not to get so distraught over their troubles, if I am to be around to enjoy their reemergence into life through eventual recovery. I say eventual, because my heart cannot dance without hope, as long as the music of life is still playing.

Ending our dependence on drugs is not just a problem in the United States; it is a global concern. The ravages of the drug wars seep through layers of our lives, and the futures of our offspring. It is not just in my own family, our communities, our state, and our country, but in other countries as well. It affects our relationship with the rest of the world. We need to teach our children to fight for human rights and dignity, and to believe in the importance and sanctity of human existence. We must advocate for an end to the war on drugs, and begin policies of tolerance, compassion, restoration, harm reduction, and healing that are directed to positive solutions for the future of our children.

Endnotes

1. Jenifer Warren, *One in 100: Behind Bars in America* (Washington, DC: PEW Center on the States, Public Safety Performance, 2008), 5.
2. William J. Sabol, Todd D. Minton, and Paige M. Harrison, *Prison and Jail Inmates at Midyear 2006* (Washington, DC: Bureau of Justice Statistics, 2007).
3. Roy Walmsley, *World Prison Population List*, 8th ed. (London: International Centre for Prison Studies, School of Law, King's College, 2009).
4. Legislative Analyst Office (LAO), California Department of Corrections and Rehabilitation, *Overview of CDCR Budget*, presentation to the Senate Budget Subcommittee, No. 4 on State Administration, March 19, 2009, 4.
5. G. Ryken, J. Petersilia, and J. Lin, "Parole Violations and Revocations in California," UC Irvine, October 13, 2008, 6, www.ncjrs.gov/pdffiles1/nij/grants/224521.pdf.
6. NIH MedlinePlus, "The Science of Addiction: Drugs, Brains, and Behavior," *MedlinePlus* 2, no. 2 (Spring 2007): 14–17; www.nim.nih.gov/medlineplus/magazine/issues/spring07/articles/spring07pg14-17.html.
7. D. Urada et al., *Evaluation of Proposition 36: The Substance Abuse and Crime Prevention Act of 2000*, Report, UCLA Integrated Substance Abuse Program, 2008, 45, www.adp.state.ca.us/SACPA/PDF/2008 Final Report.pdf.
8. Office of National Drug Control Policy, *National Drug Control Strategy FY 2001: Budget Summary*, 2000, 2, www.ncjrs.gov/ondcppubs/publications/policy/budget00/index.html.

9. Mothers and Children of the Drug War: A View from a Women's Prison in Quito, Ecuador

by Jennifer Fleetwood and Andreina Torres

Introduction

The "war on drugs" harms women and their children worldwide. Mandatory minimum sentences for drug possession have driven the dramatic increase in the number of women in prison, not only in the United States but across the globe wherever a war on drugs is being fought. This chapter looks at the case of Ecuador where the number of women imprisoned has soared since 1991. The chapter draws on ethnographic research conducted by both authors in the largest women's prison, located in Quito, the capital city of Ecuador. The first section looks at the supply-side interdiction policies implemented in Ecuador and demonstrates that women are not collateral damage but intended targets. Next, it describes how the war on drugs has changed prison and the profile of inmates as a result of interdiction efforts. The second section describes the effects of these policies from the perspective of two groups of women imprisoned in Quito: Ecuadorians and foreign nationals. We conclude that while these women's experience as mothers/prisoners differs greatly, the war on drugs produces a number of outcomes that disproportionately punish women and their families.

Women Mules: Targets of the "War on Drugs"

Women drug mules are often described as "collateral damage" of the war on drugs.[1] However, the situation in Ecuador clearly demonstrates that interdiction efforts focus disproportionately on low-level offenders, where most women in the drug trade are positioned. Furthermore, international policies have had indirect consequences that have negatively affected women and their families, both locally and internationally.

International interventions have promoted a "head count" logic to drug interdiction in Ecuador. In 2005, Ecuador and the United States signed a bilateral agreement stipulating that for an investment of $15.7 million in the security of the country, the United States demanded a 12 percent increase in the capturing and processing of "narco-traffickers" and a 10 percent increase in the capture of drugs in relation to the year 2004.[2] This logic of quantification directs interdiction efforts to interventions where large numbers of people can be arrested; in short, toward mules instead of middlemen or managers. This has disproportionately affected women.

These internationally set quotas are "topped up" with street-level drug users and dealers. The majority come from marginal populations; many are homeless, ethnic-minority women, and men of color who are arrested with insignificant quantities of drugs.[3] Since there is only one drug law, users and dealers are sentenced as if they were international traffickers.

Sentencing practices also fail to take into account the reasons for women's offending, or the outcomes of imprisoning women for very long periods of time. In Ecuador, the *Law of Narcotic Drugs and Psychotropic Substances* (Ley 108) was passed in 1991. The minimum sentence was originally ten years. In 2003 this was increased to twelve years, one of the highest sentences for drug trafficking across the continent.[4] Mandatory minimums rule out the relevance of mitigating circumstances. In 1997, the law was modified to allow judges to take into account some extenuating circumstances such as terminal illness, age, and good behavior but not child care.[5] Judges adhere strictly to standard penalties to avoid potentially career-ending accusations of bribery and corruption. Thus, family situations, such as being the sole caretaker of children or parents are not taken into consideration. This disproportionately affects women, insofar as many drug mules become involved in response to poverty as a way to provide for their families. The only way to reduce one's sentence is to provide information to the police, something few mules are able to do.

Women's Prisons in the Epoch of the "War on Drugs"

The war on drugs has had a dramatic effect on the structuring and functioning of prisons in Ecuador. The 1980s marked the beginning of a radical change in the profile of the female prison population, a process that took place throughout Latin America.[6] Women's involvement in drug trafficking replaced traditionally "feminine" criminalization—murders enacted in the private sphere, usually against husbands, brothers, or sons. Between 1936 and 1941, these crimes constituted 82 percent of those committed by women in prison, while 18 percent were property crimes.[7] By 1980, 38.2 percent of imprisoned women had committed drug-related crimes, while homicides represented only 21.8 percent of offenses and property crimes, 20.4 percent.[8] In 2004, the proportion of women imprisoned for drug-related charges had risen to 77 percent, many of whom were "mules,"[9] making the increase for such charges much more significant in women's prisons than in men's. By 2004 the proportion of men imprisoned for drug offenses was just 33.5 percent, while property crimes represented 36.4 percent and homicides 15.8 percent.[10] Consequently, the female prison population increased dramatically in recent decades; by 2004 it represented 10 percent of the total prison population, while in the 1970s it was only 4 percent. Such an increase can only be understood in the context of the aforementioned policies that have promoted a "head count" logic to drug law enforcement, often leading to the use of women as scapegoats in sentencing processes under Ley 108.

One of the most visible consequences of this population increase is the current state of women's prisons, characterized by overcrowding, lack of funding, and generally precarious living conditions for inmates. This research was conducted in "El Inca," the second largest women's prison in Ecuador. Women's prisons (like men's prisons) suffer from chronic underfunding. State funds barely cover the cost of low-quality food (the prison spends an average of 75 cents per prisoner per day on food) and the salaries of underpaid prison guards and administrative staff. Consequently, inmates routinely complained about deficiencies in personnel that often led to mistreatment:

prison guards here lack any formal training, they are ignorant and don't know how to treat inmates. . . . We know we are prisoners but we are human beings and they treat us as if we were the "worst," even though some of us have a university education. (Interview with Teresa, El Inca, January 2005)

Overcrowding, lack of resources (including staff) meant that much of prison management was done by inmates. Improvements in infrastructure (mainly cells) and the provision of basic utilities, such as gas for the kitchens in each pavilion/block, are obtained either through collective fundraising or individual resources that usually come from family support. In this context, "rehabilitation" efforts also become the responsibility of imprisoned women:

> *if it weren't for us, we would not have anything, our own initiative has allowed us to have sewing workshops, dance, theater, and choreography groups, the choir . . . but this is only possible because of our own enthusiasm, if it weren't for us we would only have the labor workshop in which we are exploited. (Interview with Luisa, El Inca, January 2005)*

Depending on which prison block an inmate lives in (there are three), life at this women's prison can be more or less expensive.[11] Moreover, inmate designation to the different pavilions responds to class and ethnic rather than "technical" criteria, such as crimes committed, time of sentence, past offenses, and so forth.

> *We try to group inmates according to a certain degree of affinity or homogeneity for them to be able to share a very small space. . . . We believe we can strive for a "progress" regime for those with a higher status, better customs, and who play an important role in prison and excel. These people are placed in the new pavilions and obviously have certain privileges, such as sharing a room only with one more person.[12] (Interview with prison psychologist, El Inca, February 2005)*

Interrupted Motherhood in "El Inca"

Conventional conceptions of motherhood center on the notion of the family that lives together, has shared priorities, and in which the mother is the primary caregiver.[13] For all women interviewed for this research and their children, being arrested and imprisoned caused a sudden, unanticipated interruption in their lives, relationships, and identities. Motherhood is a central aspect of Ecuadorian and foreign national women's experience of imprisonment. A survey of inmates showed that most of the women imprisoned for drug trafficking were married or in common-law marriages.[14] About 40 percent of respondents were mothers, half of them shared parenting duties with their partners and the other half were single mothers.[15] A large proportion of mules and women involved in international drug trafficking were single mothers, but these groups were primarily composed of foreign nationals. Imprisonment posed specific challenges to Ecuadorian and foreign national women. These will be examined in turn.

Mothering on the Inside: National Women and Their Children

Faced with little or deficient state responses for their children's situations, Ecuadorian women make difficult decisions about continuing to be mothers after imprisonment. Some who choose to have their children imprisoned with them experience the pain of seeing their children grow up in a highly negative environment. Others choose to leave them in the care of relatives and try to maintain contact with their children through visits. Some women prefer to cut themselves off entirely from the life of their children to spare them from the stigma attached to criminalization. None of these are easy decisions.[16]

"Shared" Parenting

In contrast to foreign nationals, Ecuadorian women are more likely to maintain their romantic relationships once in prison. In fact, many couples "do their time" in prison together. Through a series of interviews conducted with women drug mules it was possible to identify the importance of women's romantic relationships in their decisions and motivations to get involved in drug trafficking. Many women saw their involvement in drug trafficking as an opportunity to "save" a relationship troubled by a difficult economic situation, as well as an opportunity to provide a better future for their children.

> *there really aren't any jobs, there are no jobs . . . it's not easy to find a job and even though it is hard for many of us to get involved in drug trafficking, it's something easy, and you can get money, this is the most important thing, that you can get the money you need to support your children, to support your family, that's why as head of our households we are immersed in all of this. (Teresa, mother of two, El Inca)*

In other cases women become the victims of their partner's illegal activities and enter drug-trafficking activities without having full knowledge of their partner's role. In these cases they are legally incapable of accusing their spouses and are charged with the same punitive sentences. As a result many women put an end to their relationships.

For the majority, however, maintaining contact with their partners after imprisonment becomes paramount. Having their partners' emotional and economic support may facilitate motherhood while in prison. The possibility of having a weekly or monthly conjugal visit is an important element in maintaining family unity and support. At El Inca, inmates fought for the right to have a weekly visit to the men's prison in Quito, where many of their spouses were imprisoned. In order to make this possible they had to pay collectively for the bus ride, given prison authorities' reluctance to provide this service.

While maintaining contact with spouses provided women with hope and made them feel they were not alone in motherhood, often their partner's lack of interest and responsibility for their children's upbringing generated anxiety and resentment, especially when they did not help financially. Following persistent gender patterns, when both parents are in prison, women or relatives (especially mothers or grandmothers) are ultimately responsible for the care of children.

Imprisoned Children

Women at El Inca are also allowed to live with their children in prison. The majority of women who opted for this arrangement were Ecuadorians who did not have the resources or family support to arrange for the care of their children outside the prison. For many of these women the only other option was to leave their children in the streets. Other women simply did not trust state or privately funded services available for their children's care. Institutional ambiguity regarding the age limit of children allowed to live in prison with their mothers generated complex situations. This was illustrated by the case of a seven-year-old boy who suffered from learning disabilities and whose sexual behavior (as well as inmates' behavior toward him) was beginning to concern the authorities.

Prison authorities did not make any adjustments to assess and meet the needs of mothers. Since children were not considered part of the prison population, there was a lack of basic services such as food and accommodation. Many women had to share prison food with their children or make arrangements to buy additional food. Mothers along with their children were also concentrated in one of the most crowded pavilions, characterized by concentrating a large number of poor black and indigenous women. This pavilion was the most problematic in terms of general lack of coverage of basic necessities, intensity of conflicts and fights, drug consumption, and other issues. Many children had to grow up and live their childhoods in this environment. This was a large price to be paid by women who fought to be close to their children or simply had no other choice.

Institutional support for imprisoned women's children was deficient. The only service available was a day-care center for infants (four to five months up to two years old) in which they were able to spend the day until lockup time (from 8 a.m. to 4 p.m.). Additional resources for Ecuadorian women were provided by private foundations, religious organizations, or state-funded programs. Nonetheless, imprisoned women have developed strong distrust regarding the services provided by these outside institutions. There is a general fear about the way their children are treated by strangers, and reports of actual cases of abuse and mistreatment. This fear and distrust explained why some women preferred to have their children inside the prison, despite the harsh reality that prison life entailed for them.

At the day-care center children received general supervision and food. However, this center was severely underfunded and depended largely on charity. During a visit to this center we were informed that much of the food provided to children came from discarded produce donated by large supermarkets. The caregivers also demonstrated a lack of sensitivity toward the mother's situation and continually expressed disapproval of their care practices. Children were viewed as victims of their mothers' "wretched" behavior and lack of responsibility. While this was particularly emphasized in the case of drug users, who were often accused of trading goods such as clothes, diapers, or formula in order to obtain drugs, very little attention was given to the rehabilitation of drug users inside the prison.

Imprisoned women's ability to be "good" mothers was called into question. Their efforts to stay close to their children were seen as selfish and irresponsible. These judgments were also made regarding women who became pregnant after being imprisoned. In fact women were required to be practicing contraceptive methods in order to be granted the conjugal visit. As the director of the day-care center expressed:

> We need to make mothers realize that they cannot have any more children. Their children are future criminals. (Interview with director of day care "La Macarena," El Inca, January 2005)

Thus, women's desire to be and become mothers while in prison was seen as irrational. Such accusations failed to understand motherhood as a source of pride and a reason for women to maintain a sense of purpose. Borrowing from Bourgois's account of the meanings of motherhood among women living in El Barrio (East Harlem, New York), it is precisely the "wretched living conditions" of imprisonment that make "motherhood so appealing."[17] In a context in which women are considered to have transgressed the law but also the gender norm, reclaiming femininity becomes an important way to achieve redemption and forgiveness. For women involved in prison politics, motherhood gave female prisoners a moral advantage (regarding their male counterparts) and became a source of legitimating their claims as imprisoned women but above all as imprisoned mothers.

Mediated Motherhood

Continued family support is also an important element for Ecuadorian mothers doing time at El Inca, especially for those who prefer to leave their children in the care of relatives. Women at El Inca were allowed three visit days per week (Saturday, Sunday, and Wednesday). These days were extremely important for prisoners as they represented an opportunity to stay in touch with relatives, their children, and their partners. During visits relatives brought in food and general goods (hygiene, cleaning products, money, etc.) essential for survival inside the prison. Visits lasted all day.

Even though these visits may represent an advantage for Ecuadorian women, life in prison undoubtedly took a toll on family relationships and motherhood. With time, visit days generated anxiety and sadness in those who noted with melancholy how visits gradually became more scarce and irregular. Thus, maintaining contact with their children through visits and the help of relatives could become a fragile and ephemeral enterprise for imprisoned women.

Mediated motherhood was not possible for all Ecuadorian women. Some of them did not have relatives or friends who lived close enough to be able to visit regularly, or at all. Others had relatives who condemned their incarceration and preferred to isolate children from their imprisoned and "immoral" mothers.

In one visit my relatives told me that my sister resented me, that she didn't understand how could I have done this, how could I become involved in something like this, and she didn't want to

CHILDREN OF THE DRUG WAR

come, she didn't want anything to do with these type of things. (Teresa, mother of two, El Inca)

In other cases, women themselves prevented their children from knowing that they were imprisoned. Many told their children they were working or studying far away. These women could only stay in touch with their children through phone calls. Many Ecuadorian women felt as isolated from their family as foreign nationals. In turn they had to develop similar strategies to stay in touch or reinvent their role as mothers while being far away.

Interrupted Motherhood: Foreign National Women and Their Children

At the time of this fieldwork (2005–7) approximately one-third of women in El Inca were foreign nationals. They came from all over the world (Europe, North America, Africa, and Southeast Asia) but most were Colombian. As noted above, almost all of the foreign women imprisoned in El Inca were drug offenders, the majority of whom were drug mules. Women mules became involved in the international drug trade through diverse routes. A minority had been coerced through violent threats (toward them and their families); many worked as drug mules in response to relative deprivation. This section looks at how foreign national women in prison managed being mothers and coping with motherhood while imprisoned far from home for long periods of time.

Arrest and Interruption

All of the foreign national women were arrested as they were leaving Ecuador. Most had stayed in the country for a short amount of time and had left their children at home, usually with friends and family temporarily since many were single parents. Most claimed to be going to visit a relative or friend in another city or to be working away. All expected to be back in a few days time. Of the many worries women experienced once they were arrested, those with children were immediately concerned with the urgent issue of child care:

I was frightened. And I was thinking my God, my life is over. . . . My children, what's gonna happen to them? Are they gonna go into my house and take all my family away? (Sarah, mother of two)

Most respondents urgently needed to contact their family after they were arrested. However, there was no provision for arrestees to phone home. Some respondents had to wait several days before they could telephone (usually through a guard or lawyer). In some cases, families were notified by their national embassy. Donna remembers her first phone call home:

> One of the policemen . . . made me call my mom. He hid me in the cell . . . and I called my mom and said please forgive me. She says, "you're really in jail?" I said "yes, in Ecuador, in Quito". . . I was like crying and I was flipping out going please don't tell my daughter. She goes, "Your daughter heard me." So my daughter knew I was in jail but she didn't know why. (Donna, mother of one)

In the short term, children usually moved in with godparents or relatives since most women were single parents; in the long term, most women lost their family home.

Children of drug mules lost their parents suddenly and in secretive circumstances. Women experienced an acute sense of shame and most kept the reasons for their arrest hidden from family. Some claimed to be at college or imprisoned for less problematic crimes such as incorrect immigration documentation. However, due to the high-profile nature of the crime, children sometimes found out why their parent was in prison from other sources. Children of drug mules experienced additional stigma in relation to their parent's crime. Older children often figured out that their mother was in prison and had to keep it a secret from younger siblings. Although there are important differences according to the offense committed, the effects of having a parent imprisoned are well known. Children often experience behavioral difficulties, and may become withdrawn and feel abandoned and rejected.[18] Children of drug mules experienced additional confusion and trauma due to the sudden and secretive nature of their parent's disappearance compounded by not being able to visit prison. Those who did know that their mother was imprisoned in Ecuador were very worried that something bad would happen.

Many women were the sole earner supporting children and/or parents before they were arrested, and loss of the breadwinner caused financial difficulties for the family. Additionally, many of the costs of imprisonment were passed on to the family: especially legal and health care costs. Although lawyers were formally provided by Ecuador, they were notoriously unreliable and corrupt. Already poor families had to raise sums, sometimes several thousand dollars, to get a fair trial. As described above, most inmates had to pay their own way while they were in prison. This included health care, and sometimes even meals and taxis for the guards who accompanied them to hospital. Foreign national prisoners were often perceived to be rich and were tricked or bribed by corrupt guards as well as their fellow inmates.

Long-Distance Motherhood

Drug mules served long sentences of about six to eight years. Exiled from the context in which they had learned to mother, imprisoned women invented new ways to be part of their child's daily life and to maintain their identity as mothers. Nonetheless, women's attempts were severely limited by physical distance from home and the lack of resources available to support their efforts.

Since visits were impossible, phone calls were elevated to a new level of importance as an opportunity to maintain the parenting bond and reassure children that they still cared about them:

When I talk to them on the phone you know, they know that their mommy still loves them and one day I'm gonna get out of here safe and sound and things, you know, for me to go home and take care of them, they're depending on me, their father left them, I'm a single parent: they're my first priority. (Amanda, mother of four)

However, the prison made no provision for inmates to maintain contact with their children. The small number of public telephones in prison were identical to those on the outside in price and function.[19] Calls to the United States were some of the least expensive but calling farther away (to Africa or the Far East) was more expensive. Inmates were not monitored by staff but had little privacy as a result of prison overcrowding. Considerable effort was put into raising the funds to be able to call home. Many foreign national women worked in a greeting card-workshop run by an international group of missionaries. Some managed small "businesses" such as cutting hair, sewing, or selling crafts as well as cooking and cleaning. Thus, inmate mothers replaced the everyday labor of parenting with the labor of raising funds to maintain contact with children.

Women struggled to make sense of ways to be a mother when they were so far from home when their family was facing a crisis. This was especially the case if a family member died. Two women lost their children while they were in prison. Women, either individually or collectively, had no way to deal with the death of a child. Women spoke of feeling powerless to do anything for their families. Praying took on a new importance as something that was not weakened by either distance from children or lack of economic resources. Women prayed together as an act of solidarity. For many women prayer was seen as a strong enough force to effect material change in their children's lives.

In addition to the daily task of raising resources to maintain contact with children, women embodied motherhood in daily life. In their rooms, they proudly displayed photos of their children and drawings or letters from children. Others had their children's names tattooed on their bodies: a permanent reminder of their identities on the outside. Furthermore, women cared for children who were resident or visiting prison. Renewing their identity as (and ability to be) a mother was constructed in light of the crisis in identity experienced when they were arrested. The mothering-caring identity, as the opposite of the criminal identity, was for many to form the basis of a renewed identity when they would leave prison.

Planning and preparing for their release from prison was an important aspect of being a mother in prison. Many commented that they were in prison for a higher purpose. In particular, those with drug addictions used imprisonment as an opportunity to get "clean" so that when they returned home they could be better mothers than they had been. Nonetheless, the very small drug rehabilitation unit was underfunded and overcrowded. Its success was largely dependent on inmates who ran it themselves. Furthermore, there was almost no training or education for women in prison. The only classes available were high school classes that were of little use to foreign national women.

Finally, while this chapter has focused on mothering, this was one of many "caring" relationships and responsibilities in women's lives. In the same way that women felt anxiety for having "abandoned" their children, many women (not all of whom were mothers) felt ashamed that they could not fulfill their duty to care for parents and grandparents, especially as they grew older.

I want to go home to see my kids, my husband and all, but most of all, my mother. Jennifer, it's like please, please do not die when

I'm here. You know, (voice starts to break) the way she's sick 'n everything is like, God, don't let anything happen to her while I'm here! Let me go home to hug her, just to hold her. You know, cause she's getting weaker every day. She can't walk anymore, and you know, I think my mom's the most special person to me. And if she did die while I'm here, I know I wouldn't be able to deal with it. (Sarah)

Conclusion

Men and women do not forfeit their right to parent their children because of involvement in drug trafficking. The women we spoke to in El Inca fought hard to be mothers in very difficult circumstances. Nonetheless, it is clear that motherhood and families are brutally interrupted and reconfigured by imprisonment. It would be easy to conclude here with a set of recommendations. Women's prisons should be better resourced to take into account the needs of families and it is clear that deporting foreign national women to serve their sentences at home where they can be closer to their families would give families a chance. However, we offer a more radical conclusion. As stated at the start, the large number of women imprisoned worldwide as a result of the "war on drugs" is not "collateral damage" but rather supply-side policies premised on a "head count" logic that makes women intentional targets. Such policies have disproportionately affected women and their families.[20] Furthermore, mandatory minimum sentences that do not take mitigating circumstances into account punish women disproportionately.[21] Moreover, we contend that the suffering of women in prison that we witnessed served no purpose. Women mules did not need to spend eight years in prison to prevent them from reoffending. They did not become rehabilitated or better able to provide for their family as a result of imprisonment.

However, positive directions for the future can be found in Ecuador. Since finishing fieldwork in 2007, some significant changes have occurred. At the end of 2008, about 1,500 "micro-traffickers" were released (those arrested with less than two kilos of drugs).[22] By September of 2009, the number had risen to 2,570.[23] The "pardon for drug mules" approved in July 2008 had a significant effect on women. El Inca experienced a dramatic drop in its prison population. While in 2007 the population had risen to 507,[24] by 2009 this figure had fallen to just 296.[25] The pardon recognized that a large portion of people imprisoned for drug crimes were not appropriate targets, but rather minor players who were being punished as scapegoats. This measure, however, will have lasting effects only if it is accompanied by a broad reform of drug legislation, a process that seems to be brewing but has yet to materialize.[26]

Author's note:

Jennifer Fleetwood revisited the prison in October 2010. The pardon for "micro-traffickers" has had a dramatic effect on conditions in the prison. The prison is visibly and audibly calmer. Women reported that they had been sentenced quickly, were accommodated in humane conditions, and even had access to a small number of rehabilitation programs. Nonetheless, sentences remained high (around six to eight years), the effects of the pardon are not permanent, and the number of women in prison for drug trafficking is slowly increasing.

Endnotes

† The authors would like to formally thank the inmates of El Inca women's prison in Quito, Ecuador, who participated in research and kindly shared their stories with us. Jennifer's Fleetwood's research was supported by a 1+3 studentship from the Economic and Social Research Council [PTA-030-2004-00460].
1. M. Norton-Hawk, "Exporting Gender Injustice: The Impact of the U.S. War on Drugs on Ecuadorian Women," *Critical Criminology* 18, no. 2 (2010): 132–46.
2. J. Pontón and A. Torres, "Cárceles del Ecuador: los efectos de la criminalización por drogas," *URVIO: revista Latinoamericana de Seguridad Cuidana* 1 (2001): 55. See also U.S. Department of State, *International Narcotics and Law Enforcement: FY 2008 Program and Budget Guide*, September 2007, Bureau of International Narcotics and Law Enforcement Affairs, www.state.gov/p/inl/rls/rpt/pbg/c24130. htm.
3. S. Edwards, *Illicit Drug Control Policies and Prisons: The Human Cost* (Washington, DC: Washington Office on Latin America, 2003).
4. Ibid.
5. Fredy Rivera Velez, "Ecuador: Untangling the Drug War," in *Drugs and Democracy in Latin America: The Impact of U.S. Policy*, ed. C. Youngers and E. Rosin, 231–62 (London: Lynne Rienner, 2005).
6. B. Kalinsky, "Social Anthropology in Sensitive Research Contexts. A Case Study: State Prisons, Province of Neuquén, Argentina," UNESCO, *International Social Science Journal* 56, no. 179 (2004): 153–70.
7. J. Barrera, "La mujer y el delito," Archivos de Criminología, Neuropsiquiatría y Disciplinas Conexas. Quito: Facultad de Jurisprudencia, Ciencias Políticas y Sociales de la Universidad Central del Ecuador. Vol. 6 and 7, 1942–1943 (manuscript).

8. V. Vega Uquillas, "El sistema penitenciario ecuatoriano: estudio de diagnóstico," Registro Oficial, num. 132, Diciembre 31 de 1970, Archivos de Criminología Neuro- Psiquiatría y Disciplinas Conexas, Quito, Facultad de Jurisprudencia, Ciencias Políticas y Sociales de la Universidad Central del Ecuador, 1982.
9. Direccion Nacional de Rehabilitacion Social, *Boletín Estadístico, El sistema penitenciario ecuatoriano en cifras 2004–2005* (Quito).
10. Ibid.
11. Each prison block had a different price scale for entry fees and monthly or weekly gas and cleaning fees.
12. At the time of our research at El Inca, each room hosted three to four inmates. The "old" blocks, however, could have more than five people including children.
13. S. Enos, *Mothering from the Inside: Parenting in a Women's Prison* (Albany: State University of New York Press, 2001).
14. J. Nuñez and C. Gallardo, "Una lectura cuantativa del sistema de cárceles en Ecuador," Programa de estudios de la cuidad, Facultad Latinoamericana de Ciencias Sociales, 2006.
15. A. Torres, "Drogas, cárcel y género en Ecuador: la experiencia de mujeres mulas," master's thesis, FLACSO, Quito, Ecuador, Serie Tesis, 2008.
16. The following is based on ethnographic research conducted over six months in 2005.
17. P. Bourgois, *In Search of Respect: Selling Crack in El Barrio* (Cambridge: Cambridge University Press, 1995), 273.
18. R. Wolleswinkel, "Children of Imprisoned Parents," in *Developmental and Autonomy Rights of Children: Empowering Children, Caregivers and Communities*, ed. J. Willems, 191–207 (Oxford/New York: Intersentia, 2002). See also J. Murray, "The Effects of Imprisonment on Families and Children of Prisoners," in *The Effects of Imprisonment*, ed. A. Liebling and S. Maruna, 442–65 (Cullompton: Willan, 2005).
19. For a description of phoning home from prisons in the United States, see M. Mauer and M. Chesney-Lind, "Introduction," in *Invisible Punishment: The Collateral Consequences of Mass Imprisonment*, ed. Mauer and Chesney-Lind (New York: New Press, 2002).
20. J. Sudbury, "Introduction," in *Global Lockdown: Race, Gender, and the Prison-Industrial Complex* (London: Routledge, 2005), xi–2.
21. M. Chesney-Lind, "Imprisoning Women: The Unintended Victims of Mass Imprisonment," in Mauer and Lind, *Invisible Punishment*, 79–94.
22. P. Metaal and S. Edwards, *Pardon for Mules in Ecuador: A Sound Proposal*, (Washington, DC: Washington Office on Latin America, 2009), www.tni.org/sites/www.tni.org/files/download/dlr1.pdf
23. Fiscalía General de la Nación, *Revista de Estadísticas Criminológicas N. 2*, 2009.
24. J. Pontón, "Mujeres, cuerpo y encierro: acomodo y resistencias al sistema penitenciario," in *Estudios sobre sexualidades en América Latina*, ed. K. Araujo and M. Prieto (Ecuador: FLACSO, 2008), 309–30.
25. The proportion of women also dropped to 8 percent of the prison population. Dirección Nacional de Rehabilitación Social, 2009 Statistics, www.dnrs.gov.ec.
26. S.G. Edwards and C. Youngers, *Ecuador Memo: Drug Law Reform in Ecuador: Building Momentum for a More Effective, Balanced and Realistic Approach* (Washington, DC: Washington Office on Latin America, Transnational Institute, 2010), www.druglawreform.info/images/stories/documents/ecuador%20memo.pdf.

10. Between Diego and Mario: Children, Families, and the Drug War in Indonesia

by Asmin Fransiska, Ajeng Larasati, and Ricky Gunawan

Introduction: Incarceration, Family, and the Best Interests of the Child

Indonesia ratified the UN Convention on the Rights of the Child (CRC)[1] in 1990.[2] Twelve years later, Child Protection Law No. 23 was adopted to incorporate the CRC into the domestic legal framework. According to the convention, the best interests of the child must be "a primary consideration" in all matters concerning children (Article 3). When laws are adopted, policies developed, or decisions made in specific cases, the best interests of the child (determined with reference to the facts of the case and the full range of the rights of the child)[3] must be foremost in the conclusions reached.

The role of the family, and the importance of the family environment for the development of the child,[4] is explicitly stated in the convention. The preamble, which reflects the ethos of the document, though it is not legally binding itself, recognizes the family as "the fundamental group of society and the natural environment for the growth and well-being of all its members and particularly children." It says that the family "should be afforded the necessary protection and assistance so that it can fully assume its responsibilities within the community" in order that the child "for the full and harmonious development of his or her personality" may "grow up in a family environment, in an atmosphere of happiness, love and understanding."

The binding articles of the treaty follow from this. Article 5 requires states to "respect the responsibilities, rights and duties of parents or, where applicable, the members of the extended family . . . to provide, in a manner consistent with the evolving capacities of the child, appropriate direction and guidance in the exercise by the child of the rights recognized in the present Convention." Article 7, unique to the CRC within the UN human rights treaties, states that the child has the right "as far as possible to know and be cared for by his or her parents." Article 8 states that the child's "identity, including nationality, name and family relations" shall be respected without unlawful interference. Article 18 is specific to the family and requires, among other guarantees, that "For the purpose of guaranteeing and promoting the rights set forth in the present Convention, States Parties shall render appropriate assistance to parents and legal guardians in the performance of their child-rearing responsibilities and shall ensure the development of institutions, facilities and services for the care of children" (Article 18.2).

The family is therefore strongly protected within the Convention as an essential condition for the full realization of the rights of the child.

Imprisonment of a parent is specifically referred to in Article 9 in the context of the separation of a child from his or her parents. The article requires that children should be informed of the whereabouts of their parents where this is in their best interests (Article 9.4). While it is not explicitly stated in the CRC, it seems clear that the effect on the child or children of the accused (or dependent siblings or other children dependent on the accused), must be taken into account in criminal proceedings and sentencing. This may not be determinative, but without such consideration, the best interests of the child, and the protection afforded the family in the CRC, are not being given due regard.

Indonesia is a country that strongly adopts the war on drugs approach. The government has made drugs the first and foremost enemy and made it a top priority to eliminate drugs from Indonesia to the extent that visitors entering the country are greeted with signs reading "death penalty for drug traffickers."[5] This hard-line approach has been reflected in law and policy for decades. The Narcotics Law states that all drug-related offenses shall be punishable by penal sanctions. A provision exists to permit offenders to be diverted to a rehabilitation center, but this is at the judge's discretion and as such is rarely used. For most it remains simply words on paper. There is, however, little attention to the consequences for children when a parent or sibling is imprisoned in this way. Law enforcement bodies tend to strictly enforce the laws in a legalistic manner, and pay no attention to the social background of a defendant. How the law, as applied, can somehow affect a dependent child's life has never been taken into consideration.

In Indonesia, bonds within a family are strong. Family, as Indonesians are taught from elementary school, is the primary environment for the development of the child and from which people are prepared to enter into society. One's behavior is a reflection of one's family. The problems of one member of the family will affect the other members. It should be understood that incarceration for drug-related cases is not just a punishment for defendants—it also affects their families. If they have children, young sisters or brothers, or parents living with them, imprisonment will cause them considerable harm, including reduced economic security, reduction in psychological and emotional well-being, and stigma within the community or in school.

Some crimes, of course, are serious and require imprisonment. But in the context of drugs, the vast majority are sentenced for nonviolent drug offenses or simply for personal possession. The price, paid by the defendant and the family, is extremely high.

The following two stories, based on interviews with the families involved, highlight the negative emotional, economic, educational, and psychological effects of incarceration on children. They show how the best interests of the child and the protection of the family are ignored in the war on drugs in Indonesia. They are just two of many, many similar stories.

Diego: A Boy with a Big Dream

Diego[6] is a twelve-year-old boy. He is a sixth grade student at a public elementary school. Just like many other children he likes to play football [soccer]. His favorite player is the famous Cristiano Ronaldo. He has always been a huge fan of Ronaldo, but although he adores an international football player, he never forgets where he came from, and that is Bandung, West Java, Indonesia. He is a diehard fan of Persib, a local football club. At school, perhaps like many other children, he does not like mathematics, but he likes Indonesian and nature science, particularly astronomy. "But he doesn't want to be an astronaut or astronomer" says Diana, his grandmother, with whom Diego lives, "he wants to be a football player, just like Ronaldo."

In addition to football he is also crazy about rock music. He likes Linkin Park, a modern-rock band from the United States. This is nothing strange for a twelve-year-old boy, but what is surprising is that he is so fanatical about Metallica, a legendary rock band. This is odd because Metallica is not that popular among others of Diego's age. But this is not strange for him—his father was a vocalist in a famous underground, heavy metal band in Bandung. His father, a drug user, died of cephalitis on July 26, 2006.

Diego and his mother have lived with his grandmother since he was born. However, since last year, his mother, Rose, has not lived with them. She was put on trial for drug use, incarcerated, and later placed in a drug-dependence hospital located in Cibubur, outside Jakarta.

Rose has been using drugs for more than ten years, during which she has been arrested a number of times. On January 23, 2009, she was arrested by the police, and after a lengthy legal process, received a court decision on July 27. The court ordered her to be imprisoned for one year and eight months, but to begin with a period of rehabilitation for six months. This meant that once she got out of rehab she would still have to stay in prison for one year and two months. Since she had already served six months in detention waiting for her court hearing, however, that would be deducted from the total sentence. However, as it happened, Rose had to endure imprisonment first and then rehabilitation.[7]

Rose was transferred from Pondok Bambu Detention Center to Cibubur Drug Dependence Hospital (RSKO Cibubur), on Monday, February 8, 2010. It took months after her July sentence for the corrupt detention system to actually move her to the hospital. Once she arrived, hospital staff examined Rose regarding her addiction, and gave her some medication. They charged a fee of around US$42. Lembaga Bantuan Hukum Masyarakat (LBH Masyarakat) argued on Rose's behalf that she was transferred to the hospital by court order, and that she came from a poor family. Therefore, she should be released from any fees. The administration officer at the RSKO Cibubur responded that in order to get free drug treatment, a health insurance card (*jamkesmas*—insurance for poor people) would be required. Otherwise, Rose would be liable for the fees of about US$270/month for six months—an astronomical sum for an impoverished Indonesian family. After a lengthy, tortuous, and bewildering process, Rose was finally accepted for treatment at the hospital without any cost.[8]

It has been a tough and difficult year for Diego since Rose was arrested, imprisoned, and placed in rehabilitation. When Rose was at home, she liked to take Diego to school and pick him up afterward. She liked to help him with his homework. "She is very caring when it comes to studying together. She helped me a lot," says Diego. Often, Diego slept in the same room with Rose because it helped to comfort him, especially having lost his father. He was particularly upset that he could not celebrate his graduation to junior high school with his mother. Since the trial, Diego has seen Rose only once after she was transferred to the drug dependence hospital. When Diego came to visit his mother, Rose advised him to study well and obey his grandmother's guidance. "I was told not to play around and [that I] should study more often," said Diego.

Diana shared her grief about the change in Diego's behavior since Rose has been absent. He has become "dispirited" ever since, and "indisposed to study." He is reluctant to listen to his Grandmother's guidance and his schoolwork has deteriorated. Diana has to give extra attention to Diego, and she needs to get tough in order to ensure that he complies with her direction.

The family's income has been badly affected. Before Rose was arrested, Diana had run a small kiosk to support the family needs, but since the arrest, Diana has had to close it to pay full attention to Diego's development.

Diego does not know why his mother is staying at the hospital. He has been told she works there. He also does not understand the connection between Rose's case and the hospital. Once Diego attended a hearing, but thought that Rose was on trial for a traffic offense. Diana has sought to protect him from the stigma associated with having a parent who is a drug user. She kept Rose's addiction from him to protect him emotionally and psychologically and to ensure that he would not be bullied at school. It is widely known that drug users or addicts in Indonesia are portrayed as morally corrupt. A number of government-initiated advertising campaigns depict drug users as an evil that needs to be eliminated from earth, and other such messages. This is a result of the government's so-called war on drugs policy. As a natural consequence of the narcotics law and the advertisement campaigns, discrimination against drug users is a common feature in Indonesian public life.[9] "I don't want my grandson to suffer stigma and be ridiculed by his friends at school because of his mother. He has enough of it," said Diana.[10]

Mario: The Hope of a Family

Mario is twenty-one years old and grew up in a dense, grubby, slum area. His house, along with hundreds more, is located next to a railway in Roxy—one of many highly populated places in Central Jakarta. From the main street, it is about ten minutes' walk to reach his house. The street is not paved. At the end is a traditional market that makes the streets wet and attracts flies. At the end of this street market, Mario lives with his sister, Kate (age fifteen), three brothers, Mike (ten), Tony (five) and Andy (two), and his parents. Kate has a four-month-old baby named Jane. Mario's house is only two floors of six square feet, consisting of one room, where they watch television in the afternoon and sleep at night, and a very small bathroom on the first floor. The second floor is wooden and crosses from one side of the street to another side, like a bridge. It is also used as a bedroom.

Mario's father, John, works as waste plastic scavenger. He spends most days collecting waste, such as water cups and plastic drink bottles. In a week, he could collect approximately twenty kilos, earning about IDR 10,000 per kilo from scrap dealers—about US$1. Meanwhile, his mother, Mary, works as a coconut seller at the market, just five meters away from their house.

As the oldest child, Mario's family has huge expectations of him. Since finishing high school, Mario has helped his parents to earn money by working as an *ojek* (motorcycle taxi) driver. He is the backbone of his family.

Unfortunately, Mario was entrapped by the police not far from his house in March 2009.

Mario and his friend were sitting on a couch in front of his house having returned from work. It was almost two o'clock in the morning when another friend arrived asking if they wanted to use *shabu* (methamphetamine). Mario himself is an occasional drug user, using drugs only when gathering with friends who also use. Mario was given IDR 100,000 (about US$10) and asked to buy the *shabu*. The dealer's house is not too far from Mario's but moments after knocking on the door, two police officers arrested him. He was charged with drug (psychotropic) possession despite the fact that he had not yet paid for the drugs.[11] On July 13, 2009, Central Jakarta District Court found him guilty of possession and sentenced him to one year and four months imprisonment and a fine of IDR 2 million (about US$220). If a defendant cannot pay such a fine, he or she must spend two more months in prison. This was the case with Mario, taking his sentence to a year and a half.

During the process, Mario was detained in Salemba Detention Center, and that was when the family's misery began. For rich people, going into a detention center will render them poor, and poor people will become poorer. That is what happened to Mario's family. His income as an *ojek* driver was eliminated and the costs of visiting him in prison and keeping him safe inside placed enormous burdens on the family.

Mario's family visits him once a week or once every two weeks. They take public transportation and travel quite a distance to see him. Even though it costs only about IDR 3,000–5,000 (about US$.50 cents) per person for the transportation, this is still a large amount for this family. On arrival, more money must be spent. Every door they pass requires money: to allow Mario to come out of his cell to a hall in which he can meet his family. Every time they visit Mario, they have to spend more than IDR 300,000. This money is spent to buy decent food for Mario because of the poor quality of food in the prison. They give daily allowances of about IDR 100,000 so he can buy essential items and mobile phone vouchers costing approximately IDR 10,000–25,000 every two days (this is despite the fact that mobile phones are prohibited). This voucher is used to be resold again inside. In a month, the total expense for Mario is approximately IDR 700,000–1 million (about US$900).

Spending an extra IDR 700,000–1 million is extremely difficult for this family. Their monthly income is only about IDR 1.5–2 million. Sometimes, the income is less if the parents do not sell coconuts or cannot go out to collect plastic waste. Half of the income is consumed by Mario's needs. The other half is used for the family. It is a very small amount with seven people to care for including two young children in school, a preschool-age child, and a baby. Every family member, including the children, faces hardship and must forgo not just treats, but essentials such as milk, clothes, and books.

Added to this, and perhaps the saddest aspect for Mario's siblings, is the feeling of being neglected. Since Mario was arrested his parents have had to give their full attention to him. Even though they do not visit Mario every day, most of their days are preoccupied with worrying about his condition. Before the arrest Mario's parents loved to play with their daughter, sons, and granddaughter. Now, the children are often left behind at home when the parents visit Mario, with no one to watch them.

The children have also lost Mario, and he was very much relied upon. Even though Kate can sometimes substitute for Mario's role as the oldest, she has a baby to take care of. Andy, the youngest, is always asking about Mario. "When will aa (brother) come home, mom?" he asks.

Conclusion

It is informally known that every police officer has an arrest target of a minimum of five drug cases a month. This quota makes drug users primary targets, not to mention those innocent people who also become targets because of the need to reach quotas. Entrapment is common. Based on the Narcotics Law, entrapment and undercover purchasing of drugs is permitted. Illegal entrapment (i.e., without a superior's explicit permission as per Article 79 of the Narcotics Law) is a widespread occurrence.

Arrest quotas, entrapment, and these high conviction rates increase the number of people in already overcrowded prisons. One chamber is often occupied by 10 to 20 people, while the actual capacity is only half that. Food is poor, sanitation even worse. If a prisoner falls ill, the medical center inside cannot provide the appropriate treatment. This includes, of course, people who are drug dependent. These conditions are what Mario faces in prison. This, too, is what Rose faced. Meanwhile, Mario's family has suffered and Diego and Diana have suffered along with them.

The verdicts in these two cases failed to consider the best interests of the children who would be affected by the decisions. In Rose's case, the judges did not take into account the fact that she is a mother. In Mario's case, his importance as a breadwinner and emotional and practical support within a poor family was not considered. These factual backgrounds must be taken into account as a matter of priority if the best interests of the child as enshrined in the Convention on the Rights of the Child and Indonesian Law are to be given due regard. In this context, there is no evidence that the war on drugs has led to a decrease in drug use and/or criminality. Indeed, the evidence appears to point in the opposite direction.

According to the National Narcotic Agency (BNN) annual report for 2010, 35,299 people were convicted of drug offences from 28,382 cases. Most are for non-violent or possession offences like those above.

Based on the two cases presented here, one can only imagine the scale of harm caused to their families, their dependents and their children.

Endnotes

1. Convention on the Rights of the Child, G.A. res. 44/25, annex, 44 U.N. GAOR Supp., No. 49 at 167, UN Doc. A/44/49 (1989), entered into force September 2, 1990.
2. Presidential Decree 36 of 1990 (Keppres 36/1990).
3. The Convention on the Rights of the Child is a comprehensive human rights treaty covering civil and political rights, economic, social and cultural rights, juvenile justice, and humanitarian law. It also contains various rights unique to children, including the right to know and be cared for by one's parents (Article 7). It is the only UN human rights treaty to refer to drugs (Article 33), taking a strong focus on protection instead of criminalization and punishment. Indeed, the UN Committee on the Rights of the Child, which monitors implementation of the convention, has repeatedly stated that children who use drugs should be treated as victims and not as criminals.
4. Article 6 protects the right to life, survival, and development. It is construed broadly, relating to physical, psychological, emotional, social, and spiritual development.
5. See www.humanrightsanddrugs.org/?p=166/. See also P. Gallahue, *The Death Penalty for Drug Offences: Global Overview 2010*, International Harm Reduction Association, 2010, www.ihra.net/files/2010/06/16/IHRA_DeathPenaltyReport_Web1.pdf.
6. Diego's name has been changed to protect his identity, as have all the names in this chapter.
7. Ricky Gunawan, "Addicted to Corruption in Indonesia," http://asiacatalyst.org/blog/2009/12/addicted-to-corruption-in-indonesia-1.html.
8. Ricky Gunawan, "Indonesian Odyssey: A Drug Users Request for Treatment," http://asiacatalyst.org/blog/2010/02/indonesian-odyssey-a-drug-users-quest-for-treatment.html.
9. Martin Lundqvist and Ricky Gunawan, "War on Drugs in RI: Demonizing the Most Vulnerable," www.thejakartapost.com/news/2008/12/12/war-drugs-ri-demonizing-most-vulnerable.html.
10. [Following submission of this piece, on August 6, 2010, Rose finished her drug treatment and was released. She returned to Bandung, and now continues her life with her only son and her mother.—Ed.]
11. During this time, the Indonesian government had two regulations on drugs: Narcotics Law No. 22, 1997 and Psychotropic Law No. 5, 1997. In 2009 both acts were integrated into Narcotics Act No. 35, 2009.

11. "Ants Facing an Elephant": Mothers' Grief, Loss, and Work for Change Following the Placement of a Child in the Care of Child Protection Authorities

by Kathleen Kenny and Amy Druker

Introduction

Society most often associates the combination of illicit drugs and parenting with neglected children and inadequate parenting. This school of thought is deeply entrenched in the political ideology of the war on drugs and abstinence-based frameworks, and ignores the social, economic, and cultural realities shaping parental drug use.[1] It fails also to mention strategies parents may use to mitigate risks of drug use. Though placing children in the care of child protection authorities (CPA) may in some cases be necessary or requested by a parent, the long-standing fracturing of family relationships resulting from this practice can have far-reaching and devastating impacts on children and parents.

This chapter will shed light on the complicated grieving experience of mothers who have lost custody of their children to CPA. First, we present relevant research on this topic, including findings from community-based research conducted in 2008 in Toronto, Canada. Drawing on this research, we share women's insights into the connection between diminished mental health and feelings of hopelessness, anger, isolation, loneliness, and suicide and how these affect drug use and relationships with their children. Second, we describe a recently established project that brings women together to support each other, to discuss coping strategies, and to learn and share experiences through telling stories, consciousness raising, art making, and social action. Finally, we discuss steps taken by the group to establish a dialogue with CPA, and how it is hoped this ongoing dialogue can contribute to a growing shift in practice within the CPA from an abstinence-based framework toward a harm reduction approach.

Background Research

While some forms of socially induced suffering perpetuated by the war on drugs (e.g., militarization, police violence, drug overdose deaths, and incarceration of drug users), may be more readily identifiable, parental grief following the loss of a child to CPA remains largely hidden and unacknowledged in society. Though grief is a beneficial response in processing loss, a mother's grief following the loss of a child to CPA can be complicated by a host of factors rooted in society's judgment of those who transgress gender-appropriate mothering norms; ambiguity and confusion as to whether the loss is temporary or final; lack of societal acknowledgment and understanding of the loss; the resulting trauma and its compounding effects; and finally, systemic demands placed on mothers by CPA following the loss of custody.

There is a paucity of research and information on suffering experienced following the loss of a child to CPA. Socially unacknowledged grief has been referred to as "disenfranchised," defined as a grief that is not openly acknowledged, socially accepted, or publicly mourned, and where the griever is unrecognized and often cut off from social supports in dealing with her loss.[2] Rather than the traditional ritual of the community gathering to support each other in the aftermath of a loss, in the case of losing a child to CPA, the mother is often avoided and shamed for having deviated from mothering norms of caretaking and selflessness. A leading grief theorist, William Worden, whose work informs much of the practice of bereavement counseling and support groups in North America, describes the "tasks of grief" in four steps: to accept the reality of the loss; to experience and work through the pain of grief; to adjust to an environment in which the lost one is missing; and to emotionally relocate and memorialize the lost one and to move on with life.[3] Traditional funeral rites facilitate and validate the grieving process. The loss is announced; there is recognition of the deceased person's relationship to others; there is allowance for public expression of grief; there is support for the bereaved; and there is an opportunity for members of the community to gather and to support each other. In contrast, when a mother loses a child to CPA, the significance of the loss often goes unrecognized and there are no rituals to acknowledge it.

The uncertainty of permanence surrounding losses of children to CPA also complicates grieving experiences. Pauline Boss labels losses that are not clear or final as "ambiguous." She explains experiences of ambiguous loss as when a loved one is physically present but psychologically absent (e.g., the experience of caring for a loved one who has Alzheimer's disease) or when a loved one is physically absent but psychologically present (e.g., the experience of parents with "empty nest syndrome" in the aftermath of a young adult moving out of the family home). When a woman experiences losing a child to CPA, the loss can be harder to resolve because the mother may be psychologically preoccupied with the absent child. The loss may also be perceived as reversible, and therefore Worden's first task in accepting the loss is far more challenging and obscured by a mother's hope for reunion with her child. This can have the effect of placing the mother on an emotional rollercoaster alternating between hope and hopelessness. The lack of formal rituals and recognition of grief can further increase one's risk of continuously reexperiencing the loss as a trauma for years after the original event. It can also result in negative health outcomes such as depression, anxiety, psychic numbing, distressing dreams, and symptoms similar to posttraumatic stress disorder.[4]

The loss of a child to CPA may be framed as "both the loss of a loved person and the loss of an abstraction—one's ideal image of oneself as a competent mother," which for some women can lead to their feeling so depressed or hopeless that they are at risk of suicide.[5] De Simone has examined variables that obstruct grieving for women who previously relinquished an infant for adoption, and found higher levels of grief among mothers who believed they had been coerced by others into giving up the child.[6] Similarly, Holli Ann Askren and Kathleen Bloom's review of twelve studies of mothers who had their children adopted, found that mothers' initial grief reactions were "normal" (anger, guilt, depression) but observed these emotions to persist over time and to lead to chronic and unresolved grief.[7]

Research on Women's Experiences of Losing Children to Child Protection Authorities

In our community of South Riverdale, Toronto, Canada, a community-based study conducted in 2007 with women who use illicit drugs and engage in sex work found that a majority of participants did not have custody of their children.[8] In 2008, we aimed to gain a better understanding of women's experiences of custody loss and its lasting effects. We conducted a qualitative research inquiry with a small group of women who had lost custody of their children. We asked them what had been helpful and unhelpful following the placement of their children in care, and what could be done to support them now.[9]

Two focus groups and three semistructured interviews were conducted with nine women who currently use illicit drugs and are street involved. Participation was voluntary and participants were provided anonymity. There was variation in the number of children women had lost custody of, as well as in the custodial arrangements with CPA and in the time period since children were placed in care. Overarching themes emerging from the data found that almost all those involved in the research project experienced increased mental health struggles and marginalization as a result of losing children to CPA. Participants also provided insight into what had been/would be helpful in terms of dealing with the loss. Significantly, many women expressed how the research process represented the first time they had been invited to share their experiences.

In our analysis, women's experiences are described on two levels, comprising both *individual* and *structural* dimensions of grief and loss.(see Figure 1) At the individual level, the women expressed a range of emotionally destabilizing factors that contributed to declines in mental health following the loss of their child(ren). Almost all of the participants described increased drug use or reinitiated drug use to cope with pain, and to numb feelings such as hopelessness and lack of purpose following the sudden and often unanticipated shift in parenting roles. As one woman recalled of her experience following the loss of her child:

> *My life was empty. There was nothing else to live for. That was the purpose of my life. I had no purpose. My drug use got worse. I felt hopeless. Nothing helped.*

The women described the importance of holding on to memories of their child(ren) and viewed memories to have both negative and positive effects on their mental health. Half of the women expressed having suicidal ideation in trying to cope with the immediate aftermath of losing a child. One woman described the emotional impact of the experience as far-reaching and negatively affecting her mental and physical well-being:

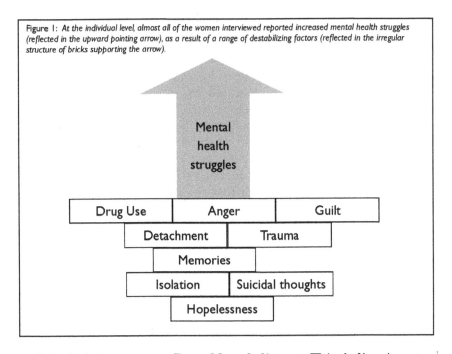

Figure 1: At the individual level, almost all of the women interviewed reported increased mental health struggles (reflected in the upward pointing arrow), as a result of a range of destabilizing factors (reflected in the irregular structure of bricks supporting the arrow).

I don't feel any more. I'm cold and distant. This feeling is not going away . . . I got into prostitution, drugs, I was suicidal . . . I don't give a fuck.

Guilt was also identified as a source of anguish and diminished self-worth for some women, while others associated structural barriers as the target of their anger and blame rather than burdening the guilt upon themselves. A small number of women reported feelings of detachment from their child following apprehensions that took place directly after the child's birth. They described feelings of guilt because of the absence of an emotional bond with their children. For the majority, the trauma experienced following a child apprehension by CPA and the continuous reexperiencing of this event was viewed as debilitating and as having compounding effects on mental health problems. All of the women had extensive histories of trauma in their lives. One woman recounted her experience:

It seemed like she just came out of my belly and these people were ripping her away from me . . . I lost my housing; I couldn't be in the house without my kid . . . I couldn't walk by her room to go to the bathroom and see the room empty. It was devastating.

A consistent experience was the lack of support in dealing with the emotional pain, deep-rooted anger, and social isolation following the loss of custody, while concurrently facing great demands from CPA. Individual-level experiences following the loss of child(ren) were found to be largely mediated by structural forces such as poverty and unresponsive social service agencies. Commenting on their experiences of systems following loss of child custody, all of the women spoke about ways in which structural forces resulted in instability, feeling judged by society, and loss of parental rights. They expressed that they either had not been offered social support to deal with the loss of their children or that the support offered was largely unhelpful. They also shared a small number of initiatives considered helpful, and these included kinship custody arrangements through CPA, as well as harm reduction services and programs targeting pregnant women/mothers who use drugs and/or alcohol (see Figure 2). In terms of unhelpful experiences with systems, women expressed feeling powerlessness, as well as negatively and unfairly judged in their encounters with CPA:

> If you're poor, you're a bad parent . . . you're classified . . . belittled by [CPA]. . . . You're judged.

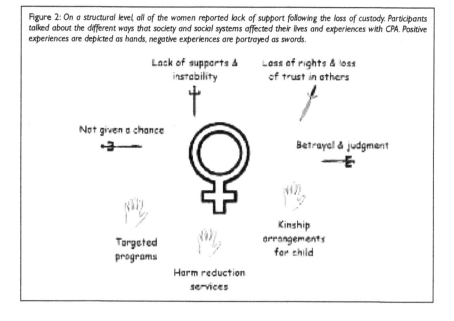

Figure 2: On a structural level, all of the women reported lack of support following the loss of custody. Participants talked about the different ways that society and social systems affected their lives and experiences with CPA. Positive experiences are depicted as hands, negative experiences are portrayed as swords.

Lack of supports & instability

Loss of rights & loss of trust in others

Not given a chance

Betrayal & judgment

Targeted programs

Kinship arrangements for child

Harm reduction services

The experience of having a child placed in care had destabilizing effects on the participants' lives, including losses of housing and employment. Many demands were also placed upon them at a time when they considered themselves least capable of compliance. Such demands included urine screening appointments (often supervised by a stranger and not necessarily a woman), hair-strand testing, drug use counseling or treatment programs, housing appointments, parenting courses, and psychological testing.

A majority of the women considered CPA's role to be adversarial and felt they were not provided with opportunities to prove themselves as parents or to establish collaborative relationships with CPA workers. One research participant explained:

I would have liked [CPA] to have given me a chance to prove myself. . . . Any mother who wants her children should be given a chance before putting her child up for adoption.

Feelings of betrayal were also identified and were pointed to as a source of distrust felt toward CPA and other service providers. Three women reported how their children placed in the care of CPA had been raped, assaulted, and/or murdered. These women spoke about not being able to come to terms with having been unable to protect their children from harm. CPA had removed children from family situations considered to be high risk, but it was felt that these children faced far greater risk within the CPA system.

Through our research process, insights were also provided into what would be helpful to support the grieving process and to address the ongoing impacts of custody loss on mothers. Group support and one-on-one support were considered to be equally beneficial. In discussing the possible group structure, emphasis was placed on the importance of a small group size, art-based activities, and advocacy initiatives. One woman suggested:

Groups would be helpful to share with people going through the same thing. We are all mums whether we have just lost custody or our kids have been adopted. Holding a discussion group for each CPA office would be good, to have them listen to parents and to understand what parents are dealing with, so they give the support parents need and are considerate of what parents are dealing with.

In response to these recommendations, and with their active

involvement we began planning a pilot that would serve as a space for discussion of experiences, validation of grieving, and advocacy for social change. In June 2009 our planning culminated with the start of a fifteen-week pilot group called the "Grief and Loss Education and Action Project."

The Grief and Loss Education and Action Project

The Grief and Loss Education and Action Project is a partnership project between South Riverdale Community Health Centre and the Jean Tweed Centre in Toronto and is facilitated by a community worker from each of these agencies (the authors of this chapter). At present, the project has recently begun a third fifteen-week group with women who use illicit drugs and are street-involved. Each two-hour session begins with a ritual of meal sharing (with seasonally available foods) and check-in (where women share how they are feeling), and concludes with a check-out (where women evaluate the session) and the provision of public transportation tokens and a $10 honorarium for each participant. During our initial meetings, we invite participants to create group guidelines, which include a "no judgment policy" related to drug use (in other words, women are always welcome to join us regardless of whether they are using or not). We also focus on having the women identify topics of interest for further exploration and we create a list of possible guest speakers (e.g., representatives of CPA, a family lawyer).

In response to the women's interests and reinforcing the empowerment orientation of our group model, the group is planned around the central themes of telling stories, consciousness-raising, art making, and social action. Safer coping strategies and self-care are also regular topics at each group meeting, and each session typically includes the practice of grounding exercises, mindfulness meditation, or discussion of strategies for growing compassion toward self and others. The ongoing option of one-on-one support from a social worker or group facilitator is also available to participants if needed. We conclude the fifteen-week group with a celebratory lunch at a restaurant during which the women are presented with a certificate of participation. In response to participants' expressed interest project "graduates" continue to meet on a monthly basis with facilitators, where they provide support to one another, carry on action-oriented work aimed at outreach to other mothers, and raise awareness and advocate for changes in how CPA works with mothers who use drugs.

Telling Stories

Heavy is the heart whose story has not been told. My heart is lighter because you listened.

Scottish parable

We live in a world full of stories. Stories tell us who we are and where we belong. Stories help us make meaning of our lives. Sometimes stories become saturated with problems, but there are always openings to create new meanings or ways of viewing ourselves in relation to others. Narrative therapy conceptualizes our identity as being shaped by narratives or stories shared about ourselves, and in this endeavor aims to expose alternative stories of resistance and resilience alongside problem-saturated stories. As a starting point in this process, we invite women early on in the group to bring with them something to share that is symbolic of their grief. One woman brought in lyrics of a song, another brought in photographs of her children, and another pointed to her tattoo. The activity creates an initial opening for stories of grief and loss to be told.

A second storytelling activity involved mapping out experiences of grief and sharing them. In this activity, we describe Worden's tasks of grief (explained earlier in this chapter) and explore how the grieving process unfolds in the absence of ritual or acknowledgment of the loss. We then invite the women to creatively represent their own stories of grief and to share these with the group. Feelings of anger, numbness, sadness, and guilt were strongly shared, as were love and hope to escape the cycle of grief in the future. Following this, women from one group brought together their grieving cycles and collectively represented their experiences in an explanatory brochure to share with others.

A third storytelling activity borrowed from narrative therapy, involved letter writing to a feeling (such as anger, hopelessness, etc.) that women identified as most affecting them in the aftermath of their loss. This technique aims to externalize the "problem" from the individual, and in so doing, allows women to reconsider their relationship to the "problem" and its range of influences in their lives—thus the narrative motto: the person is not the problem, the problem is the problem. In discussing what to do with the letters, one group decided to discard their letters into the lake—a symbol of closure and desire to move forward from these feelings.

Consciousness Raising

Con-scious-ness raising n. an intentional focused awareness on a social or political issue, usually involving the linkage of personal troubles to larger societal factors.

Consciousness raising, often associated with the social and cultural "revolution" of the 1960s, is integral to the process of critically analyzing societal forces (e.g., classism, racism, sexism, drug policy) contributing to drug use and dependence and the loss of custody of a child. It is through group discussion that insights are shared and women deepen their social analysis of power and social justice, and how these intersect with individual and collective experiences with CPA. To further facilitate this process, we draw upon an art-based activity called The Road Travelled, a variation of a community development activity from the Elsipogtog First Nation, a Mi'kmaq community in New Brunswick, Canada. The objective of the activity is to examine the intersection of individual, community, and system-level factors contributing to CPA apprehensions.

The backdrop of The Road Travelled consists of a painted mural of a winding road with mountains, a sun in the background, and trees in the foreground. The road symbolizes the women's journeys of losing custody of their child(ren). A series of symbols are then used to represent the many factors (individual, societal, or systemic) that have had positive or negative influences along the way:

Boulders represent barriers to keeping families together. Women identified a range of barriers including low self-esteem; childhood abuse; lack of parenting role models; low self-control; relationship problems; poverty; judgment concerning responsible drug use; lack of support; unfair bias toward parents who were raised in CPA foster care; power imbalance between parent and CPA; and loss of parental rights once a child is taken into care.

Turtles represent sources of healing for women following the loss of child(ren) to CPA, and included holding on to good memories; forgiving oneself; having faith their child will grow up and understand; opening up to one's feelings; and feeling loved by child(ren).

Bears symbolize those strengths that have helped women to survive and overcome barriers. These included supportive friends; having faith in oneself; having a job; supportive community organizations; talking and sharing stories of children; and helping other women.

And finally eagles symbolize those commitments women are prepared to make to effect change either on a personal, community, or systemic level, such as building relationships with foster families to stay connected with children; finding hope and courage for reconnection with children; sharing experiences with others; and helping CPA to understand the trauma experienced by those who have lost custody of their child(ren).

Through this activity women gained more awareness of the social realities shaping parenting experiences, and were challenged to delineate between individual and societal-level forces that resulted in losing custody. Insights gained through this re-visioning exercise are summarized in a brochure developed by group members, which aims to educate service providers and CPA workers about women's experiences.

Art Making

We believe that the arts are a means of communication, education and liberation, answering the need to express common values, concerns and experience; that through the sharing and development of creative activity, people—who because of [the way that society is structured, pushing some to the margins] are seen as receivers and consumers—can become contributors and sharers.

Fran Herman and James Smith, 1988[10]

Throughout the project women responded positively to opportunities to make art. These included ongoing availability of art supplies for doodling or drawing during meetings, as well as art-based activities such as grieving cycles and The Road Travelled. Body mapping, however, was enthusiastically embraced as the favorite activity.

Body mapping's effectiveness as a storytelling tool was first documented in sub-Saharan Africa, where women living with HIV sketched and painted stories of their journey with the virus. After explaining this activity, women were invited to outline their bodies on large sheets of paper and then artfully represent their stories of grief, loss, and hope for the future with paints, words, photographs, fabric, and so on. The timing of this activity (about midway through the fifteen-week group) was in response to our sense that women seemed to be in different places, while some seemed to be wanting to keep telling their stories of grief and loss, others seemed ready to "take action." We felt body mapping could meet both of these needs, in terms of the process of doing the activity (storytelling), and the outcome (the body maps themselves used as advocacy tools). Women were invited to write a narrative explanation to accompany their body maps. Those who wished, placed their body maps and narratives in a brochure with the objective of sharing their stories so that other women might not feel so alone in their struggles with CPA, and to help service providers gain insight into women's experiences.

Social Action

Ac-tiv-ism n. a doctrine or practice of taking direct intentional action to achieve a social, political, economic, or environmental change.

Early in the project, group members identified action-oriented goals aiming to change how CPA and other service providers work with parents who use drugs. We discussed different ways this might begin to happen. The women suggested that the group arrange a meeting with a CPA representative to tell their stories of loss and to share their ideas about how the child welfare system could change to better meet the needs of families affected by illicit drug use. Toward the end of our first group cycle, a meeting was arranged with a supervisor from Metro Toronto Children's Aid Society (the largest board-run child welfare agency in North America).

The women were surprised at the respectful dialogue that ensued with CPA. During the exchange, women spoke about their experiences with CPA, both positive and negative, as well as their recommendations for change. Group members drew attention to the belief that poor families were unduly targeted, that families with histories of drug use were prejudged as unfit parents, as were those parents who themselves had been in the custody of child protection as children. The intrusiveness of child protection services was also identified as feeling belittling and unfair toward families. In terms of positive experiences with CPA, one woman identified having a worker "who believed in me" and worked from a harm reduction perspective. For this woman, it was these two factors that made the biggest difference in mitigating the effect of having her child apprehended. On a macro level, women flagged issues of deep-rooted discrimination against people who use drugs, as well as the lack of affordable housing, and poverty. One woman discussed how society "assumes that women who use [drugs] don't love their children," and that "parents who use are bad parents" and highlighted the inherent injustice and incorrectness of these assumptions. Women also shared educational resources they had developed and addressed the urgent need for more child care respite to support parents, better screening of foster-care parents, as well as support for mothers before, during and after a child goes into CPA's care.

The need for parents to be involved and consulted as much as possible in the process of taking children into care was also stressed. One woman proposed that a support person be selected by the parent to provide immediate support, as well as to inform parents of their rights, and to seek out safe housing and mental health support for the mother during and after the loss of custody.

The CPA representative listened to women and affirmed their grief, anger, and frustration with the system. She also reported on new directions being undertaken by CPA, including a "Best Practice" document for CPA intake workers on how to work with families affected by drug use. At the end of the meeting, the women were invited to consult in the development of this document. The women unanimously agreed to participate in an ongoing dialogue with CPA concerning this issue and the meeting, they described the experience as both positive and empowering, and felt their stories, concerns, and ideas were heard and validated.

Learning from the Project

Drawing on quantitative and qualitative measures of grief, self-esteem, anxiety, depression, social support, and drug use, pre- and postevaluations were completed by almost all participants in the project. While a comprehensive review of our evaluation findings is beyond the scope of this chapter and the number of mothers ($n = 10$) who completed the program is small, participants spoke about the strength derived from sharing their stories and receiving support from group members to deal with their pain. Women further reported a positive effect of the project on their mental health, including increased self-esteem, hopefulness, resiliency, and personal agency, as well as reduced isolation, shame, and guilt. Though reunification of the family was not an intended outcome of the group, it is also notable that almost half of the women in the project have taken steps, with the support of group members and facilitators, to reconnect with their children in different capacities.

Two key themes of "dead alone" and "ants facing an elephant" emerged from women's stories shared in the group and are explained below.

Dead alone was a poignant phrase one woman used to describe her feeling of isolation after losing her child, and this theme was unanimously agreed upon as a term that captured women's experiences. Numbing was also identified, and increased drug use was viewed as a way of forgetting feelings of shame, guilt, "dead aloneness," sadness, and anger. Women also described self-punishing behaviors, including unsafe drug use and sex work, and even the deliberate placement of themselves in harm's way, as a means of coping with isolation, shame, and pain associated with their loss.

Ants facing an elephant was another striking phrase one woman articulated to describe the feeling of powerlessness in relationships with CPA. Women identified feeling powerless for many reasons—from the deeper issues of poverty, race, gender, and social environment, to the system's failure to support mothers in the traumatic aftermath of losing custody, as well as exclusion from the legal process due to ineffective legal counsel. Group members also discussed the challenging power dynamics with CPA workers who consider illicit drugs to be more dangerous than licit drugs and equate parental illicit drug use with inadequate parenting. The women also reported difficulties with CPA workers who were not versed in (or plainly disagreed with) harm reduction approaches, including methadone maintenance treatment.

Looking Forward

We began a third fifteen-week group cycle in January 2011 with nine women. In response to women's interest, project "graduates" from the previous two groups continue to meet on a monthly basis to support each other and to work on projects centered around outreach to other mothers, awareness raising, and advocacy efforts to support a shift in CPA from an abstinence-based framework toward a harm reduction approach. We have also been exploring a historical timeline of the child protection system and have begun public-speaking training with women to prepare for presentations and educational workshops that we hope to offer to social service providers, social work students, health practitioners and local CPA organizations.

Despite the turbulence of daily life and the challenge of working through one's own grief, the women in the project have demonstrated remarkable strength to support others who are experiencing similar pain. In this capacity, the women have opened up new spaces for dialogue with other mothers in our community whose families have been involved with CPA. Far exceeding our initial expectation for the project, the women have gained much momentum in working toward their goal of a transformed child protection system in Canada—where all women who want to parent their children are supported in their efforts to do so. Recognizing the complex factors shaping drug use and associated harms in Canada (e.g., poverty, drug laws, colonization of Aboriginal peoples, violence, and inequalities of race, class, sex, and gender), it is timely that we introduce alternate and nonjudgmental views of mothers who use drugs, particularly mothers who are poor and/or from racialized communities, who are most vulnerable to state intervention and intersection with the war on drugs. As for recommendations toward achieving this aim and realizing women's vision for systemic change, these are best set out in the words of the women themselves, who created a manifesto addressed to the Children's Aid Society (CAS) the Canadian equivalent of Child Protection Authorities:

A Hope for Things to Change: Mothers & CAS

1.   **We are ants facing an elephant.** We are women who have survived abuse, poverty, lack of parenting role models, and have been negatively labelled by society. These experiences make us strong and we want workers to see the positives in our lives.

2.   **Programs and support should be available to keep our families together.** We need more affordable child care options, safer housing, and health and social services which meet our families' unique needs. Crisis counselling/grief counsellors should be present at time of apprehension to offer support to parents (and children).

3.   **CAS workers should be trained on harm reduction.** We need workers who are knowledgeable about illicit drugs, methadone and other prescription drugs. We want workers who recognise ways in which women's drug use can be shaped by social factors, such as poverty, abuse, drug laws, and inequalities of race, class, gender, and sexuality. We need workers who believe in harm reduction and who respect us as people who practice harm reduction. We need workers to be considerate of our feelings as mothers and as human beings.

4.   **CAS workers should see our strengths and be trained on anti-oppression.** We need workers who do not want to exert power over us. We want workers who see and want to build on our strengths, and work with us to figure out steps to reconnect or keep our families together.

5.   **More rigorous and mandatory screenings and reviews of foster parents.** Too many children have experienced trauma and abuse while in foster care. Parents have rights to know where kids are and how they are being treated. We want the right to request a hearing if we suspect that our child is being mistreated in foster care.

6.   **Parents should be provided with regular updates on their kids** (including report cards, activities, medical information). Kids have a right to know about their identity—their parents, grand-parents, cultural background, and medical history. Parents should be able to participate with CAS and foster parents in decision-making that affects their kids.

7. **Visitations should be more personal.** Parents should feel comfortable and not feel humiliated when visiting children. Parents don't always know how to act on supervised visits and should be given tips to relax and get the most out of each visit. Ideally, recreational programmes should be available to parents and children during access visits.

8. **Mothers should be offered well-informed and committed lawyers.** Women should be informed about their legal rights as parents, and workers should encourage a parent's right to have a lawyer to address issues with CAS.

9. **Mothers need parent-advocates within CAS.** Women need parent-advocates to support them and ensure they understand what is going on with their child and custody arrangement.

10. **Loosen the chains.** As women make progress to stabilise their lives, CAS should seek out and acknowledge positive changes and be open to re-negotiating custody and visitation arrangements.

11. **More support groups and counselling for women involved with CAS.** Governments should give money to support different community programmes for women who have been involved with CAS both pre and post apprehension. Free transportation should be available to ensure women have opportunities to share their grief and trauma, and to work for change.

Endnotes

† This chapter is dedicated to the courageous women who have participated in the Grief and Loss Education and Action Project. It has been a privilege to learn from your immeasurable wisdom, strength, and vision. We also wish to acknowledge Molly Bannerman as a supportive force behind this project.
1. See Susan C. Boyd, *Mothers and Illicit Drugs: Transcending the Myths* (Toronto: University of Toronto Press, 1999); and idem, *From Witches to Crackmoms: Women, Drug Law, and Policy* (Durham, NC: Carolina Academic Press, 2004).
2. Kenneth J. Doka, *Disenfranchised Grief: Recognizing Hidden Sorrow* (New York: Lexington Books, 1989 [updated, 2002].
3. J. William Worden, *Grief Counseling and Grief Therapy* (New York: Springer, 2002 [updated, 2008].
4. Pauline Boss, *Ambiguous Loss* (Cambridge, MA: Harvard University Press, 1999).
5. S. Novac, E. Paradis, J. Brown, and H. Morton, "A Visceral Grief: Young Homeless Mothers and Loss of Custody," Research Paper 206, Centre for Urban and Community Studies, University of Toronto, 2006.

6. Michael De Simone, "Birth Mother Loss: Contributing Factors to Unresolved Grief," *Clinical Social Work Journal* 24, no. 1 (1996): 65–76.
7. Holli Ann Askren and Kathleen Bloom, "Postadoptive Reactions of the Relinquishing Mother: A Review," *Journal of Obstetric, Gynecologic and Neonatal Nursing* 28, no. 4 (1999), 395–400.
8. Molly Bannerman, "Women's Harm Reduction and Community Safety Project," South Riverdale Community Health Centre, Toronto, 2007.
9. M. Bannerman, K. Kenny, and C. Judge, "Women and C.A.S.: Experiences of Grief and Loss," South Riverdale Community Health Centre, Toronto, 2009.
10. F. Herman and J.C. Smith, *Accentuate the Positive! Expressive Arts for Children with Disabilities* (Toronto: Jimani, 1988), 5.

Discussion Questions

1. The costs to individuals incarcerated for drug offenses, and to their children and families, are outweighed by the benefits gained by society. Discuss.

2. Arrest quotas feature in two of the chapters in this section. What is the role of such quotas in law enforcement? Are they a legitimate incentive, or do they lead to corruption and a focus on "soft targets"?

3. Fransiska, Larasati, and Gunawan call for the impact on child dependents to be considered in sentencing for nonviolent drug offenses. Do you agree? Which considerations could be taken into account? Above what threshold of seriousness might this consideration be disregarded?

4. The best interests of the child are always best served by removing children from the custody of a parent who uses drugs. Discuss.

Part 4:
Justification: Children, Drug Use, and Dependence

Part 4 focuses on the policy justification of protecting people, especially children, from the harmful effects of drugs, including drug dependence. This premise is not challenged. Let us take it as read, and agreed by all, that it is not a good idea for children to use drugs, and that the use of drugs at an early age can be especially harmful— physically, socially, and psychologically.[1] This is clear from a number of the chapters in this section. But policies aimed at dealing with this concern must be interrogated. Is the desire to protect children from drug use and dependence justification for the measures that have been adopted? And what does a closer look say about future strategies? In this section, five very different chapters ask searching questions of the policy responses that have been put in place to deal with drug use among children and young people, and of some of the assumptions underlying prevailing views of drugs, drug use, and dependence.

The first chapter in this section is "Youth Drug-Use Research and the Missing Pieces in the Puzzle: How Can Researchers Support the Next Generation of Harm Reduction Approaches?" by Catherine Cook and Adam Fletcher. The chapter cuts to the root of this central justification for the war on drugs, challenging what we really know and do not know about drug use among young people.[2] It explores the extent of our knowledge regarding drug use among young people around the world, concluding that far too little is known about emerging patterns of drug use in low- and middle-income countries, rendering the global picture incomplete. It goes on to challenge data collection methodologies and the predominance of "war on drugs" discourses that inhibit a deeper understanding of routes into problematic use and potential drug-related harms. According to the authors, the result is that the most vulnerable young people are excluded from the existing empirical evidence and their needs are ignored. The chapter concludes with recommendations for a new research agenda to inform more appropriate and effective youth-centered harm reduction interventions.[3]

Michael Shiner's chapter, "Taking Drugs Together: Early Adult

Transitions and the Limits of Harm Reduction in England and Wales," focuses on recreational drug use among young people. According to Shiner, the potential of the harm reduction approach has not by any means been explored because of a focus on problematic drug use, including injecting, and the prevalence of abstinence-based messaging. For most young people, the majority of drug use is closely tied to the "nighttime economy," and it is here, claims Shiner, that interventions should be focused if the harms associated with club drugs such as ecstasy and the consumption of alcohol are to be mitigated. In relation to alcohol, this has included "air conditioning, ventilation, the availability of drinking water, the demeanor of door staff, transport home, the availability of information and outreach services, and access to health services." But for other drugs this approach may require a level of tolerance that many are not willing to accept. The controversy surrounding "pill testing" to inform clubbers of what they have purchased is testament to this, as authorities see it as conflicting with messages that condemn drug use.[4]

Prevention is often seen as the most important aspect of policies aiming to address drug use among children.[5] Year after year, UN member states report to the UN Commission on Narcotic Drugs about the antidrug and prevention campaigns that have been undertaken.[6] Yet despite this, all raise their ongoing concerns about drug use among children and young people in their societies. What is clear is that prevention campaigns are at best limited in effect. They have not, by very definition, worked for young people who do use drugs, recreationally or otherwise. Adam Fletcher's second contribution to this section "Drug Testing in Schools: A Case Study in Doing More Harm Than Good," challenges a more direct and intrusive form of prevention. In many countries random school drug testing is employed both to weed out young people who are using drugs and, more important, to act as a deterrent to others who may be thinking about starting. Fletcher argues that such programs are lacking not only any solid evidence base but also any central theory to explain their aims and methods. As a result, he argues, random school drug testing can result in more harm than it seeks to prevent, such as school absences, distrust of school authorities and teachers, and pushing young people toward more dangerous drug use. Meanwhile, he demonstrates, they do not reduce drug use.[7] For Fletcher the answer is more holistic. Far more effective in reducing overall levels of substance use have been "school-wide interventions that promote school engagement and positive connections between staff and students, and reduce disaffection."

Jovana Arsenijevic and Andjelka Nikolic, meanwhile, provide a fascinating insight into the lives of heroin users in a very different part of the world—Serbia. Their chapter, "'I've Been Waiting for This My Whole Life': Life Transitions and Heroin Use," challenges many of the stereotypes attached to people who are drug dependent by considering the complex factors contributing to initiation into drug use and to drug dependence. The chapter considers the socioeconomic status of young drug users attending harm reduction programs, and through interviews charts the life trajectories of eight heroin users, all of whom started using when they were very young. What emerges is an engaging and complicated psychosocial picture against which simplistic "just say no" prevention messages and claims that "addiction is a choice" are rendered redundant. As the authors succinctly state, "There is no universal explanation for heroin addiction" but what is an almost universal barrier to addressing it is the social stigma it attracts.[8]

The final chapter in the section, "Why Should Children Suffer? Children's Palliative Care and Pain Management," by Joan Marston, changes direction from reducing drug use to ensuring access to drugs. In this case, the drugs in question are essential medicines for child palliative care, including morphine. Access to the medicines under international control is not often a focus of drug policy discussions,[9] but according to the World Health Organization, about 80 percent of the world's population has no access or insufficient access to opiates for pain relief.[10] This affects millions suffering from terminal cancer, late-stage AIDS, and other conditions. For children, the situation is even worse, as child palliative care lags far behind that for adults. In most countries there is next to no child palliative care. The reasons for this are complex, and Marston sets out many of them as well as the range of measures required simultaneously to deal with this problem. Important barriers to overcome include overly restrictive narcotics laws and regulations, compounded by fears about diversion of medicines into the illicit market, and, of course, addiction. According to Marston "Where governments see control of illegal trafficking and diversion as more important than the relief of suffering, children will continue to suffer. We must set our priorities straight."

Endnotes

1. See European Monitoring Centre on Drugs and Drug Addiction, thematic page on young people, www.emcdda.europa.eu/themes/young-people/.
2. See also UN Office on Drugs and Crime, *World Drug Report 2009* (Vienna, 2009), 23–29, 265–86.
3. Harm reduction for young people can be particularly controversial as it is seen by some to tacitly endorse or tolerate drug use among this group. The reaction tends to be to place age restrictions on harm reduction services. See, for example, Eurasian Harm Reduction Network, *Young People and Injecting Drug Use in Selected Countries of Central and Eastern Europe* (Vilnius: EHRN, 2009).
4. On ecstasy testing, see, for example, J. Johnson et al., "A Survey of Regular Ecstasy Users' Knowledge and Practices Around Determining Pill Content and Purity: Implications for Policy and Practice," *International Journal of Drug Policy* 17, no. 6 (2006): 464–72.
5. See, for example, International Narcotics Control Board, *Annual Report for 2009*, UN Doc. No. E/INCB/2009/1, 1–13.
6. See www.cndblog.org, run by Harm Reduction International and the International Drug Policy Consortium, which records the statements of Member States of the UN Commission on Narcotic Drugs.
7. Proponents claim that random school drug testing works. See, for example, Office of National Drug Control Policy, *What You Need to Know About Drug Testing in Schools*, www.ncjrs.gov/ondcppubs/publications/pdf/drug_testing.pdf.
8. See, for example, C. Lloyd, *Sinning and Sinned Against: The Stigmatisation of Problem Drug Users*, UK Drug Policy Commission, August 2010, www.ukdpc.org.uk/resources/Stigma_Expert_Commentary_final.pdf. "Problem drug users are a very strongly stigmatised group and this has a profound effect on their lives, including their ability to escape addiction," 11.
9. See, however, the recent Human Rights Watch reports: *Needless Pain: Government Failure to Provide Palliative Care for Children in Kenya*, 2010, www.hrw.org/en/reports/2010/09/09/needless-pain-0; and *Please Do Not Make Us Suffer Any More: Access to Pain Treatment as a Human Right*, 2009, www.hrw.org/en/reports/2009/03/02/please-do-not-make-us-suffer-any-more-0/.
10. World Health Organization, *Access to Controlled Medicines Programme*, "*Briefing Note,*" February 2009, www.who.int/medicines/areas/quality_safety/ACMP_BrNoteGenrl_EN_Feb09.pdf.

12. Youth Drug-Use Research and the Missing Pieces in the Puzzle: How Can Researchers Support the Next Generation of Harm Reduction Approaches?

by Catherine Cook and Adam Fletcher

Introduction

Young people's use of substances, both illicit and licit, is a global phenomenon. Young drug users predominantly use substances recreationally with friends, and for many, drug use will not lead to negative health, social, or economic harms. However, a small but significant proportion of young people who use drugs will experience harm and can be particularly vulnerable to health harms for several reasons. They are more likely to take risks in their drug-taking behavior and may have a poor awareness of their own tolerance to substances.[1] Young people are also often the first to experiment with new substances (including new "legal highs" sold via the Internet) and to adopt new drug-taking methods, and they are often strongly connected to dense drug-supply networks.[2] As with adults, drug-related harms among young people are also determined by a complex of individual, social, and structural factors, such as poverty and social exclusion, which can further increase vulnerability and may mean that the harms are more profoundly experienced.

Despite these vulnerabilities, harm reduction interventions are rarely tailored to young people's needs and they are often denied access to evidence-based interventions such as needle and syringe exchange and opioid substitution therapy. In Central and Eastern Europe, for example, there are strict age restrictions on access to sterile injecting equipment and opioid substitution therapy.[3] Even in Australia, where harm reduction has a long tradition, an audit found that specialist services for young people were "thin on the ground" and identified several barriers to their accessing harm reduction and drug treatment services, including homelessness, appointment-based service provision, and a lack of youth-work expertise among practitioners.[4] The lack of youth-focused harm reduction services represents a missed opportunity to protect and improve the health of the next generation of people who use drugs.[5] It is also a fundamental human right of every young person around the world to have access to the highest attainable standard of health, including harm reduction.[6] While this standard continues to be left unmet for the majority of young people, their human rights are being violated.

In order to respond with appropriate evidence-based and human rights-based approaches, it is necessary to have a clear picture regarding the nature and extent of youth drug use, routes into problematic use at a young age, and the drug-related harms to which young people are vulnerable. Much research is undertaken to study youth drug use, but this is not to say the evidence base needed to inform harm reduction programs for young people is complete: several key pieces in the puzzle are missing. To date, although significant attention has been given to reviewing the theoretical literature and "organizing pieces of the puzzle" in order to understand the determinants of youth drug use,[7] limited attention has been given to the incompleteness of the empirical evidence base and the limitations of the research methods and ideologies that inform data collection.

This chapter explores the extent of our knowledge regarding drug use among young people around the world, and the implications of this for the next generation of harm reduction. First, far too little is known about emerging patterns of drug use in low- and middle-income countries, thus the global picture remains incomplete. Second, school-based surveys are the dominant method used to study prevalence and trends in youth drug use and these have several major limitations, which are outlined. Third, most "war on drugs" discourses continue to focus research as well as policy and practice on prevention, thus inhibiting a deeper understanding of routes into problematic use and potential drug-related harms. With all three of these limitations, the result is that the most vulnerable young people are excluded from the existing empirical evidence and their needs ignored. The chapter concludes with recommendations for a new research agenda to inform more appropriate and effective youth-centered harm reduction interventions.

An Incomplete Global Picture

At the global level, limited surveillance from many of the world's most populous nations makes it impossible to accurately estimate the total number of drug-involved young people. Many of the best available data are restricted to youth drug use in high-income countries of Europe and North America. In these countries, cannabis remains by far the most widely used drug among school-age youth, although levels of use are stabilizing.[8] European surveys report that more than one in four fifteen- to sixteen-year-old school students have smoked cannabis in the United Kingdom, Italy, France, Switzerland, the Netherlands, and the Czech Republic.[9] Rates are even higher in the United States and Canada where nearly one in three young people have smoked cannabis by the age of sixteen.[10]

While overall rates of cannabis use among school-age young people have stabilized in high-income countries, ecstasy and amphetamine use have increased, converging on—and in some cases overtaking—the high rates of "club drug" use first observed among young people in the UK in the mid-1990s. In 2007 a survey of tenth-grade students in the United States (aged fifteen to sixteen) found that 11 percent had used amphetamines and 5 percent had taken ecstasy, and similar levels of ecstasy use (6 percent) have been found among twelve- to seventeen-year-olds in Canada and sixteen-year-olds in Australia.[11] Although reports of cocaine use among school students remain much rarer than cannabis and "club drug" use, this stimulant is increasingly entering the landscape of youth drug cultures, and by the end of the 1990s, 8 percent of U.S. tenth-graders had used cocaine.[12]

However, these young people in Europe, North America, and Australia represent only a fraction of the total global youth population as more than four-fifths of the world's children and young people live in low- and middle-income countries in Asia, Africa, and South America. In many parts of these regions there is evidence that illicit drug use among young people is rising. As a result, recent United Nations reports have drawn attention to "historic highs" of global youth drug use.[13] For example, in Kenya 19 percent of young people now report having smoked cannabis.[14] As in the world's wealthiest countries, youth drug use in low- and middle-income countries also goes beyond cannabis use, with new practices emerging in some regions. In East and Southeast Asia, increased use of methamphetamine among young people is of growing concern,[15] and recent data suggest that cocaine use is increasing among school-aged youth in South America.[16]

Despite these insights into the prevalence and patterns of youth drug use around the world, data on young people's drug use in Africa, Asia, and South America remain scarce. Monitoring trends in global youth drug use is therefore extremely difficult without annual survey data from low- and middle-income countries. At present, strategic information from such countries is "patchy" with no harmonization of methods or measures.[17] The surveys that are undertaken in developing regions are carried out irregularly and have sampled young people differently, often recruiting different age groups, across countries and over time, which limits the scope for cross-national and temporal analyses. This is the case with the existing mechanism for collecting information on young people's health-related behaviors via the World Health Organization's (WHO) Global School-based Health Survey (GSHS), whereby surveys are developed locally and undertaken by ministries of health with the assistance of the WHO, a process that results in different indicators and sampling frames being used between countries.

The WHO GSHS also fails to capture information on problematic drug use and drug-related harms experienced by young people in low- and middle-income countries, instead focusing on how many young people have "ever used" drugs, and at what age drugs were first used. For instance, one question asks participants to state how many times in the past twelve months they have used a particular drug, with options ranging from never to ten or more times.[18] However, this provides no indication of whether or not using the drug has resulted in any harm to the young person and does not distinguish between occasional, relatively "normalized" patterns of youth drug use[19] and more problematic and chaotic polydrug use. The information currently collected is therefore not instructive for informing the design and implementation of appropriate harm reduction strategies. This represents a wasted opportunity to use a global mechanism of data collection to examine more problematic use and the extent of drug-related harm experienced by young people.

Inadequate Data Collection Methods

Across high-, middle-, and low-income countries, the majority of studies examining the prevalence of drug use among young people rely on self-reporting from an accessible group of young people, normally school students. These school-based surveys are often cost-effective, drawing on a large number of participants, and when the same methodologies are used researchers can make cautious comparisons over time and between countries. For example, within Europe, similar national reporting mechanisms have allowed some cross-national comparisons of patterns in young people's drug use.[20]

However, there are important limitations to the reliability and representativeness of data collected via school-based surveys. These limitations include practical problems in using school-based surveys to collect reliable self-report data about students' use of drugs.[21] For example, a fear of a lack of anonymity, or of potential repercussions for an admittance of drug use may bias results due to underreporting. A recent American study comparing data collected via self-completion questionnaires with biological markers found that teenagers' hair specimens were *fifty-two times more likely* to identify cocaine use than their self-reporting of drug-use behaviors.[22] In addition, while large-scale surveys provide the "big picture" in terms of the prevalence of youth drug use, they are depersonalizing and largely ignore the meaning and social context of young people's actions: drug use is now an extremely important source of recreation and identity for many of these young people.[23]

Perhaps most significantly, school-based surveys provide insights only into the drug-taking behaviors of young people *attending school*, therefore omitting those who are not attending school or have been excluded from school. Where studies have surveyed vulnerable young people they find much higher levels of drug use. In the Netherlands, for example, researchers found that while 8 percent of twelve- to sixteen-year-old school students reported recent cannabis use, this increased significantly among students referred to truancy projects (35 percent) and homeless young people (76 percent).[24] It is these most vulnerable groups of young people—such as those who are not in education or training, and homeless, runaway, and street youth— whose drug use is less likely to be transitory and subject to norms of self-control, and more likely to progress to more problematic patterns of use, such as injecting drugs and sharing injecting equipment, which can transmit infections such as HIV and hepatitis B and C. Surveys of "street" youth in the United States found that 45 percent had injected drugs,[25] while in Canada, this figure was 36 percent.[26]

Street-based surveys of young people, such as the Sydney Street Intercept Survey[27] and the Vancouver Youth Drug Reporting

System,[28] are extremely rare at present but could be more widely implemented to complement existing monitoring systems. Countries in Eastern Europe—which are experiencing a process of social and economic transformation, including high unemployment and poverty rates—using such street-based survey methods, have begun to identify very high rates of HIV infection among young people as a result of shared injecting equipment and unsafe sexual practices.[29] For example, a recent citywide survey of more than 300 street youth in St. Petersburg, Russia, found 37 percent HIV prevalence.[30] These drug-involved young people who are living and working on the street, and who are at risk of HIV and hepatitis C, also often report a history of parental drug use, incarceration, and "survival sex."[31]

Another potential source of data on young people's drug use is routine records kept by drug-treatment and harm reduction service providers. When a new client comes to a facility, their age may be recorded and this can later be used to examine which drugs and methods of use are bringing people of different ages into contact with services. These types of data are particularly useful for analyzing problematic drug use among young people at the population level. However, it is clearly limited to assessing patterns among those young drug users who are able and willing to access services, and this, again, may leave out the most vulnerable young drug users who for a variety of reasons may not be able to access services. Indeed, age restrictions applied to harm reduction services may inhibit such data collection outright.

The "War On Drugs": Prioritizing Prevention and Hiding the Harms

Responses to drug use among young people continue to be dominated by individually focused and group-based prevention strategies, such as school-based drugs education, mass media campaigns, and youth development programs.[32] In turn, surveys on young people's drug use focus on those questions most pertinent to informing such *drug prevention* efforts, such as "have you ever used an illegal drug?" And herein lies a further, major problem for informing the next generation of harm reduction approaches. Prioritizing prevention through policy and practice inevitably means that it tends to be similarly prioritized at a research level, especially where research is funded through governmental sources. This has led to a situation where a full and accurate assessment of harm reduction needs is not available.

From those rare studies that have focused on understanding and uncovering drug-related harms experienced by young people, it is apparent that many young people require a harm reduction approach *tailored to their needs and the nuances of youth drug use.* For example, problematic drug use is often defined as encompassing injecting and/or long-term heroin or cocaine use, but a recent UK report by the charity DrugScope on drug use among vulnerable young people concluded that the definition should be revisited for this population.[33] Heroin and crack cocaine were less common among this group than polydrug use, particularly the mixing of alcohol with cannabis and other drugs. Cannabis is now the most frequently reported "main drug of misuse" by under-eighteens attending drug-treatment agencies in the UK: in total, 11,582 young people (75 percent of all clients) received treatment for cannabis misuse in 2005–6.[34]

However, these crude population-level data regarding young people's "main drug of misuse" provide only limited insights and, more important, DrugScope's consultation recommended a review of data-collection practices in order to gather more valid and responsive information on problematic and harmful drug use within the youth population.[35] Another important recommendation made in this report was the establishment of a new national "radar" service to provide early warnings of new youth drug trends and emerging harms, enabling policymakers and services to make timely, effective responses. Such systems would have uses outside of the UK, and perhaps at a regional or global level, given the ever-evolving nature of drug use, particularly among young people.

In ninety-three countries around the world, harm reduction is featured in national policies (often in relation to HIV prevention) or is used in practice,[36] and there is a wide-ranging body of evidence that harm reduction services such as needle and syringe programs have been effective in preventing unsafe injecting and the transmission of blood-borne viruses such as HIV, including among young people.[37] However, without adequate research into problematic drug use and drug-related harms among young people, public health policymakers and practitioners lack the data necessary to inform, and provide impetus to and support for, these highly effective harm reduction interventions. The extent of drug-related harm and young people's needs remain hidden in the fog of the "war on drugs."

The Next Generation of Research

Currently, evidence regarding young people's drug use is focused on certain regions of the world, and particularly concerned with preventing experimental and recreational drug use. This leaves significant pieces of the puzzle missing. Furthermore, the extent to which young people are experiencing harms associated with their drug use is largely unknown. Nonetheless, small-scale studies from low- and middle-income countries have powerfully illustrated how young people are engaging in problematic drug use and the resulting need for new support and treatment services. In particular, in Central Asian and East European countries, it is thought that a quarter of all people who inject drugs are now under age twenty,[38] and a recent assessment found that initiation into injecting begins as young as age twelve in countries such as Romania, Russia, and Serbia.[39]

By missing crucial pieces of evidence, the current research agenda and the methods and ideologies underpinning it further reinforce existing inequalities in health. The research process could itself be conceptualized as part of the broad "risk environment" in which drug-related harms occur within the youth population. Globally, there is a need for a mix of national surveillance and complementary small-scale studies focusing on the most vulnerable young people and problematic drug use, with three particular priority areas needing to be addressed urgently.

First, emerging data from low- and middle-income countries indicate that youth drug use is a present and growing concern in many regions. In the short term, the WHO GSHS provides the opportunity for more reliable monitoring of patterns of drug use behaviors around the world, but greater attention needs to be focused on how these surveys are undertaken. Further high-quality large-scale epidemiological studies are also needed.

Second, the focus on school-based surveys means that those young people who are most "at risk," such as those who experience school exclusion and homelessness, remain largely invisible in official statistics—as does their involvement with drugs. Street-based surveys are feasible and should be implemented more widely to complement existing monitoring systems, including in those developing countries where street-based drug-using youth are a particularly neglected and vulnerable group.

Third, "war on drugs" discourses translate into drug policies, practices, *and research* that are largely centered on prevention, *particularly in relation to young people.* There is a need to break this cycle and to increase the focus on problematic use and the harms associated with it, in order to fuel and inform the necessary harm reduction responses. Definitions of what should be termed "problematic" will vary according to drug trends and this should be monitored at the population level, with early warning systems in place to quickly highlight new patterns of drug use among young people.

The limitations of current insights into young people's drug use directly inhibit an effective response, particularly in relation to the most problematic kinds of drug use. Young drug users worldwide remain extremely vulnerable to harm, a situation that is unacceptable from both public health and human rights perspectives. It is imperative that policymakers and those funding and conducting research address the gaps in current investigatory approaches into drug use among young people, in order to build and support an effective harm reduction response.

Endnotes

1. T. Legget, "The Cannabis Potency Question," *Drugs and Alcohol Today* 7 (2007): 5–9.
2. R. MacDonald and J. Marsh, *Disconnected Youth? Growing Up in Britain's Poor Neighbourhoods* (Basingstoke: Palgrave Macmillan, 2005).
3. Eurasian Harm Reduction Network, *Young People and Injecting Drug Use in Selected Countries of Central and Eastern Europe* (Vilnius, 2009).
4. T. Szirom et al., *Barriers to Service Provision for Young People with Substance Misuse and Mental Health Problems* (Canberra: NYARS, 2004).
5. S. Merkinaite, J.P. Grund, and A. Frimpong, "Young People and Drugs: Next Generation of Harm Reduction," *International Journal of Drug Policy* 21 (2010): 112–14.
6. Article 12, International Covenant on Economic, Social and Cultural Rights G.A. res. 2200A (XXI), 21 UN GAOR Supp., No. 16, at 49, UN Doc. A/6316 (1966), 993 U.N.T.S. 3, entered into force January 3, 1976.
7. For example, J. Petraitis, B.R. Flay, and T.Q. Miller, "Reviewing Theories of Adolescent Substance Use: Organizing Pieces in the Puzzle," *Psychological Bulletin* 117, no. 1 (1995): 67–86; and C. Spooner, "Structural Determinants of Drug Use: A Plea for Broadening Our Thinking," *Drug and Alcohol Review* 24, no. 2 (2005): 89–92.

8. UN Office on Drugs and Crime, *World Drug Report 2009* (New York: United Nations, 2009).
9. B. Hibell et al., *The 2007 ESPAD Report. Substance Use Among Students in 35 European Countries* (Stockholm: Swedish Council for Information on Alcohol and Other Drugs, 2009).
10. European Monitoring Centre on Drugs and Drug Addiction, *Statistical Bulletin 2009*, www.emcdda.europa.eu/situation/cannabis/3/.
11. UN Office on Drugs and Crime, *World Drug Report 2009*; Australian Institute of Health and Welfare, *Statistics on Drug use in Australia 2002* (Canberra, 2003).
12. L.D. Johnston et al., *Monitoring the Future National Results on Adolescent Drug Use: Overview of Key Findings, 2008* (Bethesda, MD: National Institute on Drug Abuse, 2009).
13. For example, C.B. Lloyd, *Growing Up Global: The Changing Transitions to Adulthood in Developing Countries* (New York: Population Council, 2005).
14. UN Office on Drugs and Crime, *World Drug Report 2009*.
15. M. Farrell et al., "Methamphetamine: Drug Use and Psychoses Becomes a Major Public Health Issue in the Asia Pacific Region," *Addiction* 97 (2002): 771–72.
16. UN Office on Drugs and Crime, *World Drug Report 2009*.
17. G. Patton et al., "Mapping a Global Agenda for Adolescent Health," *Journal of Adolescent Health* 47 (2010): 427–32.
18. World Health Organization, *Global School-based Health Survey*, www.who.int/chp/gshs/en/.
19. H. Parker, J. Aldridge, and F. Measham, *Illegal Leisure: The Normalisation of Adolescent Recreational Drug Use* (London: Routledge, 1998).
20. A. Fletcher et al., "Young People, Recreational Drug Use and Harm Reduction," in *Harm Reduction: Evidence, Impacts and Challenges*, ed. T. Rhodes, 357–76 (Lisbon: European Monitoring Centre for Drugs and Drug Addiction, 2010).
21. J. McCambridge and J. Strang, "The Reliability of Drug Use Collected in the Classroom: What Is the Problem, Why Does It Matter and How Should It Be Approached?" *Drug and Alcohol Review* 25 (2006): 413–18.
22. V. Delaney-Black et al., "Just Say 'I Don't': Lack of Concordance Between Teen Report and Biological Measures of Drug Use," *Pediatrics* 126, no. 5 (2010): 887–93.
23. For example, S. Henderson et al., *Inventing Adulthoods* (London: Sage, 2007).
24. European Monitoring Centre for Drugs and Drug Addiction, 2010, www.emcdda.europa.eu/attachements.cfm/att_33728_EN_Dif10en.pdf.
25. T. Martinez et al., "Psychosocial Histories, Social Environment, and HIV Risk Behaviours of Injection and Non-injection Drug-using Homeless Youth," *Journal of Psychoactive Drugs* 30 (1998): 1–10.
26. E. Roy et al., "Injecting Drug Use Among Street Youth: A Dynamic Process," *Canadian Journal of Public Health* 89 (1998): 239–40.
27. C. Spooner et al., "Illicit Drug Use by Young People in Sydney: Results of a Street Intercept Survey," *Drug and Alcohol Review* 12, no. 2 (1993): 159–68.
28. C. Duff, C. Chow, E. Ryan et al., *Vancouver Youth Drug Reporting System: 2006 Preliminary Findings* (Vancouver: Vancouver Coastal Health, 2006).
29. J. Busza et al., "Street-based Adolescents at High Risk of HIV in Ukraine," *Journal of Epidemiology and Community Health*, September 23, 2010, http://jech.bmj.com/content/early/2010/09/23/jech.2009.097469.full.pdf.
30. D.M. Kissin et al., "HIV Seroprevalence in Street Youth, St Petersburg, Russia," *Aids* 21 (2007): 2333–40.
31. A.A. Gleghorn et al., "Association Between Drug Use Patterns and HIV Risks Among Homeless, Runaway, and Street Youth in Northern California," *Drug and Alcohol Dependence* 51 (1998): 219–27.
32. Fletcher et al., "Young People, Recreational Drug Use and Harm Reduction."
33. DrugScope, *Drug Treatment at the Crossroads: What It's for, Where It's at and How to Make It Even Better* (London, 2010).

CHILDREN OF THE DRUG WAR

34. National Treatment Agency for Substance Misuse, *Drug treatment activity in England 2006/07. National Drug Treatment Monitoring System* (London, 2007).
35. DrugScope, *Drug Treatment at the Crossroads.*
36. C. Cook, *Global State of Harm Reduction at a Glance* (London: International Harm Reduction Association, 2010).
37. J. Toumbourou et al., "Interventions to Reduce Harm Associated with Adolescent Substance Use," *Lancet* 369 (2007): 1391–401.
38. UNAIDS Inter-Agency Task Team on Young People, *At the Crossroads: Accelerating Youth Access to HIV/AIDS Interventions* (New York: UNFPA, 2004).
39. Eurasian Harm Reduction Network, *Young People and Injecting Drug Use.*

13. Taking Drugs Together: Early Adult Transitions and the Limits of Harm Reduction in England and Wales

by Michael Shiner

Introduction

The failings of prohibition and the need for alternative modes of regulation were highlighted by British sociologist Jock Young some forty years ago. Drug laws, he argued, had proved "damaging" and "unworkable" because they cannot stamp out consumer demand or illicit supply and inadvertently create spirals of "deviancy amplification." "The problem in a nutshell is that if there is strong demand for an illicit activity, then legislation, far from removing that demand, will merely pervert and distort it."[1] "Like it or not," Young insisted, "we live in a society which makes extensive and repeated use of psychotropic drugs. Effective controls must be instituted if we are to avoid a vast amount of unnecessary misery and hardship."[2] "We must," therefore, "learn to live with psychotropic drug use" because "it is only by treating citizens as responsible human beings that any sane and long-lasting control can be achieved."[3] Drug policy did not, of course, move in the direction Young favored. In the very year his work was published, Richard Nixon, then president of the United States, declared a "total war on drugs," while in Britain the introduction in 1971 of the Misuse of Drugs Act signaled a shift toward a more explicit enforcement-led approach. Even without the benefit of hindsight, this move was noted with a sense of foreboding by liberal critics. Young warned that more punitive policies could only exacerbate the problem, while Edwin Schur maintained: "It is reasonable to predict that if the British do move significantly in the direction of American policy, the consequences of doing so will be unhappy ones."[4]

The past four decades of global prohibition have confirmed that the criminal law cannot stamp out consumer demand or illicit supply. Despite a flurry of activity that aimed to strengthen international prohibition in the early 1970s, there followed an "explosive worldwide growth in the production and trafficking of virtually all types of illicit drugs."[5] Consequently, the drug trade is now "a global problem of enormous proportions,"[6] providing "the largest and most successful form of criminal activity ever developed."[7] According to recent estimates, illicit drugs account for 3 percent of world trade, making it the third largest sector behind oil and arms.[8] International comparisons also indicate that the global distribution of drug use is not straightforwardly related to drug policy, since countries with stringent regimes do not have lower rates of use than those with liberal regimes.[9] In the United States, for example, the "war on drugs" has been escalated by almost every presidential administration since Nixon's[10] and yet it has a drug problem worse than that of any other wealthy nation.[11] A similar paradox is evident in Britain, which has developed one of the harshest drug regimes in Europe, yet is host to one of its largest drug markets.[12] This paradox is examined below, first, by considering the place and meaning of illicit drug use among young people in England and Wales, and second, by considering the narrowness of official approaches to drug prevention.

Taking Drugs Together: From Counterculture to Consumer Capitalism

The now well established link between young people and drugs can be traced back to the 1960s. This was, lest we forget, a decade of unprecedented visibility for British youth, during which society's defenses against drug use were "decisively breached."[13] When Mick Jagger and fellow Rolling Stone Keith Richards were prosecuted for drugs offenses in 1967 the case became "symbolic of a wider contest between traditionalism and a new hedonism, the focal point of which was society's attitude towards recreational drugs."[14] As youth culture became more visible and increasingly permeated by drug-friendly references, official policy began to take the form of a recurring "moral panic." After the "sixties drugs" of amphetamines and LSD, a string of substances were added to the list: "designer drugs, PCP, synthetic drugs, ecstasy, solvents, crack cocaine and the new associations: acid-house, raves, club culture and 'heroin chic' supermodels."[15] With the rise of ecstasy culture, and related talk of the "democratization" of drug use, a raft of surveys during the early 1990s began to show that youthful drug use was no longer a minority experience.

The emergence of widespread youthful drug use in Britain, and across much of the late industrial world, has been facilitated by broader processes of social change.[16] Accelerating globalization has stimulated supply, while various factors have combined to accentuate demand. Crucially, the expansion of postcompulsory education beginning in the mid-1950s, augmented by the collapse of the youth labor market during the 1970s and 1980s, created the conditions for an extended adolescence. As a result, young people from all social classes began to experience a greater gap between leaving school and "settling down," providing more room for hedonistic pursuits. Having previously made little effort to court the youth market, moreover, the drinks industry began to target young people from the early 1960s, with the result that "pub culture" and alcohol were quickly installed as "central pillars" of youth-oriented leisure.[17] The economic pressures that undermined the youth labor market also served to elevate the significance of leisure, both as a form of consumption and source of economic growth. Repeated urban-regeneration initiatives stimulated a massive expansion of the nighttime economy, which was, by the end of the past century, responsible for creating one in five of all new jobs.[18] Greater competition between outlets resulted in heavy discounting, making alcohol much more affordable, while various marketing strategies (such as happy hours, chasers and shots, etc.) actively encouraged the transgression of traditional drinking norms. With an explicit emphasis on adventure, intoxication, and release, the nighttime economy has become the primary site of "subterranean play" and its expansion has encouraged the growth of a distinctly hedonistic leisure style, which has, in turn, helped to create a platform for accelerating rates of illicit drug use. As a result, recreational drug use has become firmly established within the late industrial leisure complex, offering young people a means of celebrating freedom from adult roles and responsibilities.

Patterns of youthful drug use have changed somewhat since the high tide of dance culture in the early 1990s.[19] Overall rates of use plateaued toward the end of the decade, with prevalence rates for most substances leveling off or falling during the years that have followed (see Figure 1). What has caused these fluctuations is not entirely clear though it is likely to have involved an interplay of multiple factors, including changing tastes and fashions. While much of the overall decline in drug use has been driven by reductions in cannabis use, neither law enforcement nor prevention programs appear to have played a significant role in this regard.[20] LSD and amphetamine use have fallen sharply as ecstasy and cocaine have become the party drugs of choice for young adults,[21] though they may, in turn, be losing out to alcohol as the expansion of the nighttime economy and the liberalization of licensing laws have been accompanied by an increase in "binge" drinking and "determined drunkenness."[22] Reduced availability and purity of ecstasy and cocaine have also been linked to the recent emergence and rapid growth in the use of "legal highs" such as mephedrone (now banned) and methylone.[23]

Even allowing for recent reductions, large numbers of young people continue to engage in illicit drug use. According to recent estimates nearly two and a half million sixteen- to twenty-four-year-olds in England and Wales have used cannabis, with more than a million having done so in the past year and more than half a million having done so in the past month.[24] In addition, an estimated three-quarters of a million sixteen- to twenty-four-year-olds have used cocaine, with 374,000 having done so in the past year and 175,000 having done so in the past month. Young people from all social classes are well represented among those who engage in such drug use, though the vast majority stop doing so by their mid- to late twenties as they form stable relationships and start families of their own.[25] From a developmental perspective, illicit drug use is, for the most part, one of a range of behaviors that make up the dominant trajectory of "adolescent limited" offending, through which young people test boundaries and assert their independence. As an "adaptation" to the "maturity gap" between biological maturity and the acquisition of adult status, such behavior is "ubiquitous" and it is "statistically aberrant to refrain from crime during adolescence."[26] There may even be something reassuring about rule breaking during this phase of the life course as such behavior is indicative of social integration with peers. Nonengagement in deviance, by contrast, may be suggestive of interpersonal difficulties: young people who abstain from trying drugs, for example, have been found to be "relatively tense, overcontrolled, emotionally constricted . . . somewhat socially isolated and lacking in interpersonal skills" while those who had experimented, mainly with cannabis, were said to be "the psychologically healthiest subjects, healthier than either abstainers or frequent users."[27]

The prevalence rates shown in Figure 1 are indicative of a clear hierarchy of use, which is, in part, a function of perceptions of harm. Normative concerns about managing risk and reducing the potential for harm inform various decisions that young people make about what to use, what not to use, when to use, and how to use. Such concerns have also been found to constitute a more significant source of self-regulation than symbolic or instrumental concerns about

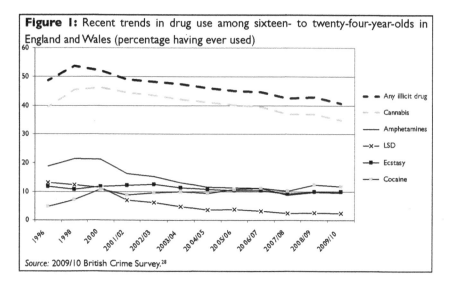

Figure 1: Recent trends in drug use among sixteen- to twenty-four-year-olds in England and Wales (percentage having ever used)

Source: 2009/10 British Crime Survey.[28]

the law.[29] Youthful drug use typically involves a limited repertoire of substances, most of which are less harmful than alcohol.[30] Cannabis is both the least harmful and most widely used illicit drug, while ecstasy and cocaine tend to be used more fleetingly in the context of a "calculated hedonism" regulated by boundaries of time, space, company, and intensity.[31] Use of the more harmful illicit drugs, such as heroin and crack cocaine, remains much more limited. Most young people continue to be thoroughly convinced of the potential harmfulness of illicit drugs other than cannabis,[32] and many disapprove of, even, recreational drug use.[33]

Tackling Drugs Together: The Limits of Harm Reduction

Drug policy has toughened into a "war" at a time when increasing levels of consumption point to a less inhibited popular culture.[34] The 1971 Misuse of Drugs Act was implemented in the wake of the newly emerging drug "problems" of the 1960s and has been central to British drug policy ever since. Under the terms of the act, controlled substances are divided into three classes (A, B, and C) according to their perceived harmfulness, and are linked to a sliding scale of legal penalties. Substances that are newly identified as a risk can be slotted into the established classification, so, for example, amendments were recently made to include "legal highs," such as mephedrone and

CHILDREN OF THE DRUG WAR

naphyrone, in Class B.[35] Since the mid-1980s, what was already an enforcement-led approach has been codified in a series of strategic documents, including *Tackling Drug Misuse* (1985), *Tackling Drugs Together* (1995), *Tackling Drugs to Build a Better Britain* (1998), and *Drugs: Protecting Families and Communities* (2008). While combining enforcement and prevention, the national strategy clearly prioritizes enforcement.[36] Prevention has been defined in fairly narrow terms and, though significant steps have been taken toward harm reduction, the vast potential of this approach has "barely been explored."[37] Officially sanctioned harm reduction practices were introduced as a pragmatic response to the threat of HIV and are almost entirely configured around the needs of injecting heroin users, with needle exchange, opiate substitution treatment, and some innovative moves toward heroin-assisted treatment and drug-consumption rooms.[38] The overriding policy imperative driving the national strategy remains one of "demand reduction," which, applied to young people, means enforcement, primary prevention, and "treatment." There is, in short, no official conception of harm reduction responses to recreational drug use. Remarkably, the 2008 drug strategy makes no reference to "pubs," "bars," "clubs," or "licensing."[39]

Given that recreational drug use is so strongly tied up with the activities of the drinks industry, it follows that the nighttime economy should provide one of the main focal points for youth-oriented harm reduction efforts. While some moves have been made in this direction, toward something we might call situational harm reduction, these remain largely informal. "Best practice" guidance has been issued for those concerned about drug use in the nighttime economy, which addresses issues such as overcrowding, air conditioning, ventilation, the availability of drinking water, the demeanor of door staff, transport home, the availability of information and outreach services, and access to health services.[40] While such guidance highlights many useful interventions, the lack of enforcement remains significant. According to a review of the health-care implications of clubbing:

> There are easily identifiable initiatives that could significantly reduce the impact of clubbing on the NHS [National Health Service]. They include the use of unbreakable drink containers, the elimination of discarded glass in or around clubs, a national registration and training scheme for club doormen, improved first aid provision at larger venues, limitations on crowding in clubs, and the abolition of drinks promotions that target young people.

All of these measures form the basis of voluntary codes of practice (such as that published by the London Drug Policy Forum, Dance till dawn safely). We suggest that they should urgently become a national legal requirement if good clubs are to thrive.[41]

Best practice could be enforced through various mechanisms, including by-laws, health and safety legislation, and/or licensing conditions.[42] Consider, for example, that recent amendments to the Licensing Act 2003 ban "irresponsible promotions," including the dispensing of alcohol directly into the mouth, and require that customers have access to free tap water so they can space out their drinks.[43] The revised conditions also ensure that customers have the opportunity to choose small measures of beers, ciders, spirits, and wine.

As well as being largely voluntary, good practice guidance has been limited by a narrow conception of harm reduction. Despite concerns about drug purity and adulterants, for example, the original "Safer Clubbing" guidance refused to recommend the use of ecstasy testing kits because, among other things: "It is hard to maintain a policy that discourages drug use at the same time as offering a pill testing service."[44] Such a stance seems strangely at odds with the legalized distribution of injecting paraphernalia and the prescription of heroin substitutes. A similar tension is evident in the way the Select Committee on Home Affairs supported the piloting of heroin prescribing and safe-injecting houses, but refused to endorse the principle of legally regulated supply more generally on the grounds that to do so would be a "gamble" and a "step into the unknown."[45] While recognizing the need for realistic drug education, moreover, the committee singled out *Lifeline,* a voluntary sector drugs project, for particular criticism, arguing that its comic-book harm reduction materials, which promise to "tell the truth about drugs"[46] "cross the line between providing accurate information and encouraging young people to experiment with illegal drugs."[47]

Conclusion

Much like the characters in the film *Groundhog Day,* the architects of British drug policy seem to be caught in a time loop, reliving the same experiences over and over again, repeating previous mistakes and failing to learn from the past. Phil, the central character in

CHILDREN OF THE DRUG WAR

Groundhog Day, broke the cycle by doing good, which leads us to the ultimate question, what would make for a good response to young people's drug use? The central problem, it seems to me, is not so very different from the one Jock Young identified some forty years ago, and nor are the solutions. We must take seriously both the limitations of the criminal law and the harmfulness of illicit drugs. In practical terms, this means accepting that the elimination of drug use is an impossible task and focusing instead on establishing a system of regulation that concentrates on reducing harm. What is required, in other words, is a more effective system of regulation than prohibition is able to provide. It remains strongly dysfunctional to harass and undermine existing drug subcultures because to do so dislocates the most viable source of norms and controls. We should, rather, seek to maintain subcultures and encourage controlled use through the dissemination of "positive propaganda," or accurate information phrased in terms of the values of the subculture, alongside an expanded set of harm reduction practices. The ultimate solution may well require a system of state-regulated supply, which enables consumers to know precisely what they are getting, while constraining suppliers—criminal, corporate, or otherwise—from pursuing profit at the cost of human well-being.[48]

Endnotes

1. J. Young, *The Drugtakers: The Social Meaning of Drug Use* (London: MacGibbon and Kee, 1971), 217–18.
2. Ibid., 219.
3. Ibid., 222.
4. E. Schur, *Our Criminal Society: The Social and Legal Sources of Crime in America* (Englewood Cliffs, NJ: Prentice Hall, 1969), 217.
5. P. Stares, *Global Habit: The Drug Problem in a Borderless World* (Washington, DC: Brookings Institution Press, 1996), 28.
6. A. Klein, *Drugs and the World* (London: Reaktion Books, 2008), 119.
7. P. Bean, *Drugs and Crime* (Collumpton: Willan, 2002), 99.
8. Klein, *Drugs and the World*.
9. L. Degenhardt et al., "Toward a Global View of Alcohol, Tobacco, Cannabis, and Cocaine Use: Findings from the WHO World Mental Health Surveys," *PLoS Medicine* 5, no. 4 (2008): 1053–67.
10. J. Simon, *Governing Through Crime: How the War on Crime Transformed American Democracy and Created a Culture of Fear* (Oxford: Oxford University Press, 2007).
11. R.J. MacCoun and P. Reuter, *Drug War Heresies: Learning from Other Vices, Times and Places* (Cambridge and New York: Cambridge University Press, 2001).
12. Police Foundation, *Drugs and the Law: Report of the Independent Inquiry into the Misuse of Drugs Act 1971* (London, 2000); European Monitoring Centre for Drugs and Drugs Addiction, *The State of the Drug Problem in Europe: Annual Report 2008* (Luxembourg: Office for Official Publications of the European Communities, 2008).

13. A. Marwick, *The Sixties: Cultural Revolution in Britain, France, Italy, and the United States* (Oxford and New York: Oxford University Press, 1998), 4.
14. M. Donnelly, *Sixties Britain* (London: Pearson, 2005), 153.
15. S. Cohen, *Folk Devils and Moral Panics: The Creation of the Mods and Rockers* (London: MacGibbon and Kee, 2002/1972), xiii.
16. M. Shiner, *Drug Use and Social Change: The Distortion of History* (Basingstoke: Palgrave Macmillan, 2009).
17. B. Osgerby, *Youth in Britain Since 1945* (Oxford: Blackwell, 1998).
18. Home Office, *Time for Reform: Proposals for the Modernization of Our Licensing Laws* (London: HMSO, 2000), cited in D. Hobbs, P. Hadfield, S. Lister, and S. Winlow, *Bouncers: Violence and Governance in the Night-time Economy* (Oxford: Oxford University Press, 2003).
19. P. Reuter and A. Stevens, *An Analysis of UK Drug Policy: A Monograph Prepared for the UK Drug Policy Commission* (London: UK Drug Policy Commission, 2007).
20. Ibid.
21. F. Measham, "The Decline of Ecstasy, the Rise of Binge Drinking and the Persistence of Pleasure," *Probation Journal* 51, no. 4 (2004), 309–26; M. Shiner, "Out of Harm's Way? Illicit Drug Use, Medicalisation and the Law," *British Journal of Criminology* 43, no. 4 (2003): 772–96.
22. Measham, "Decline of Ecstasy."
23. These psychoactive drugs were not, until recently, controlled under the Misuse of Drugs Act 1971, and have similar effects to ecstasy, cocaine, and amphetamines. See F. Measham, K. Moore, R. Newcombe, and Z. Welch, "Tweaking, Bombing, Dabbing, and Stockpiling: The Emergence of Mephedrone and the Perversity of Prohibition," *Drugs and Alcohol Today* 10 (2010): 14–21; A.R. Winstock, J. Marsden, and L. Mitcheson, "What Should Be Done About Mephedrone," *British Medical Journal* 340 (2010): c1605.
24. J. Hoare and D. Moon, *Drug Misuse Declared: Findings from the 2009/10 British Crime Survey* (London: Home Office, 2010).
25. Shiner, *Drug Use and Social Change*.
26. T.E. Moffitt, "Adolescence-Limited and Life-Course-Persistent Offending: A Complimentary Pair of Developmental Theories," in *Developmental Theories of Crime and Delinquency*, ed. T.P. Thornberry (London: Transaction, 1997), 15, 37.
27. J. Shedler and J. Block, "Adolescent Drug Use and Psychological Health," *American Psychologist* 45 (1990): 618, 625.
28. Hoare and Moon, *Drug Misuse Declared*.
29. Shiner, "Out of Harm's Way?"
30. D. Nutt, "Estimating Drug Harms: A Risky Business?" Briefing 10 (London: Centre for Crime and Justice Studies, 2009).
31. Measham, "Decline of Ecstasy."
32. G. Pearson and M. Shiner, "Rethinking the Generation Gap: Attitudes to Illicit Drug Use Among Young People and Adults," *Criminal Justice* 2, no. 1 (2002): 71–86.
33. Voicebox, Downloads: Labels and Stereotypes, 2009, http://voicebox.vinspired.com/use_our_data/downloads/pdfs/Voicebox_-_stereotypes_and_labels_results.pdf.
34. R. Reiner, *The Politics of the Police* (Oxford: Oxford University Press, 2010).
35. See www.homeoffice.gov.uk/about-us/home-office-circulars/circulars-2010/010-2010/; www.homeoffice.gov.uk/media-centre/press-releases/naphyrone-class-b-drug.
36. Reuter and Stevens, *An Analysis of UK Drug Policy*.
37. R. Newcombe, "Injecting New Life into Harm Reduction," *Druglink* 20, no. 5 (2005): 10–11.
38. Reuter and Stevens, *An Analysis of UK Drug Policy*.
39. HM Government, *Drugs: Protecting Families and Communities* (London: Home Office, 2008).

40. R. Webster, M. Goodman, and G. Whalley, *Safer Clubbing: Guidance for Licensing Authorities, Club Managers and Promoters* (London: London Drug Policy Forum, 2002); R. Webster, *Safer Nightlife: Best Practice for Those Concerned About Drug Use and the Night-Time Economy* (London: London Drug Policy Forum, 2008).

41. L.C. Luke, C. Dewar, and M. Bailey, "A Little Nightclub Medicine: The Healthcare Implications of Clubbing," *Emergency Medicine Journal* 19 (2002): 542–45.

42. T. Newburn and M. Shiner, *Teenage Kicks? Young People and Alcohol: A Review of the Literature* (York, UK: Joseph Rowntree Foundation, 2001).

43. Home Office, *Selling Alcohol Responsibly: The New Mandatory Licensing Conditions, The Mandatory Code for Alcohol Retailers England and Wales* (London, 2010).

44. Webster et al., *Safer Clubbing*, 47.

45. Select Committee on Home Affairs, *The Government's Drug Policy: Is It Working?* (London: Stationery Office, 2002), 62.

46. See www.lifelinepublications.org.

47. Select Committee, *The Government's Drug Policy*, 49

48. S. Rolles, D. Kushlick, and M. Jay, *After the War on Drugs: Options for Control* (Bristol: Transform, 2004). [See also chapter 4, by Steve Rolles.—Ed.]

14. Drug Testing in Schools: A Case Study in Doing More Harm Than Good

by Adam Fletcher

Introduction

As drug use has spread more widely through the youth population, it has become a public health priority to reduce the harms associated with it. Secondary schools continue to be the focus for policies aiming toward reducing drug use and drug-related harm, although traditional classroom-based drugs education has proved insufficient for changing students' behavior and reducing harm. Drug testing in schools is now also a prominent part of school life for many children around the world. In the United States, school-based drug-testing programs are commonplace, and in 2004, President Bush authorized the use of federal funds for school-based drug testing in the No Child Left Behind Act, placing testing at the heart of the "war on drugs."

This practice of random, suspicionless drug testing is not confined to American high schools. A study by the European Monitoring Centre for Drugs and Drug Addiction found that drug testing in schools has become an issue for public and political debate throughout Europe, and is now implemented in schools in the Czech Republic, Finland, Norway, and Sweden, and also takes place sporadically in the United Kingdom and Ireland, Belgium, and Hungary.[1] In 2009, Russia's antinarcotics agency announced that teenagers will now be tested for drugs during regular medical examinations at school, and drug-testing schemes are being piloted in schools in Kazakhstan and Hong Kong. This chapter is critical of these policies because of the practical and ethical problems associated with them, because of the lack of evidence or logic to support them, and because they will *do more harm than good.*

School Drug Testing, Consent, and the Right to Privacy

As drug-testing programs in schools have gained political support in America and been exported to other countries, the range of technologies used to test for the use of drugs has also expanded and now includes methods for the collection and analysis of blood, urine, saliva, hair, nails, or sweat samples. These surveillance practices represent an unwelcome and expensive extension of invasive surveillance into school life. It has been estimated that programs routinely cost as much as US$70 per student tested,[2] amounting to as much as US$36,000 per school each year.[3] New "point of collection tests" for use in schools can reduce the overall costs by avoiding sending specimens to an outside laboratory, although this requires procedures for testing and storing data securely on school sites, and risks the confidentiality of results.

Nonlaboratory points of collection tests also limit the reliability and accuracy of drug testing, greatly increasing the risk of "false positive" test results, and they cannot distinguish between licit and illicit drugs. For example, codeine in painkillers or prescribed medication can cause a positive test for opiates. Over-the-counter decongestants can also produce a "false positive" test result for amphetamines. How will young people's right to privacy about medical conditions be maintained under such circumstances? Young people and parents should be consulted and asked to consent to a program of invasive testing; however, it is not unheard of for a parent or guardian's refusal to consent to equate to the same disciplinary action as would be the case if a positive test were recorded.[4]

This invasion of privacy, potential for highly misleading results, and the lack of consent often associated with mandatory drug testing have meant that schools have been subject to high-profile legal challenges in the United States and elsewhere regarding their legitimacy. Indeed, the spread of mandatory drug testing in schools is further evidence of "an international environment within which human rights violations connected to drug policies are less likely to be raised and addressed" as the "war on drugs" trumps young people's rights.[5] The UN Convention on the Rights of the Child requires that state parties take "appropriate measures" to protect children from the illicit use of narcotic drugs and psychotropic substances (Article 33). However, the process of coercive testing and the assumption of guilt where consent is withheld raises serious concerns in relation to other articles of the convention, including Article 16, which states that "no child shall be subjected to arbitrary or unlawful interference with his or her privacy," and Article 3, a general principle of the convention requiring that in all matters affecting the child, the child's best interests shall be "a primary consideration." These protections are difficult to reconcile with random school drug testing, especially given the lack of evidence of any positive health outcomes of such programs.

In Search of the Evidence

Researchers have searched for evidence of effectiveness to support the proliferation of drug testing in schools—and have failed to find any. Neil McKeganey of the University of Glasgow undertook a comprehensive search of studies published in major bibliographic databases to assess the effects of drug testing in schools. He found that the current evidence base is limited to a few small-scale, methodologically weak evaluations.[6] Where studies have suggested that student drug testing "works," they have lacked any control group, and often have also been politically motivated. A 2008 study commissioned by the Australian National Council on Drugs to review the evidence relating to drug testing in schools and its effects concluded that:

> While there is a large volume of literature about drug testing programmes for school-aged children, the overwhelming majority of articles comprise anecdotal evidence and journalistic comment. Few studies have examined specifically the effectiveness of drug testing programmes for school students and none has been conducted rigorously in a controlled, unbiased manner.[7]

The largest study to date was undertaken by Ryoko Yamaguchi and her colleagues at the University of Michigan. They draw on data collected from more than 75,000 students across 410 U.S. high schools as part of the Monitoring the Future Study to assess the effect of drug-testing practices on drug use between 1998 and 2001.[8] A total of 74 out of the 410 schools surveyed reported implementing a drug-testing program during the study *but there were no differences* in either the prevalence or frequency of cannabis or other drug use reported by students depending upon whether or not drug testing had been taking place in their school. In the absence of any prospective, controlled studies, this analysis represents the best available evidence at present regarding the effectiveness of drug testing in schools and concludes that such policies do *not* deter young people from using drugs.

Meanwhile, studies exploring the views of young people, their parents, and education and health professionals consistently find that drug testing is unpopular. Young people dislike it, with those who are subjected to it becoming more negative about school following testing.[9] A study of American parents and high school officials found that the majority opposed drug testing programs.[10] Even a survey of 359 American physicians found that 83 percent were opposed to high school drug-testing programs.[11]

In Search of a Theory

Without any evidence and little popular support to underpin further drug testing in schools, it is worth reflecting on the philosophy and theoretical justifications that have allowed such practices to gain momentum. It is not unusual for new policies and practices to emerge without a clear theory or logical model underpinning them. For example, despite its widespread adoption, peer education has been described as a "method in search of a theory."[12] Drug testing in schools is based on naive misconceptions about what influences young people's behavior, and then *further limited* by misunderstandings about the potential for and extent of drug-related harms arising due to their drug use.

The policy relies on the premise that a fear of detection and punishment will deter teenagers from using drugs, or encourage them to stop using. Like many preventive interventions, it is based on the principle of modifying individual young people's perceptions of the risks regarding drug use and assumes that they rationally weigh the costs versus the benefits of their actions in *isolation.* They do not, and therefore it is not surprising that the threat of drug testing has no impact. There are many other, more complex, social, economic, and environmental factors that are beyond young people's immediate control and that shape their attitudes and actions relating to drug use, such as who their friends are, with whom they live, where they live, and what their school experiences are.[13] We should not ignore the importance of choice and individual responsibility but we must recognize these broader social and contextual determinants. As Richard Wilkinson and Michael Marmot put it:

> *Trying to shift the whole responsibility on the user is clearly an inadequate response. This blames the victim, rather than addressing the complexities of the social circumstances that generate drug use.*[14]

Drug-testing advocates claim that such an approach is also

justified in order to refer young drug users to "treatment." Yet youth drug use is characterized by "sensible" experimental and recreational patterns of use throughout Europe, North America, and elsewhere. Drug use with friends is now relatively normal, and part of a broader search for excitement, pleasure, and a sense of identity within the context of consumer-oriented and increasingly complex transitions to adulthood. Testing for the use of cannabis or "club drugs" is not like screening for cancer: the vast majority of young people experience no serious harms associated with these drugs. Yet, school-based drug tests cannot distinguish between experimental, occasional or regular, heavy use, or determine in what context a drug was used, to assess the likelihood of harm. Furthermore, surveillance does not work unless it is underpinned by a degree of social consensus regarding what is inappropriate or "deviant" behavior; but through the process of "normalization," recreational drug use has been accommodated into mainstream youth cultures.[15]

Toxic Schools: Doing More Harm Than Good

Not only is drug testing in schools theoretically misguided but it is likely to have unintended, harmful consequences. The first way in which harm is likely to arise is via "labeling" those young people identified as "drug users" by testing and identifying them as needing additional support. This process is likely to reduce their confidence, happiness, and self-esteem at school as well as to lower aspirations, and thus may lead to escalating drug use.[16] While drug testing cannot distinguish between occasional, recreational drug use and more problematic patterns of use, there is a danger that youngsters at very little risk of harm will be "labeled" and drawn into the net of counseling services, "treatment" centers, and the criminal justice system, potentially introducing them to networks of more "risky" drug-using peers.

The consequence of a positive test result also often involves suspension or school exclusion.[17] Reduced involvement in education and early school-leaving are associated with more chaotic and problematic drug-use practices, both in the short and long terms.[18] For example, a study published in 2008 of Irish young people who were using heroin found the one thing that nearly all of them had in common (eighty-one out of eighty-six) was that they were no

CHILDREN OF THE DRUG WAR

longer attending school.[19] In many cases drug testing will punish the *most vulnerable* young people—such as those from the poorest neighborhoods or those whose parents misuse drugs—who most need a supportive school environment, and whose drug use is most likely to escalate if they are excluded from school and their economic opportunities are further limited. Drug dependence and injecting drug use is also concentrated in the most disadvantaged areas and strongly linked to economic and social exclusion, both as a cause and a consequence, in high-income countries such as the United States,[20] and also regions such as Central Asia, Eastern Europe, and Russia.[21] Excluding large numbers of vulnerable young people from schools in already disadvantaged areas will only serve to increase drug-related harms in these "risk environments."[22]

As with all surveillance systems, drug testing in schools is also vulnerable to "concealment." There is potential for such a policy to do more harm than good where young people decide to change their patterns of drug use or school attendance to avoid detection. For example, drug testing can inadvertently divert young people to substances that are likely to be more harmful but less easily identifiable than cannabis, such as alcohol, amphetamines, or volatile substances (e.g., fuel or paint). This is of particular concern given the greater acute risks and long-term harms associated with excessive alcohol consumption. Furthermore, just as young people can switch substances, they can also vote with their feet and some may skip school to avoid the possibility of being tested. This increases the likelihood that they will fall behind at school and that they may become involved with older peers and a wider range of drugs, which are likely to present much greater risks than occasional cannabis use.

Drug-testing procedures also incur costs that represent a significant and unnecessary diversion of scarce resources in any education system, and the time involved in organizing these procedures is an additional burden for school managers. This time and money would be much better spent on creating a more supportive school environment in line with the principles of the health-promoting schools movement: social support, engagement, fairness, and democracy.[23] Schools with a positive, inclusive ethos that foster positive teacher–student relationships and promote school engagement have the lowest rates of drug use.[24] But drug testing only serves to damage relationships between students, teachers, and parents, and increase psychological distress.[25] Young people may also avoid participating in out-of-school, extracurricular activities that help them to form positive relationships with teachers, and can divert and protect them from engaging in drug use at a young age.[26] These dangers associated with a poorer school ethos and diminished trust are likely to be compounded further by the harms associated with creating a false sense of a drug-free environment through drug testing, and limiting the potential for schools to create "safe spaces" for young people to learn about, and discuss issues to do with, drug use.[27]

Drug Testing in Schools: "Just Say No!"

Schools are not an appropriate battleground for the "war on drugs." The role of schools is not to police and punish young people. Schools are places where young people should be happy, build positive, supportive relationships, and have access to information about drugs, developing the skills they need to grow up safely in a world in which they face myriad risks. Drug testing breaches young people's right to privacy and is inadmissible with the principles of school-based health promotion; it constitutes a policy of *harm promotion* rather than harm reduction. It does harm through labeling students; through excluding students from school; through creating perverse incentives to switch to more harmful substances; and through the costly disruption to school life and the loss of trust, ultimately undermining the principles of a healthy school environment. It does not address the social determinants of drug use but rather reproduces the contexts via which drug-related harms occur. And as with all wars, the most vulnerable young people are most likely to be the victims in the "war on drugs."

School-based drug testing also provides *an exemplary case study of why drugs policies that do more harm than good are implemented.* It is a policy built on rhetoric and anecdotal evidence, and driven by technology rather than a coherent theory of human behavior. It is an example of *political interventionism.* As with military interventionism, such interventionism in schools involves aggressive state activities. Stephen Ball of the University of London has documented the flood of government initiatives and "concomitant interventionism" in education, highlighting how twenty-first-century schools are subject to directives from a local level and global trends, in addition to having to implement a wide range of policies and practices

CHILDREN OF THE DRUG WAR

determined by national government.[28] Reflecting on this phenomenon of interventionism, professor of pediatrics at the University of Oklahoma, Mark Chaffin, explains:

> *Once taken to scale, once institutionalised and heavily funded, and once imbued with a sense of mission and mass commitment, programs take on lives of their own and subsequent hard data on program effectiveness are welcomed only if the news is good.*[29]

Yet, we have better, evidence-based policy instruments already: school-wide interventions that promote school engagement and positive connections between staff and students, and reduce disaffection have been found to be effective in reducing overall levels of substance use and supporting students' development and well-being.[30] These health-promotion approaches, which focus on ensuring that schools are safe, trusted, and inclusive social environments and also recognize and promote the rights of the child to privacy (Article 16 of the Convention on the Rights of the Child) to education (Article 28), and to health (Article 24) should be prioritized. These, rather than new surveillance and control technologies, are more "appropriate measures" (Article 33) to protect children from drugs.

Endnotes

1. European Monitoring Centre for Drugs and Drug Addiction, *Drug Testing in Schools in European Countries*, 2004, https://wcd.coe.int/wcd/ViewDoc.jsp?id=1207521&Site=COE/.
2. R.J. Ozminkowski et al., "The Cost of On-site Versus Off-site Workplace Urinalysis Testing for Illicit Drug Use," *Health Care Manager* 20 (2001): 59–69.
3. R. DuPont et al., *Elements of a Successful School-Based Drug Testing Program* (Rockville, MD: Institute of Behavior and Health, 2002).
4. N. McKeganey, *Random Drug Testing of School Children: A Shot in the Arm or a Shot in the Foot for Drug Prevention?* (York, UK: Joseph Rowntree Foundation, 2005).
5. D. Barrett and M. Nowak, "The United Nations and Drug Policy: Towards a Human Rights-Based Approach," in *The Diversity of International Law: Essays in Honour of Professor Kalliopi K. Koufa*, ed. A. Constantinides and N. Zaikos, 449–77 (Boston: Brill/Martinus Nijhoff, 2009), 450.
6. McKeganey, *Random Drug Testing of School Children.*
7. A. Roche et al., *Drug Testing in Schools: Evidence, Impacts and Alternatives*, Australian National Council on Drugs, 2008, 71, http://drugaids.socialnet.org.hk/Documents/australia_drug_testing_in_schools%20(1).pdf.
8. R. Yamaguchi et al., "Relationship Between Student Illicit Drug Use and School Drug-Testing Policies," *Journal of School Health* 73 (2003): 159–64.
9. L. Goldberg et al., "Drug Testing Athletes to Prevent Substance Abuse: Background and Pilot Study Results of the SATURN (Student Athlete Testing Using Random Notification) Study," *Journal of Adolescent Health* 32 (2003): 16–25.

10. J. Kern et al., *Making Sense of Student Drug Testing: Why Educators Are Saying No* (New Haven, CT: American Civil Liberties Union and Drug Policy Alliance, 2006).
11. S. Levy et al., "Drug Testing of Adolescents in General Medical Clinics, in School and at Home: Physicians Attitudes and Practices," *Journal of Adolescent Health* 38 (2006): 346–42.
12. G. Turner and J. Shepherd, "A Method in Search of a Theory: Peer Education and Health Promotion," *Health Education Research* 14, no. 2 (1999): 235–47.
13. C. Spooner and W. Hall, "Preventing Drug Misuse by Young People: We Need to Do More Than 'Just Say No,'" *Addiction* 97 (2002): 478–81.
14. R. Wilkinson and M. Marmot. *Social Determinants of Health: The Solid Facts* (Copenhagen: World Health Organization, 2003), 25.
15. H. Parker et al., "The Normalization of 'Sensible' Recreational Drug Use: Further Evidence from the North West England Longitudinal Study," *Sociology* 86 (2002): 941–60.
16. C. Bonell and A. Fletcher, "Addressing the Wider Determinants of Problematic Drug Use: Advantages of Whole-Population over Targeted Interventions," *International Journal of Drug Policy* 19 (2008): 267–69.
17. DuPont et al., *Elements of a Successful School-Based Drug Testing Program.*
18. T. Rhodes et al., "Risk Factors Associated with Drug Use: The Importance of 'Risk Environment,'" *Drugs: Education, Prevention and Policy* 10 (2003): 303–29.
19. J. Fagan et al., "Opiate-Dependent Adolescents in Ireland: A Descriptive Study at Treatment Entry," *Irish Journal of Psychological Medicine* 25 (2008): 46–51.
20. P. Bourgois, *In Search of Respect: Selling Crack in El Barrio* (New York: Cambridge University Press, 1995).
21. R. Goodwin et al., "HIV/AIDS Among Adolescents in Eastern Europe," *Journal of Health Psychology* 9 (2005): 381–96.
22. T. Rhodes, "The 'Risk Environment': A Framework for Understanding and Reducing Drug-related Harm," *International Journal of Drug Policy* 13 (2002): 85–94.
23. World Health Organization, *HEALTH21: An Introduction to the Health for All Policy Framework for the WHO European Region*, European Health for All Series, No. 5 (Copenhagen, 1998).
24. C. Bonell et al., "Improving School Ethos May Reduce Substance Misuse and Teenage Pregnancy," *British Medical Journal* 334 (2007): 614–16.
25. Roche et al., *Drug Testing in Schools.*
26. A. Fletcher et al., "School Effects on Young People's Drug Use: A Systematic Review of Intervention and Observational Studies," *Journal of Adolescent Health* 42 (2008): 209–20.
27. The UN Committee on the Rights of the Child, which oversees implementation of the Convention on the Rights of the Child, has clearly stated that accurate and objective information on the harmful consequences of drug use is a requirement of the treaty in this context. See, for example, UN Committee on the Rights of the Child, *Concluding Observations: Sweden*, UN Doc. No. CRC/C/SWE/CO/4, June 12, 2009, para. 49.
28. S. Ball, *The Education Debate: Policy and Politics in the Twenty-First Century* (Cambridge: Polity Press, 2008).
29. M. Chaffin, "Is It Time to Rethink Healthy Start/Healthy Families?" *Child Abuse and Neglect* 28 (2004): 589–95, here, 592.
30. Bonell et al., "Improving School Ethos May Reduce Substance Misuse and Teenage Pregnancy."

15. "I've Been Waiting for This My Whole Life": Life Transitions and Heroin Use

by Jovana Arsenijevic and Andjelka Nikolic

Introduction

One of the most significant aspects of drug abuse is that it affects the most vulnerable of demographics, namely, youth. The transition from adolescence to adulthood is a crucial period, during which a person is most likely to begin experimenting with drugs. Drug use can strongly affect young people who start searching for their own identity and a sense of independence. This age group is more prone to several issues that make them more susceptible to drug use. Curiosity and the search for new experiences, peer pressure, resistance to authority, low self-esteem, and problems with forming and maintaining positive interpersonal relationships can all be factors that make young people more vulnerable to drug use and dependence. Furthermore, drugs can be used as a strategy to deal with problems that include neglect, unemployment, violence, sexual abuse, and shell shock.

Various research data confirm that drug use is more common among the populations of youth living in vulnerable conditions (such as families with low socioeconomic status, large families, households with conflict and violence, alcoholism, etc.).[1] This group needs support and encouragement for the development of individual capacities. At the same time, drug use is also present among socially integrated young people. This is partially caused by the fact that many young people grow up under the influence of pop culture, which has a tolerant attitude toward drug use. Growing up under this influence is becoming even more risky in combination with a lack of knowledge about the risks and consequences of this lifestyle. Moreover, there are indicators that first experiments with drugs and the initiation of young people into injecting practices is happening at earlier ages than was previously the case.[2] Considering the developmental and psychosocial characteristics of youth, they have less ability to assess the risks and possible consequences of this behavior. Therefore, the development of individual mechanisms for resolving these issues is extremely important.

According to life-course theory, life trajectories are intersected by various transitions that can affect the period of growing up—either in an affirmative way by helping us find constructive solutions to our future problems or in a negative way by causing stagnation or regression in the development of our personality. Our study presents the main aspects of transitions that take place in childhood or early adolescence and that can affect the lives of adult heroin users. Using descriptive analysis of eight life stories, we focus on the first memories from early childhood, family environment, peer relations, the beginning of sexual development and first sexual intercourse, the first encounter with psychoactive substances, and age at the time of first use of heroin. Most of the eight people on whom we focus also had experiences of war.

These life stories differ in many ways: from the environment in which childhood was spent, to the beginning of involvement with subcultural groups, to first experiences of love and sexual intercourse, and the first use of psychoactive substances. A particular factor, however, the introduction to heroin, is stable in all eight regardless of age differences among participants. The only variant involves the first encounter with heroin, which, nonetheless, is almost always connected to late adolescence.

The stations along the trip to the final destination—the world of heroin—are the main subject of this chapter. Following the tracks that led us there, we were told many stories that all ended in a similar sentiment, exemplified in the following quote:

I have only one girl, I make love to her every day. It's heroin. The risk is too great, the price you have to pay is too high for a little satisfaction that lasts an hour or two.

Characteristics of Young Injecting Drug Users

In order to better understand the characteristic behavior of this demographic we studied forty-one injecting drug users, of which thirty-four were male and seven female. Through the Get Connected! project run by the nongovernmental organization Veza, in Serbia, which targets young injecting drug users aged fifteen to twenty-one, an initial questionnaire was used to collect information on the characteristics of our clients. The average age was just over seventeen (17.66). The age at the initial ingestion of any psychoactive substance, regardless of gender, was twelve (12.21), while the average age of first use of heroin by injection was, again, just over seventeen (17.59) for thirty-four participants. At the time of the study, all of the participants were heroin users.

Just under a third of participants (31.71 percent) had used some form of psychoactive substance between the ages of nine and twelve, while over two-thirds (68.29 percent) had used some form of psychoactive substance between the ages of thirteen and seventeen. This implies a particularly young age of first usage of these substances. The majority of participants had their first experience with a psychoactive substance through marijuana (78.05 percent), followed by glue (12.19 percent), and heroin (12.10). Considering the more prevalent use of amphetamines in the club scene, however, this short survey does not accurately depict their usage.[3]

From the data gathered, the earliest case of heroin use was at age eleven. Day-to-day work with injecting drug users led us to the conclusion that individuals among the Roma population are most likely to begin using heroin at younger ages. In the general population, young people rarely, if ever, have their first experience with drugs through heroin—in most cases it is marijuana. On the other hand, the majority of young people from the Roma population are not directed toward any particular substance; rather, they begin experimenting with whatever they are most likely to encounter in their community. In the past, this was glue, but today heroin is becoming more prevalent. Upon inquiring into their family life, we concluded that the majority of participants live with their primary family (68.29 percent) and a considerably smaller proportion (9.57 percent) with their secondary family, defined as family gained by marriage. Some of those studied (7.32 percent) lived under conditions that substitute for a primary family, defined as any type of foster care. Considering the age and size of the data sample, the proportion of young people who are living on their own is significant at 14.63 percent.

In another study that took place at Veza, the social and health status of participants as well as their experiences with police were investigated. The sample size was fifty-seven participants, of whom forty-five were male, eleven female, and one who identified as transgender. One important topic that was investigated was the degree of education achieved, and why no higher education was pursued. Seven categories can be created from the responses received, one of which includes the percentage of participants who completed a form of higher education. The variance between categories is shown in Table 1.

Table 1. Reasons for Lack of Higher Education/Achievement of Higher Education	
Category	%
Problems in school and lack of motivation	27.6
Beginning drug use	13.8
Joining the workforce	17.2
War period, sanctions, and bombing	6.9
Family problems	19.0
Other transitions in life	10.3
Have completed a higher education	5.2

These data imply that regular schooling most often ceased due to problems in school and a lack of motivation. Second in significance was family problems followed by joining the workforce, which participants attributed to a poor economic situation within the family (this makes it worth debating whether or not to include this factor within the "family problems" category or to separate it out). Drug use was the fourth most likely reason.[4]

Life Trajectories of Eight Injecting Heroin Users

Following on from this snapshot of the characteristics of the relevant demographic, by using the case study method, we have mapped the life trajectories of eight individuals who told us their life stories— six male, two female. The ages of the interviewees today vary from twenty-five to thirty-two, and one who is now forty-two. To introduce these life stories, Table 2 compares the socioeconomic status of the participants while they were still living in the primary family and that in their later lives when they were living independently. The table shows a clear decline for most.

Table 2. Socioeconomic Status of Interviewees While Living with the Family and Living Independently		
Socioeconomic status	Life in primary family	Independent living
High socioeconomic status	2	1
Middle socioeconomic status	5	2
Low socioeconomic status	1	5

In order to understand the differences shown in Table 2, it is important to consider that only two of the participants were currently employed, three were homeless, two were sex workers, and three were involved in acquisitive crime to support themselves financially. The decline in socioeconomic status happens parallel to heroin use, mostly because of family rejection and unemployment.

First Memories

Each interview began with an inquiry into the participant's first memory. However, the first memory of most of those we interviewed was deeply repressed and unavailable for interpretation. As far as first memories go, family relations were often mentioned, or some knowledge the interviewee gained while growing up. This did not actually have to be a real memory, but information they considered to be memories diluted by the experiences of others, or other experiences and emotions that they had come to associate with a particular story. The answers indicated some degree of understanding that they simply could not remember events from their early childhood. The following is the only story focusing on early memories.

> *I remember a series of memories, a series . . . Very nice ones. My favourite is when I come home wet, it's snowing outside, I lean on the radiator and watch cartoon movies. . . . That was Sundays at the time.*

Family

Family descriptions and the relations within each of these microsystems[5] showed a lot of variance. In six of the eight cases, parents divorced during the participant's childhood. Complete cessation of relations with the father was present in five cases. The reasons for divorce were heterogeneous and were accompanied by new lives for the parents, leaving the children in a shadow of neglect.

Family descriptions were particularly confusing, leaving room for the interpretation that the individuals themselves were not completely clear on when their family situation transformed with the introduction of a stepfather, grandparents, or foster parents as caregivers. Their adaptation to this new situation was not complete, and several years down the line they tried to contact their biological parents.

Through two stories we found instances of attempted sexual abuse by stepfathers, and one case of rape by a biological father. The individual was fourteen years old at the time.

The remaining three recollections told the story of functional family relations. One of these included a foster father, but the story indicated a history of caring and acceptance. In all but two cases, maternal relations were unstable. Often, the mother had a passive role in the family, aiming toward a life that discontinued the primary instinct of protecting a child. It is important to note that these women were themselves the victims of abuse within the family, in multiethnic marriages, and it is obvious that they could not conquer their own trauma, which prevented them from dedicating themselves to their children.

The following excerpts exemplify some of the participants' experiences:

I have a mother . . . I have a mom, no dad. Dad's not there, I've never seen him. I'd better never see him or hear from him ever.

When I was little I had a good time, I didn't have any brothers or sisters. Only a mom and dad. They didn't really argue when I was young, but they got divorced when I was in the eighth grade. They killed my old man after the war. They killed my father. They killed him over money.

I haven't lived with my mom or dad, I am the child of divorced parents, they left me when I was six months old. Because my mom is Muslim and my dad Serbian. I grew up with my grandparents, they put me through school. My mom and stepfather lived separately from us, I couldn't live with my stepfather . . . when I came to their house before my brother was born, . . . I mentioned I was going to change my clothes, he opens the door, you know, and "Oh, I didn't know you were there." And that's how it was for a while . . . then I stopped coming.

The absence of an open conversation with my father left its mark, which will influence my future psychological development. When I confront him, his reaction was like, go on back to bed, something like that as far as I remember. Anyways, I was just shrugged off.

Peer Relations

There were significant gender differences when it came to relationships with people in their own age group. Two of the individuals interviewed were female. They described relationships with their peers as meager at best, mentioning that they had one female friend, if any. The role of friends to them was particularly significant; it was their only way of compensating for the emotional deficit caused by a lack of communication with their families, especially with their mothers.

Male subjects, on the other hand, mentioned that their friends belonged to both a subculture and the mainstream population. We found different explanations for belonging to a subculture. There was the aspect of revolt, belonging to the group due to issues of identity, or simply due to an attraction to the activities of the group. It is evident that membership in these groups lasts for an extended period of time, further alienating them from the rest of their peers. An extreme case of this was being friends with children within an orphanage, where the ability to choose with whom you spend your life is gone.

With initiation into drug use, the circle of friends narrowed significantly for those interviewed. From then on, their friends were almost exclusively drug users:

Parallel groups of friends, that I spent time with, that I met up with, well when I started doing drugs more, I started spending less and less time with the people that weren't a part of that world and that's normal, every idiot knows that.

First Love

Stories about first love were told with a different expression and a small smile, even after years had gone by. Regardless of whether their relationships with these people were long or short, it is obvious that they left a very meaningful impression. First experiences with love happened between the ages of fourteen and twenty. This was also the time of initiation into sexual relations. We consider it significant that four of the individuals had an experience with heroin not far from, or as part of experiencing love for the first time. In addition, two individuals are homosexual, and their first partners were of the same sex.

I got married right before the war, somewhere over there, more or less near the end of 1988. To my English teacher. Nine years older than me. I got high with her before we hooked up. It was really simple, drug addicts recognize each other, always.

I fell in love with him and though he wouldn't give it [heroin] to me, I asked him for it. He said no. Once I tried snorting it, I jacked my guts out. I didn't like it the first time . . . I never said that he got me hooked. I wanted to try it because I'm an idiot. You know what I said? If you're gonna kill yourself [by using heroin], I'll kill myself too.

He was a dealer. In order to spend time with him, I bought heroin and threw it away.

War

All of the subjects were of different ages but despite this their life trajectories all included war. Whether during the time that the former Yugoslavia split up or when NATO bombed Serbia in 1999, by telling their life stories it was inevitable that they all included at least one segment of war stories. Other than the stress that was caused by a constant state of danger and a lack of public services such as a police force, war exacerbated many problems, particularly within already weakly integrated and noncohesive families. This was more influential with multiethnic families and families living under multiethnic conditions. War also brought about decreased control within each individual state, and with it a decrease in societal care for young people and family care for children, and more readily available weapons, drugs, and opportunities to commit crime.

Four characteristic examples of wartime experiences are presented. The first concerns a part of the former Yugoslavia that was only indirectly affected by the war, while the next three involve territories that were more directly affected.

Her brother Fuad, me and Fudo were lying down and watching the news. It felt like it was still Yugoslavia. The speakers were Senad Erzefejdzovic, Ljubomir Ljubovic, Ivica Puric. So three nations, multiethnic. And then an argument broke out. Like Mr. President stop your green berettas. Karadjic said, why don't you stop the Chetniks, let him stop that, then Mr. President. . . . And I see clearly how the war's starting, I can hear the shooting outside. And we're inside, lying down and listening to the war start . . . What comes after the war, what then, what . . . Nobody's talking, it's awkward for everybody . . . What you did to them here, what you did to them there.

A mountain. Night, the moon makes it as bright as daytime. You can see the deer running. . . . Two girls tried to escape from Bulgaria, they have light border control there. They shot at those two girls like it was a battle at Neretva, you know, they killed the two girls, who weren't to blame for anything. You should be ashamed, how are you not ashamed?

Then in 1995 I went to Kosovo. Why did I decide to? Drugs. And it's all the same to me, I ride my bike at 3:30 a.m. as the sun is coming up. There's a guy with a broken knee, this guy with no hands, with no legs, I'm riding around on my bicycle . . . All the drugstores are mine, all the morphine you want. And I'm cruising on my bicycle, on drugs and having a good time. You come into whatever house you want and take their drinks, take whatever you want, what do you care? People are running away. I don't care. Up ahead these guys are burning Albanian houses, those guys are burning Serbian houses, burning this, burning that . . . I don't care. 'Cause I've already seen it twice, I saw it in Croatia, I saw it in Bosnia and it's all normal to me, I know what's going on, I know what's going to happen.

So I was in Tuzla during the war, for a while, the first two years, then I was in Sarajevo for a year and that's how I caught shrapnel a couple times, I was injured in the legs twice.

Initiation into Drug Use

The first contact with drugs happened for the participants between the ages of thirteen and twenty, but most at about age sixteen. This corresponds to the survey described above. Glue, marijuana, and prescription medication were listed as the first drugs they came into contact with. Only one girl did not pave her way to heroin with other drugs. Heroin was her primary choice.

Among the male participants, introduction into the heroin scene on average happened at about seventeen years of age, and within their peer group, again corresponding to the survey above. Both females who were interviewed were initiated into heroin use through young men with whom they were romantically involved. The use of heroin significantly affected their life, narrowing the friends in their social circle, and eventually completely ending relations with their family and pushing them toward criminality.

First experiences with heroin use were sometimes positive and sometimes negative, but in any case did not inhibit future use. The participants' whole world quickly narrowed and became concentrated on heroin and how to acquire money to obtain it. Attempts at abstinence and recovery were short-lived. A lack of motivation or the inability to perceive their lives without heroin influenced long years of use. Among the eight interviewed, only one had achieved long-term abstinence (four years, following seven years of heroin addiction). He was then employed, and had a family and a very active social life.

I remember that first time, of course. I thought, I've been waiting for this my whole life. I dreamed of this a long time ago, I've been waiting for this my whole life.

I remember the first time I saw it (heroin). I remember the stench of death, I'd call it like that. I remember the physical experience . . . when he opened the package, I simply felt something . . . It was a thrill. Djole was like: "Did you feel it?" "What was it?" It was the stench of death.

No one is perfect enough not to get hooked on heroin. There is no perfect person that can resist getting hooked on heroin. It can literally find something that is bugging anyone, something that makes any person feel great, something with which anyone could be bought. You will be bought very fast. At the moment you are not aware of what is happening, you are not aware that you sold yourself. You sometimes think about it, when you feel withdrawal symptoms, but you finally become aware of it when you stop using it and when some time passes.

As soon as you get caught in a circuit with the devil (heroin), strange things start happening. You decide to stop using it, you go to the seaside, where you don't know anyone and it shows up the next day. Some incredible guy appears, or dealer calls to bring you some. You don't have a chance. It is always going to find you.

First you start to compromise with yourself. You say ok, I'll do it once a month. Then you do it twice a month, then every weekend and the next second, you are taking it every day.

Criminality

A wide spectrum of reported criminality could not be completely attributed to heroin. A fair amount happened before the first use of heroin. Examples included smuggling cigarettes, committing robberies with underage gangs, violent behavior, selling psychoactive substances, and prostitution. In one very extreme case a murder was committed (explained further below). Motives for such criminal acts included gaining material possessions, rebelling against one's social circle, and lack of acceptance of sexual orientation. Heroin use, however, completely changed the motives for criminality with participants moving between two points—gaining the money for heroin and using it. Crimes specifically attributed to heroin use were robberies and prostitution.

At seventeen years old I had my first robbery. I did it with a sort of bomb, so they didn't want to run after me, to grab me by the arm, instead they shot at me. Then I realized you really shouldn't do that 'cause you can end up losing your head.

I stole and I took, that's how I supported myself. At eighteen years old, in my second robbery we stole 16 million dinars. They quickly arrested us. In jail I befriended a guy from some gang, he died in my arms. He died from heroin.

The following example refers to the murder noted above. The person involved was in a romantic homosexual relationship with the victim. The victim insisted that this individual had to accept his sexual orientation and "come out of the closet" so they could reveal their relationship in public. He rejected this but continued seeing the victim as well as his official girlfriend in their social circle. He defined their relationship as loving and full of common interests. The love he was talking about, however, turned into possessiveness and obsessive persecution.

I took a cable and strangled him . . . I sat there beside him, I don't know, a certain amount of time, five minutes, ten, fifteen minutes, I don't know how long I sat there beside him. So I sat with him without being bothered . . . I felt casual. Without any emotions,

absolutely none. He never protected himself, not this time either.
. . . Before that he told me that he loved me. I looked him in the
eyes when I strangled him.

While he was telling this part of the story, he was expressing
certain forms of sociopathic behavior: manipulating and redirecting
the conversation, shifting all blame onto the victim, and not showing
emotions. He did not seem agitated. It is important to stress that this
is a unique and extreme case. It is included here to give a full view of
the experiences that the interviews uncovered.

Conclusion

There is no universal explanation for addiction to heroin. The reason
lies in a complex range of factors that influence the development of
one's addiction. On the other hand, there are number of factors that
come up in the life stories of most users.

In order to understand the lack of the first memories, we tried
to find a connection between heroin use and memory deficiency.
Heroin is a substance that causes memory deficiency, causing
certain information to be inaccessible.[6] Merely applying any findings
regarding the effects of heroin on brain activity, however, would be
inadequate in this case. The unavailability of first memories can also
be caused by various influences such as powerful systematic defenses
including suppression, or the use of other psychoactive substances.
As was previously shown, only one individual interviewed had
particularly vivid early memories. This individual had spent his
childhood in a functional family, so the aforementioned memories
were associated with strong emotions.

Even though there are discrepancies regarding the influence of
the family setting on boys and girls during the periods of childhood
and adolescence, the general conclusion is that children from
single-parent homes, as with step-parent families, show lower self-
esteem and more symptoms of loneliness and anxiety, as well as
other dysfunctional behavior on the social and psychological levels.[7]
Parents' lack of attachment and their nonresponsiveness to the needs
of a child are risk factors that, depending on other factors, can have
differing effects. As we found through the stories of these individuals,
a need to develop parental attachment existed for many years, and
therefore, as adults, the participants yearned to compensate for this

missed period and to come to terms with their own emotional injury during their childhood.

The strategic process of selecting peers is based on certain attributes, such as similar interests, personal skills, attitudes, and behavioral predispositions.[8] Initiation into drug use happened within peer groups for all the males interviewed. For the females it was through an intimate relationship. During adolescence, young women are more prone to forming intimate relationships with their peers than young men are. In the absence of peer attachment, the potential for emotional investment emerges with first love. As with boys, drug use was seen as an accepted norm.

Regarding the social context in which these interactions take place, affiliation with a subculture was manifested in persistent clashes with accepted norms. The social context and the norms changed during the war. A system of values formed in these conditions, allowing for involvement in illegal activity, which in turn became "normal" and socially accepted. A wide spectrum of criminality is not exclusively tied to heroin use and may also be seen as the product of accepting this system of values during the period of war.

In society, drug users are, for the most part, represented as weak, with no moral values, rebellious, and incapable of fitting in. On the other hand, it is expected that these "weak" and "bad" people should change and become useful members of society. Ignoring the risk factors that influence personality development, as well as the lack of acceptance of heroin addiction as an illness, puts all of the blame on the individual. Heroin addiction is often differentiated from other illnesses in that the individual is seen as "choosing" to become ill. From this, it follows that it is up to you to decide whether or not you will be "cured."

Considering the life stories above and the multitude of factors involved, the question that arises is whether there is enough understanding and support from the family and wider social environment to assist those who decide to seek help. Based on previous experience, in most cases, such support is either unavailable or fictitious. As much as the user's personality may be "weak" and unable to fight against addiction, the personalities of people in the user's closer and wider social context are just as weak and unable to accept the stigma that their child, sibling, partner, or friend carries. Conservative views and the ignorance of society in Serbia are the main causes of intolerance toward drug users. The question that needs to be answered is whether heroin, as a substance, is so addictive that it makes dependence almost incurable, or the reaction of our social environment makes it seem that way. This is reflected in a common phrase used in Serbia: *Once a junkie, always a junkie.*

Endnotes

1. For example, *Rapid Assessment and Response Guide on Psychoactive Substance Use and Especially Vulnerable Young People* (Geneva: World Health Organization, 1998).
2. See, for example, Eurasian Harm Reduction Network, *Young People and Injecting Drug Use in Selected Countries of Central and Eastern Europe*, 2009, www. harm-reduction.org/library/1301-young-people-and-injecting-drug-use-in-selected-countries-of-central-and-eastern-europe.html.
3. [See also chapters 12 and 13.—Ed.]
4. These data were gathered from a small number of participants, but we are confident that the findings will not stray far from the conclusions of a broader study, with it being equally unlikely for the existing seven categories to be inadequate.
5. A microsystem, consists of complex relations between the person and the immediate setting (e,g., home, school, workplace). See R.E. Muuss, *Theories of Adolescence,* 6th ed. (New York: McGraw-Hill, 2006).
6. F. Nyberg, "The Role of the Somatotrophic Axis in Neuroprotection and Neuroregeneration of the Addictive Brain," Department of Pharmaceutical Biosciences, Division of Biological Research on Drug Dependence, Uppsala University, S-75124 Uppsala, Sweden.
7. N. Garnefski and R.F. Diekstra, "Adolescents from One Parent, Stepparent and Intact Families: Emotional Problems and Suicide Attempts," *Journal of Adolescence* 20, no. 2 (April 1997): 201–8.
8. T.J. Dishion, G.R. Patterson, M. Stoolmiller, and M.L. Skinner, "Family, School and Behavioral Antecedents to Early Adolescent Involvement with Antisocial Peers," *Developmental Psychology* 27 (1991): 172–80.

16. Why Should Children Suffer? Children's Palliative Care and Pain Management

by Joan Marston

There can be no keener revelation of a society's soul than the way in which it treats its children.

Nelson Mandela[1]

Introduction

Children's palliative care is a professional and compassionate response to suffering caused by life-limiting or life-threatening conditions. It is a combination of excellent assessment of the child's body, mind, and spirit; management of pain and other distressing symptoms; and emotional, developmental, spiritual, and social support of the child and the family that continues into the bereavement period. Many of these children, with conditions such as cancer, AIDS, neurological conditions, genetic anomalies, metabolic conditions, severe disabilities, organ failure, and neonatal conditions, experience pain throughout the course of the disease, and often more severely toward the end of life.

Children cannot make pain an existential issue or understand the cause and effect of why they are experiencing it. When a child has pain, that is his or her whole world, and there is no understanding, just a desire to be comforted and pain free. They also cannot advocate for themselves and need a compassionate community to see their pain and feel outrage at their neglect. Older children may have the courage and the opportunity to speak on their own behalf, but what of the neonate, the infant, and the young child?

Palliative care is an answer to childhood pain. It is not just end-of-life care, or care when "nothing more can be done," but should be available from the time of diagnosis of any life-limiting or life-threatening condition, and can be given alongside potentially curative treatment. Treatment of pain is an essential element of palliative care, and access to medicines for this is crucial. Chronic pain is common in cancer and in AIDS. Research has shown that between 60 percent and 90 percent of people with advanced cancer will experience moderate to severe pain,[2] as will about 80 percent of people with advanced AIDS.[3] While there are at present no similar studies that involve only children, we assume that the percentage of children with pain would be similar to that of adults. While they have many elements in common, however, the World Health Organization recognizes palliative care for children as different from that for adults.[4]

The special vulnerabilities of children, their right to health and freedom from inhuman or degrading treatment are recognized worldwide, as children are born into a world where most countries have ratified the UN Convention on the Rights of the Child; where the world is striving to reach the Millennium Development Goals, a number of which influence the health and development of the child; where the UN and strong international partners have a Global Strategy for Newborn, Maternal and Child Health;[5] and where most countries have special laws and policies protecting children and their rights. But in almost every part of the world, children continue to suffer with life-limiting conditions and untreated moderate to severe pain. This chapter provides a brief overview of the global state of child palliative care before considering the many barriers to improving access to controlled medicines for pain treatment, including the impact of overly restrictive or burdensome narcotics laws. It goes on to highlight the human rights case for addressing this issue, and sets out a series of recommendations necessary to ensure that children in pain have the chance of being free from unnecessary suffering.

The Global State of Child Palliative Care

The good news is that most pain can be controlled with relatively simple-to-prescribe and inexpensive drugs, all of which are on the World Health Organization's Model Formulary for Children (2010) and updated Essential Medicines for Children (2010).[6] The WHO Pain Ladder has been used as the universal guide to the management of pain, and has three steps that are followed as the pain increases.[7] At each step of the ladder, adjuvant drugs (drugs that enhance the effect of opioids and other analgesics) can be given alongside the pain-relieving medication.

Step 1 is nonopioids such as paracetamol and nonsteroidal anti-inflammatory medicines.

Step 2 is weak opioids such as codeine and tramadol.

Step 3 is strong opioids such as morphine.

All of these drugs are relatively inexpensive and easy to use. The WHO Ladder has been shown to be effective in widely different parts of the world,[8] but it cannot be implemented when any of the steps are missing because there are no medicines for that step.

The bad news is that child palliative care is severely underdeveloped worldwide. An as yet unpublished research project by Caprice Knapp of the University of Florida, Michael Wright of the International Observatory for End-of Life Care in Lancaster, England, and the Scientific Committee of the International Children's Palliative Care Network (ICPCN), carried out in 2010, indicates that, at present pediatric palliative care development in countries can be assessed at one of four levels:

Level 1   No known hospice or palliative care activity for children;

Level 2   Some capacity-building activity;

Level 3   Localized pediatric hospice and palliative care provision with some access to morphine and other palliative care drugs;

Level 4   Reaching a level of integration with mainstream health providers, with access to morphine and other palliative care drugs.[9]

Of the 192 member states of the United Nations, the researchers found that 66 percent were at Level 1; 18 percent were at Level 2; 10 percent at Level 3 and a mere 6 percent were at Level 4. Only in 16 percent of the world's countries would children have any chance of receiving palliative care that could include access to pain relief.

Europe has the best spread of palliative care programs for children, with 27.9 percent of countries at Level 3 and 11.6 percent at Level 4. Oceania has the highest percentage of countries at level 4 with 14.3 percent, but has no countries at Levels 2 and 3, and 85 percent at Level 1. Africa, with the highest burden of disease and 2 million children infected with HIV, has only one country at Level 4, South Africa, and 83 percent of countries at Level 1.

The United Kingdom is probably the most successful country in the world in implementing palliative care for children. The first children's hospice, Helen House, was started in 1982 by Sister Frances Dominica, in Oxford, and the movement has since spread across the country. The UK has two national associations working closely together and very effectively to promote children's palliative care—the Association for Children's Palliative Care ACT and Children's Hospice UK. Government has supported the movement and committed relatively large sums of funding, providing some funding to children's hospices each year. Pediatric palliative care as a discipline and as a speciality has been taught at Cardiff University and Great Ormond Street with University College London for many years. The first True Colours Chair of Palliative Care for Children and Young people was established in London in 2009; and the community in the UK is very supportive of the children's hospices. Children's hospices are places where children receive high-quality palliative care and respite, in beautiful child- and youth-friendly environments with wonderful activities and well-trained and qualified staff and volunteers.

Scotland has an excellent model of a countrywide, well-managed children's hospice movement: Children's Hospice of Scotland, or CHAS, as it is fondly known. CHAS carried out a national survey to identify the number of children needing palliative care in 2002, assessed the requirements to care for these children, and built two beautiful units (Rachel House and Robin House) to provide respite and end-of-life care for them. Both houses have outreach teams working in the community, and there is a home-care team working in the north of the country.

But it is not just rich nations where such positive developments have taken place. Belarus has a national network of branches of the Belarusian Children's Hospice. Uniquely, in this country, the children's hospice movement was responsible for developing the adult hospice movement. Poland also has an extensive network of children's hospice services throughout the country and a strong chaplaincy program. South Africa has expanded the number of children's palliative care programs from six in 2007 to 62 in 2010 thanks to the vision of the Hospice Palliative Care Association of South Africa to implement a pediatric portfolio with a national manager; the support of international donors; and the acceptance of the importance of palliative care programs for children by the member hospices.

And yet, with all that, many children are still not receiving palliative care. Why are there still barriers when, clearly, so much has been achieved?

"Mind the Gap!"

If you have traveled on the London Underground, you will have heard the voice over the loudspeakers continually warning commuters to "mind the gap" between the train and the platform. In the children's palliative care community we are aware of the gap in development between adult and pediatric palliative care. St. Christopher's Hospice in London, the first modern hospice for adults, was established in 1967, while Helen House, the first children's hospice was opened in 1982—a fifteen-year gap that we are working to close. Indeed, it must be closed if we believe that children have the same right as adults to good palliative care.

When the development of children's palliative care was compared with the development of (mainly adult) palliative care in the world as assessed by the International Observatory for End-of-Life Care, the disparity was highlighted:[10]

Level	Observatory	Pediatric
I	33%	66%
2	18%	18%
3	34%	10%
4	15%	6%

Even in the palliative care world, a world known for its compassion and commitment to the relief of suffering, children have been neglected

In the WHO publication *Achieving Balance in Opioid Control Policy*, it states that "Most, if not all, pain due to cancer could be relieved if we implemented existing knowledge and treatments. . . . There is a treatment gap: it is the difference between what can be done, and what is done about cancer pain."[11] This statement could equally refer to all chronic pain in children. The treatment gap—the difference between what is and what should be in the treatment of pain in children—can take many forms. When countries do not accurately assess the level of need, and order stock accordingly, there will be a gap in provision for pain management and the danger of too little stock to treat pain. When countries provide stock only to one or very few hospitals in the country as in Cameroon and Tanzania, patients living far from those centers will have an unacceptable gap between pain being diagnosed and pain being treated. When there is no effective supply chain there will be a gap between procurement and supply. And when pain medications are available only at limited sites in a country and families need to travel great distances to obtain the prescribed medicine, there will be significant gaps in accessibility.

So how do we close the treatment gap and go on to ensure access to all children in need?

Barriers to the Provision of Palliative Care and Pain Management

To make palliative care work, a range of complex components are required simultaneously:
- Access to opioids and palliative care drugs.
- International and national laws and policies that support access to these medicines.
- Government support for palliative care.
- National Association that supports pediatric palliative care.
- Training courses for professionals, caregivers and families.
- Donor support.
- Model children's palliative care programs for training and mentorship.
- A national advocacy strategy.
- Hospice and palliative care organizations that include children's palliative care.

With all of these components in place, a child has a *chance* of receiving palliative care and having chronic pain managed. But considerable barriers block the way. They are legion and operate at the local, national, and international levels:
- Intergovernmental forums for drug policy discussions that have neglected access to controlled essential medicines.
- Governments that do not recognize the need for palliative care and opioid availability to treat pain, and that see palliative care as an unaffordable luxury, not an essential part of the health-care system.

- Lack of health policies that include palliative care.
- Health systems that do not include palliative care.
- Failure of governments to order sufficient opioids to meet the need in the country.
- Failure of supply chains for opioids.
- Failure to take seriously international legal obligations to ensure access to medicines.
- Overly restrictive narcotics laws and regulations.
- Failure of health-care professionals to prescribe opioids, or underprescribing of opioid dosages.
- Training of undergraduate health-care professionals that does not include palliative care and has little content on pain management.
- Health professionals who have not received any training in palliative care and pain management and still have fears concerning the use of opioids, addiction, and respiratory suppression.
- Community members who retain fears of using opioids and equate the use of morphine with death.
- Beliefs that neonates and babies do not feel pain.
- Traditional health practitioners who use traditional medicines and block the use of opioids.
- Social barriers that prevent children from accessing palliative care and pain relief, such as poverty, orphanhood, homelessness, and vulnerable caregivers such as the elderly or youth.
- Traditional adult-focused palliative care practitioners who do not recognize the different palliative care needs of children, or are not trained to provide palliative care to children.
- National palliative care associations that do not ensure that children receive the same attention as adults.

We need to identify and fully understand these and other barriers that prevent children from receiving the care they require before we can move forward. But many cannot see the need, or understand the human effects of the word "pain." The issues above seem clinical and legalistic when read in isolation. It is therefore vitally important to illustrate the importance to children of surmounting these obstacles.

A Tale of Two Children (and Two Countries)

Bongani's[12] story in Bloemfontein, South Africa

Bloemfontein is the judicial capital of South Africa, situated in the center of the country in the Free State province. It is home to one of South Africa's few children's hospices, St. Nicholas Children's Hospice, which has a children's in-patient unit, Sunflower House, and a large home-based care outreach program.

South Africa's consumption of opioids is below the world mean but is still the highest in sub-Saharan Africa.[13] Morphine and all basic palliative care drugs are on the Essential Medicines List for the country.[14] South Africa has training programs for doctors, nurses, social workers, and spiritual care workers in palliative care and, more recently, pediatric palliative care. While there is as yet no adopted national policy on palliative care, a policy has been developed, and the government sits together with a number of national organizations on a National Alliance for Access to Palliative Care.

Meet Bongani—she is nine years old, diagnosed HIV positive when she was five and presented with severe pain in both feet and in parts of both hands when she was eight. Bongani was one of the 14.1 million children orphaned by AIDS in sub-Saharan Africa, and cared for by her elderly grandmother who first took Bongani to a traditional healer who was unable to manage her pain.

When Bongani came to the district hospital she was in severe pain, and both feet, two fingers on her right hand, and three on her left hand, were cold and blue. She was diagnosed with a rare circulatory problem in her extremities, and with advanced HIV disease. Bongani was seen by a medical doctor who was trained in pediatric palliative care and who was also the medical director of St. Nicholas Children's Hospice and Sunflower House, where Bongani was admitted for pain management and palliative care. Cared for by a multiprofessional team trained in pediatric palliative care, Bongani was started on antiretroviral therapy, oral morphine and other palliative care drugs, and other nonpharmacological interventions such as play therapy and massage. Bongani's pain was well-controlled and she was able to play with the other children and even go out for special treats.

However, the hands and feet did not improve and Bongani needed an amputation of half of both feet, and the affected fingers of both hands. She was supported throughout the time in the hospital, and the palliative care team ensured that she continued on her morphine and had adequate pain control. Her grandmother was kept informed of her progress and brought in to visit her granddaughter.

Bongani lived for two months after the amputations, played happily with her friends until the day she died, and died peacefully in Sunflower House, without pain, and with her grandmother and the hospice chaplain next to her. Before she died she spoke openly to the chaplain of her mother and her wish to be with her, and said that she did not fear dying.

Where opioids are available and on the Essential Medicines List and this is linked to a pediatric palliative care team whose members understand the correct use of opioids, with a doctor trained in pediatric palliative care, a child's pain and suffering can be effectively relieved and that child can enjoy and participate in life. But all elements need to be present for this to succeed. Having opioids without staff trained to use them correctly, or having trained staff without access to opioids will leave children in pain.

Michael's Story in Kisumu, Kenya

Michael[15] is eight years old, orphaned by AIDS, and living with his elderly aunt in Kisumu. He has sickle cell anemia, a life-limiting blood disorder characterized by episodes of severe pain.

The over-the-counter pain medicines that his aunt buys for him are not strong enough to relieve the pain. This causes him to lose out on schooling and he is not able to play with his friends. Michael says the pain makes him unhappy and at times he wishes he could die to get away from it. Michael is suffering in his body, mind, and spirit. Good pediatric palliative care with access to oral morphine to control his pain would give Michael back his childhood and improve his quality of life.

Kenya is a country with morphine on its Essential Medicines List[16] and a strong national palliative care association, the Kenyan Hospice and Palliative Care Association, which has made big strides in the development of palliative care in the country. Unfortunately, as with many countries in the world, government policies actually block access to morphine for pain management. According to a recent report by Human Rights Watch, *the Kenyan government has erected legal and regulatory barriers to using morphine to treat severe pain. The Kenyan narcotics law focuses on the illegal uses of morphine and other opioids and makes illicit possession punishable by life imprisonment and a heavy fine. There are exceptions for medical use, but no detailed guidelines about lawful possession by patients and health care workers. . . . Consequently, the medicine is unavailable at the vast majority of public hospitals in Kenya, in contravention of the country's international legal obligations.*[17]

In other words, the government is more concerned with controlling drug trafficking than with ensuring a supply of morphine for pain management. Added to this, pediatric palliative care is almost nonexistent, although with some interest and the support of the national association for development (Level 2). And there is inadequate training of health-care professionals in pain management of children. Meanwhile children suffer unnecessarily—Michael continues in pain and suffers from depression.

International Commitments and National Narcotics Laws

International Obligations Relating to Drug Control

The major barriers to children's receiving pain management and palliative care lie with national governments operating at home and on the international stage. There must be political will and an unwillingness to stand back and watch children suffer. But governments, especially in poorer countries, often prioritize other public-health emergencies, and fail to see that pain and suffering *is* itself a public-health emergency. They are quick to sign international conventions that protect human rights and require access to medicines, but slow to live up to these obligations. On the global level, the "international community" has been far more concerned with recreational use and supply reduction than with ensuring access to essential medicines.

The Single Convention on Narcotic Drugs was adopted in 1961 and has to date been ratified by almost every state in the world. It is a treaty best known for its approach to "illicit" uses of narcotic drugs, but in its opening paragraphs the treaty also proclaimed that narcotic drugs were "indispensable for the relief of pain and suffering." While morphine is strictly controlled under the international drug control system, the obligation relating to palliative care could not be clearer. States' parties were instructed to ensure they had sufficient stock to meet the medical needs in each country.[18] The International Narcotics Control Board (INCB) was mandated to monitor this obligation. However, in 2008, the WHO estimated that despite the international acceptance of the Single Convention, 80 percent of the world's population still had little or no access to pain relief.[19] For the past twenty years, the WHO and the INCB have reminded governments of their obligations to ensure access to medicines for pain treatment, but with little effect on children. Meanwhile, vast sums have been spent on law enforcement and supply reduction in the decades since the adoption of the Single Convention, eclipsing by far the efforts to ensure access to essential medicines. While the shortfall in access is mainly in middle- to low-income countries, it is not exclusively so. The ICPCN is, in 2010, advising some very high-income countries to develop their first children's palliative care services.

Opiophobia and the "Chilling Effect" of Restrictive Drug Control Laws

Many people fear that morphine may be addictive, and believe that it is only given when the patient is near death. Health professionals often state that they fear morphine will suppress respiration, and show a lack of understanding of use of opioids in the treatment of chronic pain. This became clear in Human Rights Watch's study in Kenya in 2010, according to which:

> *In Kenya, morphine is widely viewed not as an essential, low-cost tool to alleviate pain, but as dangerous. . . . Until recently, medical and nursing schools taught that morphine must only be administered to the terminally ill, because of unwarranted fear that it would cause addiction, and hospitals often only offer the drug when curative treatment has failed. . . . Even at the seven public hospitals where morphine is available, doctors and nurses are sometimes reluctant to give it to a child, because they believe it amounts to giving up on the fight to save the child's life, and because unwarranted fears of addiction remain.*[20]

For many years messages about opiates have, for the most part, been rooted in scare tactics aimed at deterring recreational use and preventing addiction. While that aim has not been achieved, the fears instilled in relation to these drugs remain. Those fears are closely related to narcotics laws that can act as barriers to full access to palliative care medicines. In the 1961 Single Convention, within which access to essential controlled drugs is included as an obligation, addiction to drugs is referred to as an "evil," threatening the fabric of society.[21] There is certainly an imbalance within the text, and this is reflected in international drug control efforts in recent decades. In Kenya, narcotics laws have had a "chilling effect" on access to palliative care medicines. As documented by Human Rights Watch, Kenya's 1994 Narcotic Drugs and Psychotropic Substances Control Act (Narcotic Drugs Act) regulates morphine and other opioid pain medicines and is widely seen among health-care professionals as prohibiting these drugs. Heavy penalties are imposed for illicit possession, and, for medical workers, this can mean a loss of their license. According to the Kenyan Pharmacy and Poisons Board, "Due to the punitive nature of the 1994 Act, most providers have shied away from selling opioids."[22]

While morphine is safe, effective, easy to use, and usually inexpensive, there is the potential for abuse. For this reason morphine is a controlled medicine, and the manufacture of morphine, its distribution and dispensing are controlled internationally and regulated in each country. But governments can and often do order relatively small amounts of morphine, inadequate to meet the need for pain control in their country, as they fear that it will be diverted for illegal use. This is despite the fact that the INCB states that diversion is relatively rare. Each government has a responsibility to ensure the safekeeping of morphine, to prevent or minimize diversion, but those regulations also need to facilitate the medical use of morphine and not prevent its availability and its use. Where governments see control of illegal trafficking and diversion as more important than the relief of suffering, children will continue to suffer. We must set our priorities straight.

Access to Medicines for Pain Treatment as a Human Right

Recently human rights monitors have increased their focus on access to medicines and pain treatment. The argument is, for the most part, made under two headings—the right to health, and freedom from torture or cruel, inhuman, and degrading treatment. Both, of course, are recognized in the UN Convention on the Rights of the Child as well as other international human rights treaties. Nongovernmental organizations such as Human Rights Watch and the Open Society

Foundations have made the issue a focused campaign, while UN human rights mechanisms have also begun looking more closely at the problem.

In 2009 the UN Human Rights Council adopted a resolution calling on member states to ensure access to medicines as a component of the right to the highest attainable standard of health.[23] This echoed the view of the UN Committee on Economic, Social and Cultural Rights that access to medicines is a core minimum obligation of the right to health[24] as well as previous resolutions of the UN Economic and Social Council.[25] In October 2010, the UN Special Rapporteur on the right to health, Anand Grover, submitted a report to the UN General Assembly in which he recommended that all states "amend laws, regulations and policies to increase access to controlled essential medicines"[26] in order to "improve the quality of life of patients diagnosed with life-threatening illnesses through prevention and relief of suffering."[27]

In December 2008 the UN Special Rapporteur on torture and other cruel, inhuman, and degrading treatment or punishment, Manfred Nowak, together with the UN special rapporteur on the right to health, wrote the following to the UN Commission on Narcotic Drugs in the lead-up to the adoption of the 2009 political declaration and plan of action on drug control:

Governments also have an obligation to take measures to protect people under their jurisdiction from inhuman and degrading treatment. Failure of governments to take reasonable measures to ensure accessibility of pain treatment, which leaves millions of people (including children) to suffer needlessly from severe and often prolonged pain, raises questions whether they have adequately discharged their obligation.[28]

In 2010, the commission, for the first time in its 53-year history, adopted a resolution on access to controlled medicines, calling on member states to "identify the impediments in their countries to the access and adequate use of opioid analgesics for the treatment of pain and to take steps to improve the availability of those narcotic drugs for medical purposes." It should be noted, however, that the fear of diversion and addiction was still very clear, and included in the very title of the resolution.[29]

The Open Society Foundations have taken up the challenge of access to palliative care drugs as part of a new campaign called the

"Campaign to Stop Torture in Health Care." Many children's palliative care practitioners and the ICPCN are supporting this campaign as we believe children who experience inadequate pain relief for both chronic and procedural pain are subjected to inhuman and degrading treatment. According to the Open Society Foundations:

at a time when many governments are regressing on their health commitments, using a torture framework to address human rights violations in health settings mandates immediate state action to stop them. A torture framework provides health advocates with an opportunity to connect with new, potentially powerful partners, including mainstream human rights and anti-torture organizations that may neglect vulnerable populations subjected to torture and ill treatment in health care settings, and traditional civil and political rights organizations that have yet to engage in health and human rights issues. A torture framework also places responsibility for patients' suffering where it belongs: with governments, who too often place health workers in a dynamic where they are enlisted in violations of human rights. In practical terms, the Campaign to Stop Torture in Health Care is not a campaign against individual health workers as such, but against the failure of governments to protect all people (patients and providers) in health care settings.[30]

These are strong statements, and we hope that governments will be forced to listen and to act accordingly; and that children will be among the beneficiaries of this campaign.

A Country with a Vision: Progress in Uganda

Uganda is a country in East Africa with a population of 31 million, of whom 1 million people are infected with HIV. Much of the population lives in poverty and in rural areas, and more than 50 percent of the population is under the age of eighteen.

Uganda has a government that recognized that its people had the right to palliative care and pain relief, and it became the first country in Africa to recognize palliative care as an essential part of their health service. Working together with a visionary team of advocates from Hospice Africa Uganda, and in collaboration with the WHO and nongovernmental organizations, Uganda developed a five-year National Palliative Care Strategy that included the development of nurses and clinical officers who would be able to prescribe oral morphine, and looked at introducing drug regulations to promote an adequate supply of morphine that could reach those in pain quickly and effectively. Along with most African countries, the number of health-care workers is low and the country has lost many of these professionals to more developed countries. Therefore, this was an innovative and effective way of increasing the number of prescribers to meet the need for pain control.

While there are still challenges to the implementation of this strategy, Uganda has increased access to oral morphine for adults and children, and become a model for other African countries. South Africa has a regulation at government level, supported by the South African Nursing Council, to allow nurses trained in palliative care and prescribing, to prescribe and dispense all palliative care medicines.

Conclusion and Recommendations for Action

Children and adolescents with life-limiting conditions have very specific palliative care needs that are often different from those of adults.

If the physical, emotional, social, spiritual, and developmental needs of these children and adolescents are to be met, the caregivers require special knowledge and skills.

We ask that the voices of these children and adolescents be heard, respected, and acknowledged as part of the expression of palliative care worldwide.

The ICPCN Statement of Korea on Palliative Care for Children, 2005

How do we close the treatment gap? How do we ensure access for all children in need to palliative care and pain treatment? We must start with the belief that the suffering of a child is unacceptable and that this can and must be changed. From there, we have much work to do:

- We need to continue to advocate for the rights of each child to relief of pain—with governments, educational institutions for health care providers, donors, medical and nursing associations, palliative care organisations, drug suppliers, and international agencies—working together with organisations that are advocating to improve opioid availability.

- The voice of children themselves should be the most powerful voice in that movement. It is, however, seldom heard.
- All health care workers must receive training in palliative care for children as an integral part of their undergraduate training. This training must include pain management and use of opioids; as well as assessment of pain, and communication with children.
- Governments must be held responsible for setting in place properly funded policies and procedures to ensure an adequate supply of opioids, especially oral morphine.
- These policies and procedures must take precedence over concerns about diversion (which is, in any case, rare).
- Drug control laws that restrict access to opiates for palliative care must be amended to ensure that they do not operate as a barrier to the relief of suffering.
- Where there is a lack of doctors to prescribe, the government should look at alternative models, such as nurse prescribing (e.g. as in Uganda).
- Prescription procedures should be simple and not impede access to pain relief.
- Tools used for assessing pain in children should be available, simple to use, culturally acceptable and be used correctly.
- Donors must be encouraged to provide funding for palliative care for children—at present very few do so.
- Manufacturers must be encouraged to develop child-friendly formulations.

The UN Commission on Narcotic Drugs must direct more of its attention to this issue, reflecting the true balance of its mandate.

In the words of the Beatles ballad, we have been on a "long and winding road" to get where we are in developing palliative care for children. The road ahead promises to be long and winding as well, with many obstacles along the way before we reach our vision of quality palliative care for all children wherever in the world they are. We acknowledge our failings in not advocating as vociferously as we should, whether with governments, international bodies, other nongovernmental organizations, or within the palliative care community itself. And we end with words from the community we work for, a child who had pain and who received good palliative care, morphine, and supportive therapies. Rosie is six years old, with an osteosarcoma:

"I was sad and cried because I had pain like a knife in my leg. Now I have the pain medicine and the kind nurse to visit me, I can sing again, even if I can't dance"

Endnotes

1. Statement made by Nelson Mandela to the media on the launch of the Nelson Mandela Children's Fund. 6 May 1996.
2. K. Foley et al., "Pain Control for People with Cancer and AIDS," in *Disease Control Priorities in Developing Countries*, 2d ed., ed. Dean T. Jamison et al., 981–94 (New York: Oxford University Press, 2006), 982.
3. Ibid.
4. World Health Organization, *Palliative Care for Children*, 2002, www.who.int/cancer/palliative/definition/.
5. World Health Organization, *UN Global Strategy for Women's and Children's Health*, 2010, www.who.int/pmnch/activities/jointactionplan/en/.
6. World Health Organization, *Model Formulary for Children* (Geneva, 2010), 18–25.
7. World Health Organization, *Cancer Pain Relief and Palliative Care for Children* (Geneva, 1998), 24–25.
8. J. Amery, *Children's Palliative Care in Africa* (Oxford: Oxford University Press, 2009), 115.
9. C. Knapp et al., unpublished research, ICPCN, 2010.
10. Ibid.
11. World Health Organization, *Achieving Balance in National Opioid Control Policy* (Geneva 2000), 1.
12. Bongani is not her real name.
13. Pain and Policy Study Group, University of Wisconsin, *Afro Regional Morphine Consumption 2008*, www.painpolicy.wisc.edu/internat/opioid_data.htr/.
14. Department of Health, *Standard Treatment Guidelines and Essential Drugs List for South Africa, Hospital Level Paediatrics* (Pretoria: National Department of Health, South Africa, 2006), 373–78, www.doh.gov.za/docs/factsheets/pharma/paediatrics/part1.pdf.
15. Michael is not his real name.
16. Human Rights Watch, *Needless Pain: Government Failure to Provide Palliative Care for Children in Kenya*, New York, September 9, 2010, 6.
17. Ibid., 8.
18. Preamble, Single Convention on Narcotic Drugs, March 30, 1961, 520 U.N.T.S. 204.
19. WHO Briefing Note, *Access to Controlled Medications Programme* (Geneva, 2008).
20. Human Rights Watch, *Needless Pain*, 8.
21. Preamble, Single Convention on Narcotic Drugs 1961.
22. Human Rights Watch, *Needless Pain*, 47, 48.
23. Human Rights Council, Resolution 12/24 *Access to Medicine in the Context of the Right of Everyone to the Enjoyment of the Highest Attainable Standard of Physical and Mental Health*, UN Doc No. A/HRC/RES/12/24, October 2, 2009.

24. UN Committee on Economic, Social and Cultural Rights, *General Comment No. 14: The Right to the Highest Attainable Standard of Health*, UN Doc. No. E/C.12/2000/4, August 11, 2000.
25. UN Committee on Economic, Social and Cultural Rights, Resolution 2005/25 E/2005/INF/2/Add.1, 70.
26. Anand Grover, *Report of the UN Special Rapporteur on the Right of Everyone to the Highest Attainable Standard of Physical and Mental Health*, UN Doc. No. A/65/255, August 6, 2010, para. 76.
27. Ibid., para. 43.
28. M. Nowak and A. Grover, Letter to the UN Commission on Narcotic Drugs, December 8, 2008, www.ihra.net/contents/329/.
29. UN Commission on Narcotic Drugs, *Promoting Adequate Availability of Internationally Controlled Licit Drugs for Medical and Scientific Purposes While Preventing Their Diversion and Abuse*, Resolution 53/4, E/CN.7/2010/18.
30. Open Society Foundations, *Campaign to Stop Torture in Health Care*, Concept Note (New York: January 2010).
31. International Children's Palliative Care Network, www.icpcn.org.uk.

Discussion Questions

1. "Drug addiction is a choice." Discuss with reference to children and adolescents.

2. What are the differences in the ways young boys and young girls begin using drugs? What are the implications for early intervention?

3. To what extent are laws and policies relating to drug use driven by morality? How can this be reconciled with scientific evidence-based responses?

4. The majority of young people use drugs recreationally. What are the consequences for this majority of focusing policy on problematic use? What might be involved in a harm reduction response to recreational drug use?

5. Fletcher argues that random school drug testing does more harm than good. What are the harms he identifies and what is the potential "gain" intended by such policies? Is there a hierarchy?

6. It is now a greater imperative to ensure access to controlled drugs for medicinal purposes than to restrict access for recreational use. Discuss.

CONTRIBUTORS

Damon Barrett (editor) is a cofounder and Project Director of the International Centre on Human Rights and Drug Policy. He is currently Senior Human Rights Analyst at Harm Reduction International in London.

Atal Ahmadzai is currently working as research officer at the Center for Policy and Human Development, Kabul University, Afghanistan.

Jovana Arsenijevic is the coordinator of the Get Connected! project run by the nongovernmental organization Veza, a program specially tailored for young injecting drug users in Belgrade, Serbia.

Aram Barra is a youth activist working in HIV/AIDS and harm reduction issues in Latin America. He is currently Projects Director of Espolea, a youth-led, human rights organization based in Mexico.

Gretchen Burns Bergman is Executive Director and cofounder of A New PATH (Parents for Addiction Treatment and Healing), based in California. She served as State Chairperson for Proposition 36, mandating treatment instead of incarceration for nonviolent drug offenders.

Catherine Cook is Senior Analyst for Public Health Policy and Research at Harm Reduction International in London.

Amy Druker works with the Pathways to Healthy Families Program at The Jean Tweed Centre, Toronto, Canada, providing outreach services and support to pregnant and parenting women who use drugs.

Jennifer Fleetwood finished her PhD on women in the international drug trade in 2009, and is in the process of publishing her research. She is a currently a lecturer in criminology at the University of Kent in the UK.

Adam Fletcher is a lecturer in sociology and social policy at the London School of Hygiene and Tropical Medicine, Britain's national school of public health.

Asmin Fransiska is a lecturer and Vice Dean at the Faculty of Law, Atma Jaya University, Jakarta, Indonesia. She is also coordinator of the Indonesian Coalition for Drug Policy Reform.

Erik D. Fritsvold is an assistant professor in the Crime, Justice, Law & Society concentration in the Sociology Department at the University of San Diego, and coauthor of *Dorm Room Dealers: Drugs and the Privileges of Race and Class.*

Michelle Gueraldi is a human rights lawyer and lecturer in international law based in Rio de Janeiro, Brazil.

Ricky Gunawan is Program Director of the Community Legal Aid Institute (LBH Masyarakat), based in Jakarta, Indonesia.

Jess Hunter-Bowman, Associate Director at Witness for Peace, is an expert on U.S. foreign policy in Latin America with a focus on Colombia.

Daniel Joloy is a human rights researcher working at Espolea, a youth-led organization based in Mexico. He also collaborates with Amnesty International Mexico, being responsible for the Dialogue with Authorities Program.

Kathleen Kenny works with the COUNTERfit Harm Reduction Program at South Riverdale Community Health Centre, Toronto, Canada, on community-development initiatives and wellness programming for people who use drugs and have mental-health struggles.

Christopher Kuonqui is currently Senior Policy Adviser to the United Nations Development Programme Sudan Country Office based in Khartoum, and recently served as policy research adviser to the Center for Policy and Human Development in Kabul.

Ajeng Larasati is assistant manager on legal aid and human rights at the Community Legal Aid Institute (LBH Masyarakat), based in Jakarta, Indonesia. She focuses on drug law and policy and has been involved in the organization's casework on drug-related offenses.

Joan Marston is chair of the International Children's Palliative Care Network and is based in South Africa.

A. Rafik Mohamed is the chair of the Department of Social Sciences at Clayton State University, Georgia, and coauthor of *Dorm Room Dealers: Drugs and the Privileges of Race and Class.*

Andjelka Nikolic is responsible for monitoring and evaluation of the Get Connected! project run by the nongovernmental organization

Veza, a program specially tailored for young injecting drug users in Belgrade, Serbia.

Steve Rolles is Senior Policy Analyst for Transform Drug Policy Foundation, based in the UK, and author of *After the War on Drugs: Blueprint for Regulation.*

Rebecca Schleifer is Advocacy Director in the Health and Human Rights Division at Human Rights Watch.

Michael Shiner is a senior lecturer in criminology and social policy at the London School of Economics. He specializes in drug and alcohol studies.

Deborah Peterson Small is the founder and Executive Director of Break the Chains: Communities of Color and the War on Drugs, based in the United States.

Andreina Torres is currently a graduate student at the City University of New York. In 2005, as part of her MA studies at FLACSO-Ecuador she conducted research on women in prison in the country. Her work was published in 2006 under the title of *Genero, carcel y drogas: la experiencia de mujeres mulas.*